B'CHOL L'VAVCHA

בְּכָל־לְבָבְךָ

With All Your Heart

A Commentary

by Harvey J. Fields

B'CHOL L'VAVCHA

בְּכָל־לְבָבְךָ

With All Your Heart

A Commentary by Harvey J. Fields

Elaine Rose Glickman, Project Editor

Revised by Elaine Rose Glickman with Harvey J. Fields

Illustrated by Olivia Schanzer

UAHC Press New York

Library of Congress Cataloging-in-Publication Data

Fields, Harvey J.
    B'chol l'vavcha = With all your heart / a commentary by Harvey J. Fields;
revised by Elaine Rose Glickman with Harvey J. Fields.
        p. cm.
    Rev. ed. of: Shaharit (Reform, Central Conference of American Rabbis : Sabbath).
Be-khol levavekha. New York : Union of American Hebrew Congregations, c1976.
    Includes bibliographical references.
    ISBN 0-8074-0777-1 (pbk.: alk. paper)
        1. Shaharit (Reform, Central Conference of American Rabbis : Sabbath)
2. Sabbath—Liturgy—Texts. 3. Siddurim—Texts. 4. Reform Judaism—Liturgy—Texts.
5. Prayer—Judaism. I. Title: With all your heart. II. Glickman, Elaine Rose. III. Shaharit
(Reform, Central Conference of American Rabbis : Sabbath). English & Hebrew. IV. Title.

BM675.S3 Z73 2001
296.4′5046—dc21
                                                                2001047015

Typesetting: El Ot Ltd., Tel Aviv
This book is printed on acid-free paper.
Copyright © 2001 by the UAHC Press
Manufactured in the United States of America
10 9 8 7 6 5 4 3 2

Dedication

FOR

Debra and Jonathan — Joel — Rachel and Hanan
Rebecca — Noa — Amit — Ari — Jeremy

Each child carries its own blessing into the world.

A Yiddish Proverb

Acknowledgments

Every attempt has been made to obtain permission to reprint previously published material. The author gratefully acknowledges the following for permission to reprint previously published material:

RUTH F. BRIN: "A Sense of Your Presence," "In Praise/Genesis 1, 2," "Sabbath Prayer," and "For the Blessings" by Ruth F. Brin. From *Harvest: Collected Poems and Prayer*, © 1999 by Ruth Firestone Brin. Reprinted by permission of Ruth F. Brin.

DAVID BURSTEIN: "God help us not to tolerate and be tolerated..." by David Burstein. Reprinted by permission of Rabbi David Burstein.

CENTRAL CONFERENCE OF AMERICAN RABBIS: Excerpts from *Gates of Prayer*, © 1975, are copyright by Central Conference of American Rabbis and are reproduced by permission; excerpts from *Gates of Prayer*, © 1994, are copyright by Central Conference of American Rabbis and are reproduced by permission; excerpts from *Gates of Repentance*, © 1978, are copyright by Central Conference of American Rabbis and are reproduced by permission.

JUDY CHICAGO: "Merger Poem" by Judy Chicago. © Judy Chicago, 1979. Reprinted by permission of Judy Chicago.

MARCIA FALK: "Light a Candle," "The Feast," "Blessing of Redemption," "Restoring Shekhinah, Reclaiming Home," and "Blessing of Peace." Copyright © 1996 by Marcia Falk. Excerpted from *The Book of Blessings: New Jewish Prayers for Daily Life, the Sabbath, and the New Moon Festival* by Marcia Falk (Harper, 1996; paperback edition, Beacon Press, 1999). Used by permission of the author.

RANDEE FRIEDMAN: Excerpt from letter "Dear God, I am writing this letter..." by Randee Friedman. © 1984 by Randee Rosenberg Friedman. From *Covenant of the Heart: Prayers, Poems, and Meditations from the Women of Reform Judaism*, copyright © 1993 National Federation of Temple Sisterhoods. Reprinted by permission of Randee Friedman.

Contents

Introduction

We often assume that prayer and worship are purely emotional experiences, that it is enough to arouse in the worshiper the feelings of awe, reverence, gratitude, communion, and so on.

The *emotional* experiences of prayer and worship are surely necessary—but not sufficient. There is a strong *intellectual* element in Jewish prayer, as there is in Judaism itself. Understanding and insight are necessary too, especially *before* a worship experience—and, for these, knowledge and study are operationally necessary.

And so, in addition to the full play of the emotional aspect of prayer, Rabbi Fields has also given us, in *B'chol L'vavcha,* a program for investigation, discussion, research, and debate.

He has done more. We hear much nowadays about cognitive and effective learning and their confluence or convergence for better results than from either alone. We hear too little, however, about two other learning dimensions: the psychomotor, the development of habits and skills; and the conative, decision making among recognized choices. *B'chol L'vavcha* provides ample scope for these two dimensions as well and is thus truly, as instructional material, a *kol bo,* a total approach.

It will be obvious to teachers and students that flexibility has been built into both format and procedure and that opportunity and encouragement for creativity abound.

We take pride in work that, within its subject-matter field, is so complete and comprehensive, so versatile and multidirectional. We know it will find wide use on a variety of age levels from intermediate grades to adults and for teacher education programs.

Abraham Segal, *Director*
Union of American Hebrew Congregations
Central Conference of American Rabbis
Commission on Jewish Education
June, 1975

Some Words of Thanks

B'chol L'vavcha was created over twenty-five years ago. It was born out of the realization that *t'filah,* "prayer," was not only a powerful expression of our human experience with God, but also a precious repository of the evolving values and spiritual yearnings of the Jewish people. The more I studied the art of Jewish prayer, its beautiful poetry, its constant challenge for introspection, and its daily reminder of my mitzvah responsibilities to myself and others, the more I realized that *t'filah* is a marvelous map into the spirit of Jewish living. Realizing that, I set off to share my questions and discoveries with others—particularly with those who were beginning their journey into the vast legacy of our people.

The writing of *B'chol L'vavcha* came precisely during a period of transformation and change within Reform Jewish ritual and prayer. The new prayer books *Gates of Prayer, Gates of Repentance,* and *Gates of the House* replaced the nearly seventy-five-year-old *Union Prayer Book.* Reform Jews and their synagogues discussed and decided questions of Jewish dress, the amount of Hebrew to be recited or chanted, the division between congregational song and solos by the *chazan,* and how to create gender-sensitive and inclusive language for their prayers. Many synagogues launched multiple minyanim, or worship groups, and others created *chavurot,* study-friendship groups, to probe the meanings of Jewish prayer. That such renewal continues today is an indication of the vibrancy of our Reform Movement. That *B'chol L'vavcha* enriched the spiritual journey for many liberal Jews and, now, in its revision will continue to enlarge the scope of the journey for a new generation, bring great satisfaction.

It also brings to mind how much is owing to the following teachers and associates whose devotion made possible the first edition of *B'chol L'vavcha*: Rabbis Jack D. Spiro, Joseph B. Glaser, Alexander M. Schindler, Robert I. Kahn, Samuel Glasner, Bennett F. Miller, and Daniel B. Syme. Of equal inspiration were friends: Abraham Segal, Arden Shenker, Samuel Nemzoff, Ralph Davis, Leo Glueckselig, Esther Fried Africk, and Sharon Jankowski. My beloved mentor, Rabbi Roland B. Gittelsohn, remains in a class by himself. It is he who taught me the art of combining a passion for writing with a constant enthusiasm for serving as a congregational rabbi.

I have been privileged to work as a rabbi for four congregations: Temple Israel of Boston, Massachusetts; Anshe Emeth Temple of New Brunswick, New Jersey; Holy Blossom Temple of Toronto, Canada; and for the past two decades, Wilshire Boulevard Temple of Los Angeles, California. I am grateful to all of my students, colleagues, and friends whose insights fill the pages of the first and now this revised edition of *B'chol L'vavcha*.

Special thanks go to UAHC publisher Kenneth Gesser, who urged this revision and republication, and to Rabbi Hara Person, who artfully presided over the editing process. I am particularly appreciative of Rabbi Elaine R. Glickman's devotion, wisdom, and creativity in the revision process. Her contributions have added new vitality to our quest for the meaning and power of Jewish prayer. Liane Broido did an incredible job tracking down permissions. Debra Hirsch Corman put in a tremendous effort in copy-editing the manuscript. To both I owe thanks. Thanks also to Stuart Benick and Rick Abrams for all their help.

I am truly blessed. I can conclude these thanks with the same words of conclusion used twenty-five years ago on this page of the first edition of *B'chol L'vavcha*. "My wife, Sybil, has read and sensitively criticized each page of *B'chol L'vavcha*. Her commitment to sharing a fresh insight into Jewish tradition and life with me has, more than anything else, made this project possible."

H.J.F.
Erev Pesach, 5761/2001

Additional Words of Thanks

With both excitement and trepidation I approached the task of collaborating with Rabbi Harvey J. Fields in revising *B'chol L'vavcha*. I wanted to enrich *B'chol L'vavcha* with the insights of a new generation of rabbis, scholars, and teachers, men and women—without detracting from the wisdom that already filled its pages. And I endeavored to make this remarkable book a newly valuable resource for our young people—without distancing those who have for years relied upon its guidance. I hope that I have, in some measure, succeeded—I hope that you will be instructed and inspired by the results.

I owe many thanks to many people who assisted me in my work on *B'chol L'vavcha*. Thank you to Rabbi Hara Person for entrusting to me this project and for supporting me along the way and to Rabbi Harvey J. Fields for welcoming my ideas and encouraging my efforts. I am also indebted to Michelle Shapiro Abraham, Ilona Thomson, and especially Rabbi Steven M. Gross, who provided invaluable guidance and generosity as I began this work. Finally, a most special thank you to my parents, Helen and Larry Rose and Judy and Albert Glickman, and to my wonderful husband, Rabbi Brenner J. Glickman.

I am overjoyed to dedicate my work on this revision to my son, Moses Aaron Glickman. Mo, I love you with all my heart.

E.R.G.
2001

About *B'chol L'vavcha*

The Chasidic teacher Rabbi Solomon of Karlin once said: "The greatest of all miracles is to bring into the heart of a Jew the Holy Influence whereby he may be enabled to pray properly to his Creator." That, it would seem, is certainly an appropriate statement with which to begin a book or project on prayer.

On the other hand, I wonder what Rabbi Solomon means by his observation. When one thinks about it for a moment, Rabbi Solomon's statement seems to raise more questions than it answers.

What, for instance, does Rabbi Solomon mean by "miracles"? What is a miracle? And what is the "Holy Influence"? Does he mean God or one power or aspect of God? And what could he mean when he uses the words "to pray properly"? Is there a way to pray properly? How would you describe it? Who is to judge whether or not a person is praying properly? How so?

And, with just a little חֻצְפָּה (*chutzpah*), one could even ask what Rabbi Solomon means by the phrase "the heart of a Jew." Is that different from the heart of a non-Jew? How so?

What Is *B'chol L'vavcha*?

B'chol L'vavcha was created in order to answer the questions raised by Rabbi Solomon's observation and to help us discover and accomplish the "miracle" of prayer. That, of course, will not be easy or automatic. Prayer is an art requiring the full range of our emotional and rational sensitivities and abilities. *B'chol L'vavcha* was conceived as a means that might open to us the rich possibilities of Jewish prayer. We hope that it will lead to questions, investigation, discussion, research, debate, and creativity—and that its results will be enjoyable, exciting, and inspiring.

Throughout *B'chol L'vavcha*, you will find prayers and quotations from various sources. Wherever possible, we have identified the authors or books quoted. The designation *HJF* indicates that the prayer has been written by the author of *B'chol L'vavcha*.

We are most grateful to the Central Conference of American Rabbis for permission to use portions of *Gates of Prayer* (1975). We would also like to express thanks to all the authors who allowed us to use their material. Every effort was made to find authors and obtain permission to reprint. We will gladly add author information in subsequent editions. We hope that *B'chol L'vavcha* will be a helpful commentary not only to *Gates of Prayer* but to other prayer books used by the Jewish people throughout the world. In every way, *B'chol L'vavcha* is truly pluralistic. It is meant to enrich students of prayer from all streams of Jewish expression.

Students and teachers may wish to compare translations with other prayer books. Note the differences and ask the question "Why would the translator have chosen one version over another?" You should also be aware that wherever possible, masculine references to God or human beings are not used. This should be kept in mind when translating from Hebrew to English.

B'chol L'vavcha includes several additional prayers, poems, and meditations based on the themes of our traditional prayers. These are meant to enlarge our understanding of the various ways in which Jews have interpreted and applied our ancient prayers to their joys and disappointments, to their fears and triumphs. Hopefully, they will inspire you to create your own "meditations of the heart."

Please note that Hebrew words within *B'chol L'vavcha* are transliterated and translated the first time they appear. They are also listed in the glossary, starting on page 257.

B'chol L'vavcha contains many illustrations. We hope you will enjoy and be inspired by them. Illustrating prayer books *is not* a new idea. During the Middle Ages, Jews decorated their prayer books and Haggadot (for Pesach). They often used elaborate and beautiful lettering or illustrations about their rituals, family celebrations, and community life. You may wish to take a look in your synagogue library at some of their artistic achievements. If you are moved by a particular prayer, take the next step and create a design or picture that captures its meaning for you.

The purpose of *B'chol L'vavcha* is to help us appreciate the development and artistry of Jewish prayer as well as the significant role it has played in the history and experience of the Jewish people. Because we wanted this book to involve the student in a creative exploration of the meaning of Jewish prayer, we have filled it with questions, observations from Jewish tradition, and topics for consideration.

B'chol L'vavcha asks many more questions than it answers. There are two reasons for that. First, the themes of our Jewish prayers often raise issues and insights that should be pursued and explored. Rather than closing off the opportunity to share ideas or to discover modern applications for ancient thoughts and convictions, this book often leaves a subject open for continued speculation and argument. Readers are challenged to come to their own conclusions. Second, when a problem or question is raised, there is usually not one simple answer. Accordingly, *B'chol L'vavcha* offers a variety of Jewish approaches and responses. Hopefully, this will stimulate an exciting exchange of ideas that leads not only to new understandings but also to new questions.

Suggested Ways to Use *B'chol L'vavcha*

B'chol L'vavcha was developed so that it could be used with maximum flexibility by students of the widest possible range of ages. The following suggestions grow out of several years of experimenting with the material in a number of different ways. Some of them may fit your needs; others may not. Choose those that seem helpful, and develop your own methods and approaches.

Suggestion One: *B'chol L'vavcha* can be used very effectively within the Hebrew religious school setting by fourth through seventh graders. The students can be motivated to learn the Hebrew of the prayers by looking forward to leading their peers in worship. While the commentary has been written for high school students and adults, teachers will find it very helpful in interpreting the meaning of the prayers with their intermediate-grade students. Where *B'chol L'vavcha* is used in the Hebrew religious school setting, congregations should be divided by various class levels. For example, all fifth graders would compose one congregation. In this case, one class group can be responsible for preparing and conducting a service each time the entire grade-level-congregation meets. Where such an arrangement is impossible, because numbers are either too small or too great, students could be combined and assignments divided up so that each student has the opportunity to participate. A congregation should be limited to seventy-five persons. You can also invite parents to be present and to participate. Maximum involvement is the goal.

Suggestion Two: *B'chol L'vavcha* is an exciting way for high school students and adults, either together or separately, to celebrate Shabbat morning. It raises a wide variety of subjects for sharing. You may wish to begin with a discussion of "What Is Prayer?" (see page 242) or with the controversy between fixed and creative prayer ("Creating New Prayers—A Controversy: Old and New," page 7). When working with high school students and adults, you might wish to assign people the responsibility of leading the study and allow the group to decide the order and subjects for its discussion. Spend about an hour in study and sharing, and then move on to your Shabbat morning worship.

Suggestion Three: *B'chol L'vavcha* may be used for retreats, conclaves, or summer camp programs. Use great care in selecting topics from the commentary for discussion. Encourage students or campers to select from the prayers we have included in the book or to create their own for inclusion in their services.

Suggestion Four: *B'chol L'vavcha* can also be adapted to a congregational bar/bat mitzvah program. Not only will it acquaint students with the basic Hebrew of the Shabbat morning worship and its traditional sections, but it will also allow a bar/bat mitzvah student to probe the meaning of Jewish prayer and, hopefully, enhance the bar/bat mitzvah celebration. If it is possible, create a Shabbat *chug* (group) of bar/bat mitzvah students (and parents!) that uses *B'chol L'vavcha*, meets each Shabbat morning for study and prayer, and utilizes the opportunity to prepare creatively for the ceremonies.

Suggestion Five: You may want to use *B'chol L'vavcha* for an adult education program on the meaning of Jewish prayer or as a part of your high school curriculum. If you do, it is suggested that each student have a copy of *Gates of Prayer for Shabbat and Weekdays* or a traditional *siddur*. This will allow a maximum opportunity for comparison and contrast as well as provide a valuable window into the evolution of Jewish prayer.

Shabbat Worship and the Use of *B'chol L'vavcha*

B'chol L'vavcha may be used as a prayer book. Remember, however, preparing for worship is a key to a beautiful prayer experience. As the group prepares to lead a service, first select the prayers that you are going to use. Not *every* prayer in *B'chol L'vavcha* is meant to be included. For example, at your first service, you may wish to include the Hebrew and English of the *Yotzer* prayer. The next time, you may choose to use the Hebrew and one of the creative versions provided in this volume or a prayer written by someone in your group.

Parts of the service should be assigned at least two weeks in advance so that each participant has ample time to prepare. The amount of Hebrew utilized will, obviously, depend upon the level and ability of each reader. Beginners should read or chant the opening line and closing line of Hebrew and read the rest in English. Those more advanced will prepare more Hebrew. In assigning parts, decide which are to be read or chanted by leaders and which by the whole congregation. Be sure to plan for lots of singing by the congregation. Leaders should inform the congregation when to stand, sit down, read responsively, or join in song. A simple announcement of (for example) "We join together in the *Aleinu* on page 214" is all that is required.

Music is extremely important for the success of *B'chol L'vavcha*. If possible, try to arrange for a music leader or *chazan* who can work with the group as it prepares its service and who will be present to lead singing when the congregation meets for Shabbat worship. Should you have a person who is talented in the area of dance, you may wish to add that lovely ingredient, on occasion, to some of your services. At times, the use of movies, videos, or recorded music can also be very enriching. Don't hesitate to use various media within the context of your prayer.

Carefully choose a place for prayer. You may be fortunate to have your own synagogue sanctuary or small chapel. On the other hand, you may want to create your own sanctuary by erecting such things as a reader's desk, ark, and eternal light. At times, you may wish to make your sanctuary outdoors, taking advantage of the beauty of nature, or you may choose to meet for prayer in a home. Seating is also important. Experiment until you find the arrangement that seems to spark the most involvement from the congregation. Try placing the reader's desk in the midst of the congregation or the front of the congregation, or have everyone sit in the round. If your group is small enough, you may find it better to have participants read from their seats and eliminate the reader's desk, except for the reading of Torah. The length of a service is of great importance, especially when it involves younger people.

More Ideas

Assign one or two people the task of creating a large, decorative poster of סֵדֶר הַתְּפִלָה (*seder hat'filah*), the order of prayer, which can be hung wherever your group meets for discussion and preparation for Shabbat worship. The poster should contain the following outline of the Shabbat morning service and space to record the participants' assignments. The poster will also serve as a helpful reminder of the order, sections, and prayers of the Shabbat service.

סֵדֶר הַתְּפִלָּה

Invite parents, grandparents, teachers, friends, and the rabbi, cantor, and educator to join you at worship, and if possible, assign them parts in the service. For example, you may wish to ask a post–bar/bat mitzvah to chant a portion of Torah and haftarah or decide to invite a parent to come forward for the *aliyah*. On another occasion you may want to ask two or three people to prepare a dramatic interpretation of the Torah portion.

Plan a *Kiddush* just after the service. Serve wine and challah. If there is time, you may want to include a special Shabbat program of Torah discussion, singing, poetry reading, and folk dancing.

If you are meeting regularly for discussion and worship, you might want to consider dividing your group into the following committees:

A וַעַד עֲבוֹדָה (*vaad avodah*), Committee on Worship, could be responsible for the assignment of parts for your service and for the selection of special songs and readings on holidays or other occasions. This committee may also wish to assign certain sections of the service for creative expression. It may also want to initiate projects to beautify the place of worship or to experiment with different seating arrangements.

A וַעַד תַּלְמוּד תּוֹרָה (*vaad talmud Torah*), Committee on Torah Study, might be responsible for choosing the areas of study in *B'chol L'vavcha*. In some cases, the committee itself may wish to assign the discussion leaders or even plan the lesson. Within this book, you will find suggestions for special projects. Here, too, the committee can set a project in motion and direct it.

A וַעַד קִדּוּשׁ (*vaad Kiddush*), Committee for *Kiddush*, can plan your *Kiddush* with special programs and events. On one occasion, you can have Shabbat singing; at other times, instrumental music, plays, media presentations, a hike, or other recreational activities.

All of these committees ought to be rotating in membership so that everyone has a chance to serve in a different area of leadership responsibility.

What's in a Name?

Why is this book called בְּכָל-לְבָבְךָ, *B'chol L'vavcha?*

Our title is taken from the well-known sentence that follows the words of the שְׁמַע (*Sh'ma*) in the Torah (Deuteronomy 6:5) and in every prayer book. That sentence reads: "You shall love your Eternal God with all your heart [בְּכָל-לְבָבְךָ], with all your mind, and with all your being." The second paragraph of the שְׁמַע also uses these words: "Love the Eternal your God, and serve God בְּכָל־לְבָבְךָ, with all your heart."

Once some students asked their rabbi: "What does it mean to serve God בְּכָל־לְבָבְךָ, with all your heart?" The rabbi replied: "The service of the heart is prayer."

This book is called *B'chol L'vavcha*, בְּכָל־לְבָבְךָ, because it is hoped that it will help us discover and rediscover what it means to love God and to serve God "with all our heart" and to do so with passion and joy.

The Commentary

THE *TALLIT*

Tallit   טַלִּית

בָּרוּךְ אַתָּה יי, אֱלֹהֵינוּ מֶלֶךְ הָעוֹלָם, אֲשֶׁר קִדְּשָׁנוּ בְּמִצְוֹתָיו
וְצִוָּנוּ לְהִתְעַטֵּף בַּצִּיצִית.

We praise You, Eternal God, Sovereign of the universe: You hallow us with Your mitzvot and teach us to wrap ourselves in the fringed *tallit*.

COMMENTARY

The טַלִּית *(tallit)*, prayer shawl, with its צִיצִית *(tzitzit)*, or fringes, has been worn by Jews since biblical times. Today, many Jews continue to wear the טַלִּית. Among Reform Jews the wearing of a טַלִּית at worship is optional. The commandment to wear the צִיצִית is found in the Torah, in the Book of Numbers:

> The Eternal spoke to Moses saying: Speak to the Israelite people and instruct them to make for themselves fringes on the corners of their garments throughout the ages.... Look at it and recall all the Eternal's commandments and observe them, so that you do not follow your heart and eyes to do evil.
>
> Numbers 15:37–39

Why?

Why have Jews worn the צִיצִית from biblical times until today?

We know that dress has always played an important part in the way people relate to one another. The Native American headdress, for instance, indicates the tribal position of the person wearing it. The uniform a soldier wears tells us his or her rank in the army. A Catholic priest is known by the white collar he wears.

Dress is also associated with various kinds of rituals. There is the white dress of the bride, the robes of the priest, and the animal masks worn by some Native American tribes at special festive occasions.

Often ancient people wore special garments or charms because they believed this practice would protect them from evil spirits or be pleasing to the gods. Today, many people still wear what they call "good luck" charms, believing that the charms will bring them safety, good health, success in their sport, or even protection from harm.

Originally the Hebrews, like other peoples, may have worn the צִיצִית for protection from evil or for good luck. The Torah, however, transformed these superstitious practices and gave them a higher, spiritual meaning. The Torah teaches that the צִיצִית were meant to help us "recall all the Eternal's commandments." The Hebrew word for "commandment" is מִצְוָה (mitzvah). A מִצְוָה is a Jewish responsibility. The word מִצְוָה (plural: מִצְווֹת, mitzvot) is also used for any good deed or act of piety or kindness. Later on (pages 55–57), we will discuss the variety of different מִצְווֹת in Jewish tradition.

The *Tallit* and Prayer

The מִצְוָה of prayer is one of the most important responsibilities of the Jew. Prayer is our opportunity to share our Jewish faith, to express our love of God and humanity, to judge our actions and relationships with others, and to seek ways of improving ourselves and the world in which we live.

Putting on the טַלִּית with its צִיצִית is the way some Jews "dress up" for prayer. Wearing the טַלִּית helps many Jews get into the mood for worship. When we put on the טַלִּית, we do something that Jews have done for centuries when they prayed.

Rebbe Nachman of Breslov, a great-grandson of the Baal Shem Tov, taught that "it is a מִצְוָה to be properly dressed for prayer." Would you agree with him? You may wish to arrange a discussion or debate on what is "proper dress" for prayer. Should you have such a discussion, be sure to include the טַלִּית and the wearing of the כִּפָּה (kippah), yarmulke or skullcap, and תְּפִלִּין (t'fillin), phylacteries. You may also wish to discuss if "proper dress" includes the kinds of clothes we choose to wear to services. Are there certain outfits that add to or detract from our ability to pray? Do you think that there should be standards for what "proper dress" means in the synagogue? Why or why not? If "yes," what would some of these standards be?

Who Wears the *Tallit*?

For many centuries, only the men wore the טַלִּית and כִּפָּה when they came to synagogue. The reason may have been that only the men were obligated to pray three times a day—שַׁחֲרִית (*Shacharit*), morning; מִנְחָה (*Minchah*), afternoon; and מַעֲרִיב (*Maariv*), evening. Because of the duties of the home and the rearing of children, women were not expected to be at the synagogue at the special assigned times for prayer. This may explain why it became a custom for only men to wear the טַלִּית.

When you attend services today, however, you may notice that things are very different. While you will see many men who are wearing a טַלִּית and כִּפָּה to pray, you may see that some choose to worship without טַלִּית and כִּפָּה. You will also find that the טַלִּית and כִּפָּה are now worn by women as well as men. There is nothing in Jewish law that prohibits a woman from wearing a טַלִּית or כִּפָּה, and more and more women are choosing to wear them when they pray. At Conservative, Reform, and Reconstructionist synagogues today, you are likely to see female rabbis, female cantors, and female worshipers wearing טַלִּית and כִּפָּה.

What do you think? Should "dress up" for worship include wearing a טַלִּית, כִּפָּה, or תְּפִלִּין? Why or why not? Do you find it meaningful to wear your best clothes to synagogue? Is there a benefit to "dressing up" for special occasions? Are there certain clothes that are not appropriate to wear in the synagogue? Discuss some of these questions with friends, with the rabbi and cantor, and with adults in your congregation. The differences in opinion might make an interesting debate.

Looking at the *Tallit*

If you look carefully at each of the four corners of the טַלִּית, you will notice a long fringe. It is made in a very special way out of four threads.

The four threads are drawn through a small hole at the corner of the טַלִּית and tied in a double knot. Then one of the threads, called the שַׁמָּשׁ (*shamash*), or serving thread, is wound around the others seven times and knotted; and then eight times and knotted. Then it is wound another eleven times and tied; and finally another thirteen times and tied.

Why is the long fringe tied in such an elaborate way? Because it is a symbol. A symbol is an object that represents a special meaning. When we look at it, it reminds us of an idea, hope, or great truth. For instance, the flag of our nation is a symbol. When we look at it, we are reminded of our country and of our responsibilities as citizens.

The long fringe of the טַלִית is a symbol. The special way in which it is tied reminds us of an important teaching of Judaism.

The Mathematics of the Fringe

A little mathematics will help us understand the symbolic meaning of the long fringe. Look at a טַלִית and notice the following:

The first winding equals	7
The second winding equals	8
which together equal	15

In Hebrew letters, 15 could be יה.

The third winding equals 11. In Hebrew letters, 11 could be וה. All together they spell יהוה, which is the name for God.

The final winding equals 13. The Hebrew letters אחד also add up to 13, and the word אֶחָד (echad) itself means one.

When totaled together, the windings of the fringes remind us that יהוה אֶחָד, God is One. יהוה אֶחָד forms the last two words of the sentence of the שְׁמַע (Sh'ma).

There is also another insight to be gained from the mathematics of the צִיצִית. The letter צ in Hebrew is equivalent to 90. The letter י is equivalent to 10, and the letter ת to 400. Added together the word צִיצִית has the numerical value in Hebrew of 600. If you add to that the five knots and eight strands of the completed fringe, your total will be 613. According to Jewish tradition, there are 613 מִצְוֹת, commandments, in the Torah.

When we put on the טַלִית, we are not only dressing up for Jewish prayer, but we are also recalling our people's belief in One God and our commitment to the מִצְוֹת of Jewish tradition.

The *Tallit Katan*

Traditional Jews wear the צִיצִית not only on a טַלִית at times of prayer, they wear them as a special garment at all times!

The garment used for this purpose is called a טַלִית קָטָן (tallit katan), "small *tallit*," or אַרְבַּע כַּנְפוֹת (arba kanfot), "four corners." It is similar to an undershirt with four corners.

As on the טַלִּית, there are fringes on each of the four corners. Usually the fringes are left to hang out so that the wearer may see them and be reminded of the commandments of the Torah and that God is One.

Wearing a *Kippah*

Through Jewish history, our people have dressed in many different styles, usually choosing clothing like those living around them. We are not sure just where and when Jewish men began wearing the כִּפָּה (kippah), or *yarmulke* in Yiddish, as a head covering. We are not even certain when some Jews declared it necessary for Jewish men to be wearing a head covering for prayer or when it became expected that every male wear a כִּפָּה at all times, whether at work or at prayer.

What is clear from the study of Jewish customs is that the Torah does not command the wearing of a כִּפָּה and that there were many Jewish communities where men did not cover their heads for prayer. The leading Jewish teacher of the twelfth century, Moses Maimonides, declared that covering the head was a way of demonstrating respect for God. Later, others argued that by wearing a כִּפָּה, a man proudly acknowledged himself as a Jew. In other words, the כִּפָּה became a badge of Jewish identity.

In nineteenth-century Germany and America, many within the developing movement of Reform Judaism discarded the wearing of כִּפָּה and טַלִּית. Sensitive to the dress customs of non-Jews who actually removed their hats as a sign of reverence to God when they entered their churches, they chose to copy them within their synagogues.

Over the course of the last decades, however, Reform Jews have been making different choices. More males are choosing to wear a כִּפָּה while in prayer, study, or in the fulfillment of מִצְוֹת. And what is true of males is also true of females. Increasing numbers of Reform, Conservative, and Reconstructionist Jewish women are also wearing כִּפּוֹת.

Why is this so? Why are so many Jews, men and women, choosing to wear a טַלִּית and כִּפָּה? Ask some of the adult members of your congregation. Find out whether they wear their כִּפָּה at home, at work, just when they are celebrating a Jewish ritual, or only at synagogue. Ask how many carry a כִּפָּה with them in their pocket or purse. What can such a survey teach us about Jewish celebration and the way Jews identify with their people today?

6

CREATING NEW PRAYERS—A CONTROVERSY: OLD AND NEW

Should we use prayers written by others or only those we have composed ourselves? Should we use a prayer book that gives us a fixed order for prayer or create our own order of worship each time we wish to pray?

Can a congregation exist without some order of service that it uses each time it comes together for prayer? Does a congregation need its own special fixed prayers, as a nation needs its own special anthems, in order to express feelings of unity and common concern?

Which is better, fixed or spontaneous prayer?

These are not new questions. The issue of whether prayers should be fixed or spontaneous was hotly debated by the Rabbis of the Talmud over two thousand years ago. And the debate was never really resolved. In almost every age the controversy has continued between those who wanted a fixed prayer book and those who preferred newly created prayers.

Today, the debate is as alive as ever. All you have to do is ask a group of people which they prefer, fixed or spontaneous prayer—and the sides will quickly be drawn. Below are some of the arguments on each side of the debate. In other places on the next pages you will find quotations from Jewish sources that record the variety of opinions on the issue. How do you think we can resolve the debate within our own congregation? What rules ought to be followed in our debate and why? How shall we make change and preserve our congregation?

Arguments for Fixed Prayer

1. We are a congregation, and in order for us to feel a sense of unity with one another, we need to use the same words. The more we share, the closer we will feel.

2. If we wait until we feel like composing a prayer, we might never pray or we might lose the ability to pray. Prayer demands the discipline of regular practice and the same words if we are to be successful at it.

3. Not all of us are great poets or writers. It is silly not to make use of the outstanding poetry and prayers of our tradition that have been tested by

TWO THOUGHTS

Change not the fixed form in which the Sages wrote the prayers.

Talmud

Be not rash with your mouth, and let your heart not be hasty to utter a word before God.

Ecclesiastes 5:1

time and many generations. They can express our feelings better than we ourselves can.

4.   When we use prayers composed by Jews throughout our history, we identify ourselves with the traditions and generations of our people. When we pray with the same prayers used by Jews throughout the world, we feel at one with our people no matter where they are. Fixed prayer insures the unity of the Jewish people.

5.   Often when an individual composes a prayer, it is self-centered and expresses only selfish concerns. Fixed Jewish prayer is concerned with the welfare of the community and has been carefully written so as to avoid selfish, fleeting needs.

6.   The Rabbis teach us that a person should not be hasty to utter a word before God. That temptation is eliminated by fixed prayer. Spontaneous prayer is often hastily and carelessly composed. Prayer ought to be written with concentration by individuals possessing great skill. Fixed prayer fulfills this requirement.

7.   Spontaneous prayer causes confusion among the worshipers. The talmudic sage Rabbi Zeira once said: "Every time I added new words to my prayers, I became confused and lost my place." Such confusion takes away from the beauty and meaning of the prayer experience. A fixed order of worship solves this problem.

8.   Beautiful prayers, like great poetry, never lose their meaning through repetition. The more we read them with open minds and hearts, the more meanings we can discover. The cure for dull prayer experiences is in us, not in the creation of new prayers.

Arguments for Spontaneous Prayer

1.   While the fixed prayers may be beautiful, after you have said them over and over again, they become dull and repetitive, and they lose their meaning. The Rabbis recognized this, and in the Mishnah they tell us: "Do not let your prayers be a matter of fixed routine but rather heartfelt expressions."

2. Spontaneous prayer allows us to express our feelings, hopes, and concerns. If we are bound by a fixed text, we are prevented from making our worship as personally meaningful as it should be. The Bratzlaver Rebbe, a leading teacher of Chasidism, once said to his students: "You must feel your words of prayer in all your bones, in all your limbs, and in all your nerves." When we use our own prayers, we feel deeply about that for which we are praying.

3. We are not machines, and we can't be programmed to be in the same mood as everyone else at the same time. Spontaneous prayer allows us the freedom to express our true feelings in the moment we pray.

4. We should not forget that the fixed prayers of tradition were once spontaneous expressions of individuals and their communities. Throughout Jewish history, Jews have been composing new prayers and adding them to the prayer book. We need to continue that creative process, for it has helped keep Jewish prayer meaningful and even added to the survival of Judaism.

5. In every generation our people has faced new problems and challenges. These should be expressed in our prayers. Obviously, if we are bound to a fixed text or style of prayer, we cannot include contemporary issues or forms in our worship.

Creating New Prayers

The controversy over fixed and spontaneous prayer continues in our own day. There are those who oppose any changes either in the order of Jewish worship or in any of the traditional prayers. Others favor innovation and the creation of new prayers and worship experiences. *B'chol L'vavcha* attempts to compromise between the two positions. It combines the order and prayers of our tradition with new prayers and invites us to create our own expressions.

RABBINIC OPINIONS

Only that person's prayer is answered who lifts his hands with his heart in them.

BT *Taanit* 8a

Rabbi Eliezer said: If a person prays only according to the exact fixed prayer and adds nothing from his own mind, that prayer is not considered proper.

BT *B'rachot* 28a

Rabbi Abahu would add a new prayer to his worship every day.

Rabbi Acha in the name of Rabbi Yosei said: It is necessary to add new words to the fixed prayers each time they are recited.

BT *B'rachot* 4a

Throughout B'chol L'vavcha *you will find themes entitled "Creating with Kavanah." Kavanah (כַּוָּנָה) means inner feeling, devotion, and concentration. Within the box will be a list of the themes of the prayers in that section.*

You will also find the themes explained in the Commentary passages. You may use those themes for the creation of your own prayers.

You should first master the traditional prayer and its meaning. Then use some of the other prayers in the section. Afterwards, with an understanding of the traditional prayer, you will be ready to create your own original expression.

At the time of congregational worship you can substitute the creative prayers for the traditional ones.

How Do We Create Our Own Prayers?

Just as no one has ever given a successful recipe for writing beautiful poetry, no one has ever produced an easy recipe for creating meaningful and beautiful prayer. The challenge of writing outstanding literature is both exciting and demanding. It requires thoughtful consideration, skill, patience, discipline, and an understanding of the themes and ideas we want to express.

While Jewish tradition does not provide us with a simple method of how to create our own prayers, it does offer us some very useful guidelines. These guidelines give us direction and serve as a check and balance against which we judge and evaluate our creative prayers.

Guidelines for Creative Prayer

Let Your Words Be Few

Rabbi Meir said: "Let a person's words before God always be few" (BT B'rachot 61a). A prayer does not have to be lengthy. It can be brief and still be beautiful. After you have written your first draft, study it and ask yourself which words might be eliminated in order to make the prayer easier to understand.

Don't Pray for the Impossible

The Rabbis teach us that "to pray for the impossible is disgraceful" (*Tosefta, B'rachot* 7). The Chasidic rabbi Leib Sassover explained this guideline to his students by telling them: "It is not permissible to ask God to change the laws of nature to suit your desires."

POURING OUT ONE'S HEART

Though one may be praying with fixed words, one can never predict or anticipate the true prayer of the heart—nor, it would seem, should one strive to. [A prayerful moment] is one that allows truth to be seen and heard and recognized—in whatever form it takes.
Marcia Falk, in *My People's Prayer Book*, vol. 2, *The Amidah*

Fixed prayer lacks the intensity and directedness of spontaneous prayer. But spontaneous prayer alone is insufficient because knowing how to pour out one's heart in prayer is an art that needs to be learned and practiced.
Judith Hauptman, in *My People's Prayer Book*, vol. 2, *The Amidah*

Do Not Separate Yourself from the Community

We are members of many communities. Some are more immediate and important to us than others. Our prayers ought to reflect our responsibilities and relationships to our families, the Jewish people, our nation, and all humanity. The talmudic Rabbis taught that "all Israel is responsible for one another." By this they meant that whenever another Jew is in danger or in need of help, our duty is to do all we can. Jewish prayer stresses our role in seeking peace and security for the people of Israel and for all the world. The prayers we compose should remind us of our responsibilities as human beings and inspire us to actions of love, charity, helpfulness, concern, and peace.

Judging Ourselves and Our Society

The Hebrew word לְהִתְפַּלֵּל (l'hitpaleil), "to pray," can mean "to judge oneself." One of the important purposes of prayer is to help us understand and improve ourselves and our society. We accomplish this purpose when our prayers remind us of the ideals and values of our tradition and challenge us to evaluate ourselves ethically. The Koretzer Rebbe taught: "If you feel no sense of improvement after you have worshiped, then your prayer was in vain." The prayers we create should encourage us toward the ethical examination of ourselves and the society in which we live.

Don't Pray for the Hurt of Others

We are taught: "It is forbidden to ask God to send death to the wicked" (*Zohar, Chadash* 105). Our prayers may express our anger or our feelings of not being loved or appreciated. We may even want to express our desire not to share the company of those who have caused us or others pain. To ask God, however, to bring pain or destruction to others, even though they may be our enemies, is forbidden by Jewish tradition. It is not in keeping with our Jewish values. We are taught to look for the divine image within each person and to see all people as children of God.

Give Thanks

Perhaps the earliest form of prayer was thanksgiving. The Psalmist says: "It is good to give thanks unto the Eternal" (Psalm 92:2). Life is a sacred and wonderful gift from God. Our prayers should reflect our sensitivity to everything from the drop of rain to the miracle of growth, from the natural laws,

11

which make life possible, to the human mind, which is able to explore the universe and its mysteries.

Enjoy Music, Dance, and Art before God

Words are not the only form of prayer in Judaism. The Book of Psalms tells us that worshipers in the ancient Jerusalem Temple used all forms of musical instruments along with singing to enhance their prayers (Psalm 150). Dancing and songs are also mentioned in the Torah. At the joyous time of their liberation from Egypt, Moses and the people sang a song to God, and Miriam, Moses' sister, "took a timbrel in her hand and all the women went out after her in dance with timbrels" (Exodus 15:1, 20). Today, Israeli dancing among men and women continues this tradition.

Sometimes an idea, a hope, or a feeling can be better expressed through music or dance than through words. This is also true of art, video, or films. Often a good picture will highlight an idea and help people understand something in a new way. Creating our own prayers, then, can include forms of dance, instrumental music, song, and the use of art and film.

Jewish Meditation

Rabbi Herbert M. Baumgard writes: "Before one can pray, he must realize...that [God] is here, wherever one is. We must pray where we are, with what we have. You cannot pray while frantically running. The person who wishes to pray must find a quiet place to rest.... All of us, especially in our modern, harried world, need these moments when we can walk away from our burdens and commune with the vastness of the universe" (*Judaism and Prayer*).

Rabbi Baumgard's observation speaks to those Jews who seek God not only through worship, song, and dance, but also through silent devotion and private meditation. As Jews look inward as well as outward for signs of God's presence, they may choose to delve into the practice of Jewish meditation. Although we may not think of meditation as a "Jewish" phenomenon, there is actually a rich tradition of Jewish meditation that has been nourished by centuries of Jewish mystics. Your study group may wish to ask your rabbi about participating in a session of Jewish meditation. You may wish to find a quiet place for reflecting on the meditations of Rebbe Nachman of Breslov, reproduced on page 13. Try this practice for a week, then ask: What difference has it made to me?

Why does Rabbi Baumgard believe that we need peace and quiet in order to pray to God properly? Do you agree? What have you learned from meditating on a single prayer? Are prayer and meditation the same thing? Why or why not? Do you think that meditation is a good tool for drawing closer to God?

Emphasize Sharing

Have you ever wondered why most Jewish prayers are written in the plural ("*Our* God, and God of *our* ancestors"; "*We* give thanks"; "Let *all* bless You")?

Jewish worship is a community experience that is meant to include and involve everyone who wishes to participate. When you are creating a prayer, you may want to ask yourself how others in the congregation will be involved in this prayer.

There are several ways to include the congregation in worship. One is *responsive reading,* where the leader reads a line and the congregation answers. Another is *antiphonal reading,* where one side of the congregation reads and then the other responds. Perhaps the most common form of involvement is the *congregational prayer,* where everyone reads together. A final form, and perhaps the most loved, is *congregational singing.*

This emphasis upon sharing is not meant to exclude prayers read by one person. At times we share best when listening thoughtfully to another person's feelings. The most successful worship is usually a balanced combination of individual and group participation.

Preparations for Prayer

The Tanzer Rebbe was asked by a follower: "What do you do in order to prepare for prayer?" The rebbe replied: "I pray that I may be able to pray properly!"

The pious of old used to wait an hour before praying in order to concentrate their thoughts on God (*Mishnah, B'rachot* 5:1).

Throughout the centuries Jews have created a variety of meditations to aid us in preparing for prayer. These have been collected and placed into a section at the beginning of the prayer book called פְּסוּקֵי דְזִמְרָא (*P'sukei D'zimra*), Verses of Song.

The פְּסוּקֵי דְזִמְרָא include many psalms and prayers written by Jewish poets over the last two thousand years. On Shabbat and the Festivals, Psalms 19, 34, 90, 91, 135, 136, 33, 92, and 93 are added in this order to this section of preparations for prayer.

In the following pages, you will find a selection of traditional morning blessings as well as meditations from the פְּסוּקֵי דְזִמְרָא. Use some of them, or their themes, in the creation of your own service.

בִּרְכוֹת הַשַּׁחַר
פְּסוּקֵי דְזִמְרָא

The Morning Blessings and
Benedictions of Praise

Birchot HaShachar

P'sukei D'zimra

BENEDICTIONS OF PRAISE

Birchot HaNehenin—
Blessings of Enjoyment

בְּרְכוֹת הַנֶּהֱנִין

בָּרוּךְ אַתָּה יי, אֱלֹהֵינוּ מֶלֶךְ הָעוֹלָם, בּוֹרֵא פְּרִי הַגָּפֶן.

We praise You, Eternal God, Sovereign of the universe, Creator of the fruit of the vine.

בָּרוּךְ אַתָּה יי, אֱלֹהֵינוּ מֶלֶךְ הָעוֹלָם, בּוֹרֵא מִינֵי בְשָׂמִים.

We praise You, Eternal God, Sovereign of the universe, Creator of the world's spices.

בָּרוּךְ אַתָּה יי, אֱלֹהֵינוּ מֶלֶךְ הָעוֹלָם, בּוֹרֵא פְּרִי הָעֵץ.

We praise You, Eternal God, Sovereign of the universe, Creator of the fruit of the tree.

Birchot HaMitzvot—
Blessings of Performing Commandments

בְּרְכוֹת הַמִּצְווֹת

בָּרוּךְ אַתָּה יי, אֱלֹהֵינוּ מֶלֶךְ הָעוֹלָם, אֲשֶׁר קִדְּשָׁנוּ בְּמִצְוֹתָיו וְצִוָּנוּ לְהַדְלִיק נֵר שֶׁל שַׁבָּת.

We praise You, Eternal God, Sovereign of the universe: You hallow us with Your mitzvot and command us to kindle the lights of Shabbat.

בָּרוּךְ אַתָּה יי, אֱלֹהֵינוּ מֶלֶךְ הָעוֹלָם, אֲשֶׁר קִדְּשָׁנוּ בְּמִצְוֹתָיו וְצִוָּנוּ לַעֲסוֹק בְּדִבְרֵי תוֹרָה.

We praise You, Eternal God, Sovereign of the universe: You hallow us with the gift of Torah and command us to immerse ourselves in its words.

בָּרוּךְ אַתָּה יי, אֱלֹהֵינוּ מֶלֶךְ הָעוֹלָם, אֲשֶׁר קִדְּשָׁנוּ בְּמִצְוֹתָיו וְצִוָּנוּ עַל נְטִילַת לוּלָב.

We praise You, Eternal God, Sovereign of the universe: You hallow us and command us to fulfill the mitzvah of the *lulav*.

בִּרְכוֹת הַפְּרָטִיוֹת
Birchot HaPratiyot—
Blessings for Occasions

On Hearing Good News

בָּרוּךְ אַתָּה יי, אֱלֹהֵינוּ מֶלֶךְ הָעוֹלָם, הַטּוֹב וְהַמֵּטִיב.

We praise You, Eternal God, Sovereign of the universe: You are the Source of all good.

On Seeing the Ocean

בָּרוּךְ אַתָּה יי, אֱלֹהֵינוּ מֶלֶךְ הָעוֹלָם, שֶׁעָשָׂה אֶת־הַיָּם הַגָּדוֹל.

We praise You, Eternal God, Sovereign of the universe, for the life-giving waters of the sea.

On Seeing a Beautiful Person, Animal, or Plant

בָּרוּךְ אַתָּה יי, אֱלֹהֵינוּ מֶלֶךְ הָעוֹלָם, שֶׁכָּכָה לוֹ בְּעוֹלָמוֹ.

We praise You, Eternal God, Sovereign of the universe, whose world is filled with beauty.

COMMENTARY

When the Israeli author Shmuel Y. Agnon was told that he had been awarded the Nobel Prize for literature, he recited the prayer for hearing good news. And when he arrived in Stockholm to receive the award from the king of Sweden, Agnon recited the blessing appropriate for that occasion. In both instances, the form of the prayer recited by Agnon is known in Jewish tradition as the בְּרָכָה *(b'rachah)*, benediction of praise.

Throughout the centuries Jews have developed and used בְּרָכוֹת (b'rachot), benedictions of praise, for almost every occasion in life. Why? Why should a religious Jew, according to the talmudic sage Rabbi Meir, say at least 100 בְּרָכוֹת each day? What difference do you think it would make if you said a prayer of thanks for every experience you had during the course of one day?

Try it out for one day! Make a list of your experiences and a record of what you said by way of thanks. After you have composed your list, ask yourself what effect the whole experience has had on you. Then share your thoughts with the members of your study group.

What Is a בְּרָכָה?

Prayer is meant to heighten our sensitivity to all the experiences in life. The word בְּרָכָה is derived from the Hebrew בָּרַךְ, which means to "bend the knee." "Bending the knee" is the ancient Jewish way of showing respect and gratitude to God.

The religious Jew sees God in every aspect of existence. God is in the beauty of the sunset, in the morning dawn, in the love we feel for another person, in the desire we have to provide for the poor, in the help we receive in times of trouble, in the gratitude we feel after satisfying our hunger, and in our struggles to overcome evil and suffering. The בְּרָכָה is a means through which Jews give thanks and praise to God, reminding ourselves that life is a sacred opportunity.

Three Kinds of בְּרָכוֹת

According to Moses Maimonides (1135–1204), one of the greatest of all Jewish scholars, there are three kinds of בְּרָכוֹת.

1. בְּרָכוֹת הַנֶּהֱנִין (birchot hanehenin): These are benedictions of praise in gratitude for the pleasures we derive from eating, drinking, or smelling a pleasant odor. An example of this kind of בְּרָכָה would be the blessing a Jew recites before eating:

בָּרוּךְ אַתָּה יי אֱלֹהֵינוּ מֶלֶךְ הָעוֹלָם, הַמּוֹצִיא לֶחֶם מִן הָאָרֶץ.

We praise You, Eternal God, Sovereign of the universe, for You cause bread to come forth from the earth.

2. בִּרְכוֹת הַמִּצְווֹת *(birchot hamitzvot):* These are benedictions of praise recited at the time of doing mitzvot commanded by Jewish tradition. Notice that this kind of בְּרָכָה includes the words אֲשֶׁר קִדְּשָׁנוּ בְּמִצְווֹתָיו וְצִוָּנוּ, "You hallow us with Your mitzvot and command us....'' An example of a benediction recited at the time of performing a mitzvah would be the בְּרָכָה made when placing a mezuzah on the doorpost:

בָּרוּךְ אַתָּה יי אֱלֹהֵינוּ מֶלֶךְ הָעוֹלָם, אֲשֶׁר קִדְּשָׁנוּ בְּמִצְווֹתָיו וְצִוָּנוּ לִקְבּוֹעַ מְזוּזָה.

We praise You, Eternal God, Sovereign of the universe: You hallow us with Your mitzvot and command us to affix the mezuzah.

3. בִּרְכוֹת הַפְּרָטִיּוֹת *(birchot hapratiyot):* These are the benedictions of praise recited at personal or private occasions. These may be said at times of joy, such as when Agnon received the Nobel Prize. They may also be said at a moment of sadness as an expression of affirmation and love of God. For instance, when a Jew hears of the death of a loved one, he or she says:

בָּרוּךְ אַתָּה יי אֱלֹהֵינוּ מֶלֶךְ הָעוֹלָם, דַּיַּן הָאֱמֶת.

We praise You, Eternal God, Sovereign of the universe, the Righteous Judge.

Look at the beginning of the section entitled "Benedictions of Praise" for more examples of these three types of blessings.

The בְּרָכָה and Jewish Prayer

Many of the prayers in the prayer book begin or end with the Hebrew words בָּרוּךְ אַתָּה יְיָ. Some historians of Jewish prayer believe that this formula of the בְּרָכָה was developed by the Sages of the Great Assembly during the time of Ezra and Nehemiah (421 B.C.E.). The בְּרָכָה formula, however, may actually be much older than that.

The Hebrew Bible reports that when King David prayed before the Israelites he used the words בָּרוּךְ אַתָּה יְיָ, "We praise You..." (I Chronicles 29:10). It could be, then, that this form of the בְּרָכָה is one of the oldest Jewish formulas of prayer.

Commenting on the formula of the בְּרָכָה, Rabbi David ben Joseph once said: "We begin the בְּרָכָה with the words בָּרוּךְ אַתָּה יְיָ אֱלֹהֵינוּ, 'We praise You, Eternal our God,' in order to remind ourselves that the God we worship is *our God* and the *God of all people.* Then we say מֶלֶךְ הָעוֹלָם, *'Sovereign of the universe,'* to remember that *our God* is also the *Power that sustains all of nature.''* Look again at the benedictions of praise found in the beginning of this section. How do these benedictions reflect Rabbi David's words?

ELOHAI N'SHAMAH: THE SOUL THAT YOU HAVE GIVEN

Elohai N'shamah　　　　אֱלֹהַי נִשָׁמָה

אֱלֹהַי, נְשָׁמָה שֶׁנָּתַתָּ בִּי טְהוֹרָה הִיא! אַתָּה בְּרָאתָהּ, אַתָּה יְצַרְתָּהּ, אַתָּה נְפַחְתָּהּ בִּי, וְאַתָּה מְשַׁמְּרָהּ בְּקִרְבִּי. כָּל־זְמַן שֶׁהַנְּשָׁמָה בְּקִרְבִּי, מוֹדֶה אֲנִי לְפָנֶיךָ, יי אֱלֹהַי וֵאלֹהֵי אֲבוֹתַי וְאִמּוֹתַי, רִבּוֹן כָּל־הַמַּעֲשִׂים, אֲדוֹן כָּל־הַנְּשָׁמוֹת. בָּרוּךְ אַתָּה יי, אֲשֶׁר בְּיָדוֹ נֶפֶשׁ כָּל־חָי וְרוּחַ כָּל־בְּשַׂר־אִישׁ.

The soul that You have given me, O God, is pure! You created and formed it, breathed it into me, and within me You sustain it. So long as I have breath, therefore, I will give thanks to You, my God and the God of all ages, Source of all being, loving Guide of every human spirit. We praise You, O God, in whose hands are the souls of all the living and the spirits of all flesh.

COMMENTARY

The prayer *Elohai N'shamah* was composed by the talmudic Rabbis (BT *B'rachot* 60b), and it is a part of *Birchot HaShachar*, the daily Morning Blessings. *Birchot HaShachar* are the first part of the *Shacharit*, or morning, service. According to Jewish tradition, *Birchot HaShachar* are among the first words a Jew should say after waking up in the morning. In these blessings, we give thanks to God for our bodies, our spirits, and the opportunity to greet a new day in health and peace. This prayer, *Elohai N'shamah*, praises God for the gift of our soul.

What do we mean by נְשָׁמָה (*n'shamah*), ''soul''?

The נְשָׁמָה is a person's uniqueness. It comprises our character, our personality, and our spiritual qualities. It is all of our feelings, attitudes, and expressions. Just as each of us has a thumbprint unlike any other in the world, so does each of us possess a soul unlike any other in the world.

Judaism teaches that God gives each person a נְשָׁמָה טְהוֹרָה (n'shamah t'horah), "pure soul," at the time of birth. Jews do not believe that human beings are born in sin or evil. The soul of every person can be good or evil depending upon the way we choose to live. Our task is to develop our talents and our sense of right and wrong so that our souls may become beautiful expressions of God's creation.

NISIM B'CHOL YOM: MIRACLES EVERY DAY

Nisim B'chol Yom נִסִים בְּכָל יוֹם

בָּרוּךְ אַתָּה יי אֱלֹהֵינוּ מֶלֶךְ הָעוֹלָם, אֲשֶׁר נָתַן לַשֶּׂכְוִי בִינָה לְהַבְחִין בֵּין יוֹם וּבֵין לָיְלָה.

Praised be the Eternal God, who has implanted mind and instinct within every living being.

בָּרוּךְ אַתָּה יי אֱלֹהֵינוּ מֶלֶךְ הָעוֹלָם, שֶׁעָשַׂנִי יִשְׂרָאֵל.

Praised be the Eternal God, who has made me a Jew.

בָּרוּךְ אַתָּה יי אֱלֹהֵינוּ מֶלֶךְ הָעוֹלָם, שֶׁעָשַׂנִי בֶּן חוֹרִין.

Praised be the Eternal God, who has made me to be free.

בָּרוּךְ אַתָּה יי אֱלֹהֵינוּ מֶלֶךְ הָעוֹלָם, פּוֹקֵחַ עִוְרִים.

Praised be the Eternal God, who helps the blind to see.

בָּרוּךְ אַתָּה יי אֱלֹהֵינוּ מֶלֶךְ הָעוֹלָם, מַלְבִּישׁ עֲרֻמִּים.

Praised be the Eternal God, who clothes the naked.

בָּרוּךְ אַתָּה יי אֱלֹהֵינוּ מֶלֶךְ הָעוֹלָם, מַתִּיר אֲסוּרִים.

Praised be the Eternal God, who frees the captive.

בָּרוּךְ אַתָּה יי אֱלֹהֵינוּ מֶלֶךְ הָעוֹלָם, זוֹקֵף כְּפוּפִים.

Praised be the Eternal God, who lifts up the fallen.

בָּרוּךְ אַתָּה יי אֱלֹהֵינוּ מֶלֶךְ הָעוֹלָם, הַמֵּכִין מִצְעֲדֵי־גָבֶר.

Praised be the Eternal God, who makes firm our steps.

בָּרוּךְ אַתָּה יי אֱלֹהֵינוּ מֶלֶךְ הָעוֹלָם, אוֹזֵר יִשְׂרָאֵל בִּגְבוּרָה.

Praised be the Eternal God, who girds our people Israel with strength.

בָּרוּךְ אַתָּה יי אֱלֹהֵינוּ מֶלֶךְ הָעוֹלָם, עוֹטֵר יִשְׂרָאֵל בְּתִפְאָרָה.

Praised be the Eternal God, who crowns Israel with glory.

בָּרוּךְ אַתָּה יי אֱלֹהֵינוּ מֶלֶךְ הָעוֹלָם, הַנּוֹתֵן לַיָּעֵף כֹּחַ.

Praised be the Eternal God, who gives strength to the weary.

בָּרוּךְ אַתָּה יי אֱלֹהֵינוּ מֶלֶךְ הָעוֹלָם, הַמַּעֲבִיר שֵׁנָה מֵעֵינַי וּתְנוּמָה מֵעַפְעַפָּי.

Praised be the Eternal God, who removes sleep from the eyes, slumber from the eyelids.

COMMENTARY

These blessings are part of a series of benedictions composed by the talmudic Rabbis (BT *B'rachot* 60b) to thank God for miracles we experience every day. Traditionally, Jews would recite these words at home just after waking up; later, however, the benedictions were incorporated into the daily morning service.

Giving Thanks

How do you feel when you first wake up in the morning? Are you grumpy and wishing you could go back to sleep? Are you anxious as you think about the challenges the day might bring? Are you excited and look forward to new friends and new experiences?

Our talmudic Rabbis realized that we may feel a variety of emotions as we awaken to face a new day. However, they also wanted us to feel gratitude and wonder at the miracle of life, to recognize how special it is to be alive for another day. When we first wake up in the morning, we often rush into our daily activities without pausing to savor the gift of a new day of life. These blessings remind us to set aside some time to give thanks to God for all the good we so often take for granted.

Rabbi Samuel E. Karff writes: "Why is it important to pause and count our blessings? Because of the human temptations to pray only prayers of asking for something at those times when we are aware of the pain and the unfulfilled yearnings in our life....We can only begin to accept the all of life and affirm that life is worth its price if we lift to consciousness...all the good stuff in our lives."

What do you think Rabbi Karff means by "lifting to consciousness" the "good stuff" in our lives? How might reciting these benedictions help us to begin each day with a more balanced perspective and to remember what is good and precious in our lives? How might these prayers help us to find courage and faith during difficult times?

Miracles and Responsibility

Look carefully at the first three benedictions on page 21. Why do you think our Rabbis felt that these benedictions described miracles and not just everyday occurrences? What do you think is miraculous about living in freedom and being Jewish? How might our behavior change if we reminded ourselves every morning that we are created in the image of God?

As you read the rest of the benedictions, you may think that some of them refer to acts that are definitely miraculous—for example, God's giving sight to the blind or making clothes for the needy! Actually, our Rabbis believed that these blessings apply to all of us. Though we may not be blind, we are grateful when we open our eyes in the morning and realize that we can still see. Though we may have never lacked shirts, pants, or dresses, we may remember how blessed we are to have clothes to keep us warm and dry. And though we may always feel strong and able to walk around, we thank God for renewing in us our strength and our skills. According to our talmudic Sages, sight, clothing, strength, and the ability to walk are nothing less than miracles.

You might be surprised to learn, however, that just thanking God for these everyday miracles is not enough. Judaism teaches that with gifts come responsibilities. Even as we praise God for giving us sight, clothes, strength, and the ability to walk, we should think of those who do not enjoy all of these blessings and work to assist them. How might these benedictions remind us of this responsibility? How can we help God bring sight to the blind, clothes to the needy, and strength to the weary?

OF COURAGE AND TRUTHFULNESS

Of Courage and Truthfulness

לְעוֹלָם יְהֵא אָדָם יְרֵא שָׁמַיִם בַּסֵּתֶר וּבַגָּלוּי, וּמוֹדֶה עַל הָאֱמֶת, וְדוֹבֵר אֱמֶת בִּלְבָבוֹ.

A person should always serve and respect God in secret or in public by acting honestly and speaking truthfully.

לְפִיכָךְ אֲנַחְנוּ חַיָּבִים לְהוֹדוֹת לָךְ, וּלְשַׁבֵּחֲךָ, וּלְפָאֶרְךָ. אַשְׁרֵינוּ, מַה טּוֹב חֶלְקֵנוּ, וּמַה נָּעִים גּוֹרָלֵנוּ, וּמַה יָּפָה יְרֻשָּׁתֵנוּ. אַשְׁרֵינוּ שֶׁאֲנַחְנוּ מַשְׁכִּימִים וּמַעֲרִיבִים, עֶרֶב וָבֹקֶר, וְאוֹמְרִים פַּעֲמַיִם בְּכָל יוֹם:

It is our duty to thank, bless, and praise You, Eternal God, for we are fortunate to be Jews. How beautiful and pleasant is our heritage and tradition. Happy are we who, each morning and evening, are able to proclaim:

שְׁמַע יִשְׂרָאֵל: יְיָ אֱלֹהֵינוּ, יְיָ אֶחָד!
בָּרוּךְ שֵׁם כְּבוֹד מַלְכוּתוֹ לְעוֹלָם וָעֶד!

Hear, O Israel: the Eternal One is our God, the Eternal God alone!
Blessed is God's glorious majesty for ever and ever!

COMMENTARY

Rabbi Y'hudah HaNasi (135–220 C.E.) was the editor of the first great collection of Jewish law, the Mishnah. He taught that a person should strive for the truth in private and in public—alone and with others. And he knew that the pursuit of truth was not always the easiest path to take.

Being honest with oneself is a challenge. It means recognizing faults and being ready to accept responsibility for one's actions, choices, and words.

But being truthful with oneself can mean something else as well. Often we find ourselves in situations where we are tempted to conform to the opinions or behaviors of others. Rather than doing what we may believe best for ourselves, we choose to imitate someone else.

The founder of modern Zionism, Theodor Herzl, once wrote: "The greatest happiness is to be that which one is." What do you think he meant by that observation?

Fortunate to Be Jews

Many of our prayers are not only beautiful expressions of faith; they also reflect the times in which they were written. The paragraph of our prayer that begins "It is our duty..." was composed while Jews were living under the harsh rule of the Persian king Yazdergerd II in about 452–456 C.E.

Yazdergerd II sought to destroy Judaism. He forbade worship services in the synagogue and sent spies to report on the activities of Jews. He wanted to prevent Jews from reciting the *Sh'ma*, since it proclaimed the belief in one God, while the Persians, who were Zoroastrians, believed in two gods—the god of good and the god of evil.

Rather than give in and conform to Yazdergerd II, Jews met secretly for their services. They recalled the teaching of Rabbi Y'hudah HaNasi and added to it the prayer "It is our duty...." Then, they recited the *Sh'ma*.

This prayer became so popular as a prayer of defiance and courage that even after the persecution had ceased, Jews included it in the *Birchot HaShachar* section of the service.

EVEN AT THE PRICE OF ONE'S LIFE

There are events without which one's life becomes unimportant, a worthless toy; and there are times when one is commanded to do something, even at the price of one's life.

> Hannah Senesh, the day before leaving on a mission to rescue fellow Jews during the Holocaust (she was captured and killed by the Nazis)

I am happy that I lived honestly, in peace with my conscience. I never compromised my soul, even under the threat of death.

> Former Soviet refusenik Natan Sharansky, just before a Soviet court sentenced him to prison for his work helping Jews emigrate from Russia

One who has courage and faith will never perish in misery.

> Anne Frank

Death does not frighten me....I do not fear it because I attribute little value to a life without purpose. And if it is necessary for me to lay down my life in the attainment of the goal, I'll settle for it; I will do so willingly.

> Yonatan Netanyahu, five days before he died leading a raid to rescue Jews captured by Ugandan terrorists

Divide your group and imagine you are (a) Jews living under Yazdergerd II; (b) Jews living under Hitler in 1939; (c) Jews living as Marranos in Spain; and (d) Jews living in Russia in 1985. Have each group compose a prayer to be recited before the שְׁמַע, *as did the Jews of Yazdergerd's time. Then compare the prayers and discuss their differences, similarities, and how they reflect the problems that the various Jewish groups faced.*

BARUCH SHE-AMAR: PRAISED BE THE ETERNAL ONE AND PRAISED BE THEM WHO PRAISE THE ETERNAL ONE

Baruch She-amar

בָּרוּךְ שֶׁאָמַר

בָּרוּךְ שֶׁאָמַר וְהָיָה הָעוֹלָם.

Praised be the Eternal One who spoke, and the world was created.

בָּרוּךְ הוּא.

Praised be God.

בָּרוּךְ עוֹשֶׂה בְרֵאשִׁית.

Praised be the Eternal One, Source of creation.

בָּרוּךְ אוֹמֵר וְעוֹשֶׂה.

Praised be the Eternal One who speaks and does.

בָּרוּךְ גּוֹזֵר וּמְקַיֵּם.

Praised be the Eternal One who announces and fulfills.

בָּרוּךְ מְרַחֵם עַל הָאָרֶץ.

Praised be the Eternal One who has compassion for all the earth.

בָּרוּךְ מְרַחֵם עַל הַבְּרִיּוֹת.

Praised be the Eternal One who has compassion for all human beings.

בָּרוּךְ מְשַׁלֵּם שָׂכָר טוֹב לִירֵאָיו.

Praised be the Eternal One who rewards the goodness of those who have faith.

בָּרוּךְ חַי לָעַד וְקַיָּם לָנֶצַח.

Praised be the Eternal One whose life-giving power is for ever.

בָּרוּךְ פּוֹדֶה וּמַצִּיל.

Praised be the Eternal One who redeems and frees.

בָּרוּךְ שְׁמוֹ.

Praised be the name, Eternal God.

COMMENTARY

The בָּרוּךְ שֶׁאָמַר (Baruch She-amar) was formulated sometime during the ninth century. It became so popular as a praise of God that it was placed at the very beginning of the פְּסוּקֵי דְזִמְרָה section of the service. During the פְּסוּקֵי דְזִמְרָה, Jews offer special prayers of praise and thanksgiving, exalting God as our Creator and Redeemer.

The Creator

Some prayers not only give thanks and praise to God, they also help us understand what Jewish poets believed about God. In the בָּרוּךְ שֶׁאָמַר, we find the outlines of a description of God.

The author begins this prayer by praising God as the Creator of the universe. The words recall the first chapters of the Torah, where we are told about the creation of the world. The Torah and our prayers do not give us a scientific explanation of creation. Rather, the first chapters of the Torah and the בָּרוּךְ שֶׁאָמַר help us understand the wonder of the world and God's creative power in making possible all that we see and experience.

Compare the first five sentences of בָּרוּךְ שֶׁאָמַר with the following from the first chapter of Genesis:

God said: "Let there be light." And there was light....
God said: "Let the earth put forth grass and fruit-bearing trees." And it was so....
God said: "Let the earth bring forth living creatures." And it was so....
God said: "Let us make humanity."

Why do you think that the authors of Genesis and the בָּרוּךְ שֶׁאָמַר thought of God as being able to create by "speaking" or "announcing"? Can a person "create" with speech? Note that the Hebrew root דבר means both "speak" and "thing." How do you think these two meanings are related? Rabbi Asher ben Yechiel once said to his students: "Do not allow an unworthy coin to go forth from your lips—weigh and judge carefully all your words." What do you think he meant?

The Merciful One

The second part of the בָּרוּךְ שֶׁאָמַר speaks of God's power of compassion. The Hebrew word for compassion is רַחֲמִים (rachamim). It is derived from the Hebrew root רחם, which can mean love, tenderness, and concern. רֶחֶם can also mean "womb," the place in the mother's body in which the child is nurtured before its birth. In Jewish tradition, God is thought of as הָרַחֲמָן (HaRachaman), "the Merciful One" who constantly sustains and cares for the universe.

Do we have evidence that God really "sustains and cares" for the world or human beings? What about the development of our bodies, or the order a scientist discovers in our universe, or the process of growth we find in nature? What about the way in which a child is nurtured in the womb of its mother?

A Challenge

Jewish tradition challenges us to imitate God. The Torah tells us that God is "merciful and gracious, long-suffering, and abundant in goodness and truth" (Exodus 34:6). The task of the Jew is to strive to incorporate all of these ethical traits into his or her behavior.

During the lifetime of the prophet Micah (about the eighth century B.C.E.), men and women, especially the wealthy, failed to live up to the ethical ideals of Judaism. They treated the poor with contempt, and they disregarded the rights of widows, orphans, and the impoverished sick. One day Micah went to the Temple and angrily protested the corruption and evil he saw all about him.

He asked the people questions that they would have preferred not to hear. And he told them what God really wanted from them:

> Hear this, I pray you,
> You the heads of the House of Jacob,
> And the rulers of the House of Israel,
> You who hate justice and pervert all that is right....
> It has been told you, O humanity, what is good,
> And what the Eternal One requires of you:
> Only to do justice, and to love mercy, and to walk humbly with your
> God.
>
> Micah 3:9; 6:8

What has Micah's statement to do with the בָּרוּךְ שֶׁאָמַר prayer?

How can a person imitate God? When a person works to free a captive or someone who is being persecuted by others, how is he or she imitating God? Turn to Exodus 34:6, and discuss with your study group some of the ways we can imitate God in our relationships with one another, our parents, and our teachers.

Dr. Ellen Frankel writes that "we might imagine, as we look in mirrors, God's face behind our own. After all, we are each created b'tzelem Elohim, in the likeness of God. We should daily recognize God within our own features. For if we did so, we would recognize God's face in each person we meet— and act accordingly." What do you think Dr. Frankel means by this statement? How might looking for God's image in the poor and the needy help us to live out the prophet Micah's charge?

What do you think the rabbi meant by saying: "God is really God when human beings decorate themselves with good deeds"?

PSALMS 100 AND 135

Psalm 100

הָרִיעוּ לַיָי כָּל הָאָֽרֶץ. עִבְדוּ אֶת יְיָ בְּשִׂמְחָה. בְּאוּ לְפָנָיו בִּרְנָנָה.
דְּעוּ כִּי יְיָ הוּא אֱלֹהִים. הוּא עָשָֽׂנוּ, וְלוֹ אֲנַֽחְנוּ, עַמּוֹ וְצֹאן
מַרְעִיתוֹ.

בְּאוּ שְׁעָרָיו בְּתוֹדָה, חֲצֵרֹתָיו בִּתְהִלָּה.
הוֹדוּ לוֹ,

בָּרְכוּ שְׁמוֹ. כִּי טוֹב יְיָ, לְעוֹלָם חַסְדּוֹ, וְעַד דֹּר וָדֹר אֱמוּנָתוֹ.

Raise a shout for the Eternal One, all the earth;
   worship the Eternal One in gladness;
   come into God's presence with shouts of joy.
Acknowledge that the Eternal One is God;
   God made us and we are God's,
   God's people, the flock God tends.
Enter God's gates with praise,
   God's courts with acclamation.
Praise God!
Bless God's name!
For the Eternal One is good;
   God's steadfast love is eternal;
   God's faithfulness is for all generations.

Psalm 135:1–4

הַלְלוּיָהּ. הַלְלוּ אֶת שֵׁם יְהֹוָה.
הַלְלוּ עַבְדֵי יְהֹוָה שֶׁעוֹמְדִים בְּבֵית יְהֹוָה.
הַלְלוּ יָהּ, כִּי טוֹב יְהֹוָה. זַמְּרוּ לִשְׁמוֹ כִּי נָעִים.
כִּי יַעֲקֹב בָּחַר לוֹ יָהּ, יִשְׂרָאֵל לִסְגֻלָּתוֹ.

Hallelujah.
Praise the name of the Eternal One;
   give praise, you servants of the Eternal One
   who stand in the house of the Eternal,
   in the courts of the house of our God.

Praise the Eternal, for the Eternal One is good;
    sing hymns to God's name, for it is pleasant.
For the Eternal One has chosen Jacob,
    Israel, as God's treasured possession.

COMMENTARY

The Book of Psalms, סֵפֶר תְּהִלִּים (Seifer T'hillim), is a collection of 150 prayers. Many of the psalms were sung or recited while the Temple in Jerusalem was still in existence. When the Temple was destroyed by the Romans (70 C.E.), the Rabbis incorporated many of the psalms into the service of the synagogue.

The names of the authors of the psalms are not known. Some of the psalms begin with the words "A psalm of David," as if to indicate that they were written by King David. We know, however, that they were not all composed by David but, perhaps, were given his name by authors who wanted to dedicate their poems to him, or by editors who believed that David had written them.

Throughout the ages, the Book of Psalms has been considered among humanity's greatest literature. The hopes, faith, and feelings expressed in the psalms have not only shaped Jewish prayer but also contributed to the development of Christian worship.

Psalm 100

In Psalm 100, the poet calls upon the whole earth, all that lives, to thank and praise God. For the Psalmist, prayer is a joyful experience. The poet appreciates life and all the opportunities for happiness it offers.

The Psalmist also recognizes that it is only human beings who can appreciate God's relationship to nature and express thanksgiving. No other form of life that we know of is capable of such understanding or expression.

What do you think the poet meant by the words "God's faithfulness is for all generations"? How does God's power extend to all generations? How would you compare the ideas expressed in "Other Thoughts" (page 32) to Psalm 100?

Psalm 135

In Psalm 135, the poet calls upon all who are standing in the house of God to join in praising the Eternal One. By "house of God," the poet meant the

As a house implies a builder, a dress a weaver, a door a carpenter, so the world proclaims God as its Ceator.

Rabbi Akiva

God's wisdom and power in creating an ant or bee is no less than in the making of the sun and its sphere.

Y'hudah HaLevi

[God's] goodness renews day by day the work of creation.

Yotzer prayer

Temple in Jerusalem. Today when we recite this psalm, we mean any place where people have gathered for prayer.

A Special People?

The poet refers to the Jewish people as "chosen" and God's "treasured possession." Does this mean that Jews are "better" or more favored by God than other people? Not at all!

When we speak of Jews as being "chosen" or "treasured," we have in mind our people's task to fulfill the commandments of the Torah and to help all people advance toward a day of justice and peace. To be "chosen" means to be selected for responsibilities—not for privileges!

Read the following Bible passages: Amos 5:4–15; Isaiah 42:1–6; and Deuteronomy 30:1–20. What do they tell us about the task of the Jewish people? For what are Jews "chosen"? Your study group might wish to discuss how your congregation should be fulfilling some of the tasks of the Jewish people. You may even wish to develop some projects of your own.

Nishmat: The Soul of Everything That Lives

Nishmat

נִשְׁמַת

נִשְׁמַת כָּל־חַי תְּבָרֵךְ אֶת שְׁמְךָ, יְיָ אֱלֹהֵינוּ, וְרוּחַ כָּל־בָּשָׂר תְּפָאֵר וּתְרוֹמֵם זִכְרְךָ, מַלְכֵּנוּ, תָּמִיד.

The soul of everything that lives shall praise Your name, Eternal One. The spirit of every human being shall continually uplift Your glory.

אִלּוּ פִינוּ מָלֵא שִׁירָה כַּיָּם, וּלְשׁוֹנֵנוּ רִנָּה כַּהֲמוֹן גַּלָּיו, אֵין אֲנַחְנוּ מַסְפִּיקִים לְהוֹדוֹת לְךָ, יְיָ אֱלֹהֵינוּ.

Even if our mouths were as filled with song as the sea is filled with water, and even if our tongues could sing like the waves of the ocean roar, we could still be unable to thank you, Eternal our God.

עַל כֵּן, אֵבָרִים שֶׁפִּלַּגְתָּ בָּנוּ, וְרוּחַ וּנְשָׁמָה שֶׁנָּפַחְתָּ בְּאַפֵּינוּ, וְלָשׁוֹן אֲשֶׁר שַׂמְתָּ בְּפִינוּ, הֵן הֵם יוֹדוּ וִיבָרְכוּ אֶת־שְׁמְךָ, מַלְכֵּנוּ.

Therefore, we will strike to give You thanks for the gifts You have given to us. We will praise You with clapping hands and dancing feet, with songs and words of our mouths, and with all our souls.

Commentary

This meditation is known as the נִשְׁמַת (Nishmat). It was written during Maccabean times and recited as a part of the Temple service. The נִשְׁמַת was a favorite prayer of the Rabbis who composed the Passover Haggadah. They recommended it as the concluding prayer for the seder.

It is difficult, if not impossible, to thank God for all the gifts of life!

Why is this so? Perhaps, because there are so many gifts of God that no list could contain all of them. For that reason, the author of the נִשְׁמַת reminds us that, while we cannot name all of the things God does for us, we can give thanks for what we experience and for what we have.

The modern liturgist and scholar Marcia Falk takes another view. "This poetic prayer might be seen as encouraging us to lavish praise on God's creation and to thank God ever more profusely," she writes. "But it is equally possible to interpret it differently...as an acknowledgment of the ultimate inadequacy of words. Perhaps this prayer comes to teach us that when words cannot convey the fullness of our emotions—in particular, of our gratitude—they ought to be set aside."

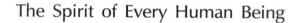

What do you think of this idea? Are there times when we can express ourselves better by keeping silent than by speaking? Do you think that it is possible to pray and communicate with God without using words?

The Spirit of Every Human Being

The נִשְׁמַת prayer speaks of every human being giving glory to God. Jewish tradition considers each person a unique reflection of God. The Torah teaches that man and woman were created in the image of God (Genesis 1:27). The Rabbis taught that just as a painting is a reflection of the artist's interests and abilities so, too, is each human being a representation of God's power, love, and creativity. This appreciation of each person's relationship with God has led to important conclusions about how human beings treat one another.

For instance, Rabbi Nehemiah taught that "God considers every human being equal in value to all of creation" (*Avot D'Rabbi Natan*, 31). In other words, the life of each person should be treated as if the future of the world depended upon it. How would you apply Rabbi Nehemiah's observation to the treatment of the elderly, the poor, the sick, and those who may be considered enemies? What changes would we need to make in society in order to treat "every human being equal in value to all of creation"?

Once you have discussed the meaning of the נִשְׁמַת, you may wish to create a prayer that incorporates your own ideas and feelings about how we should treat others as precious images of God. In your prayer, try to contrast the ways you see people treated with the ways you believe they ought to be treated.

Praise God for every drop of rain...for in it are all the waters of the earth!

Compare the following psalm with the נִשְׁמַת. *What do both prayers have in common? Where do they differ?*

O Eternal our God,

How glorious is Your name in all the earth!

When I behold Your heavens, the work of Your fingers,

The moon and the stars, which You have established;

What is man, that You are mindful of him?

And the son of man, that You think of him?

Yet You have made him little lower than Divine,

And have crowned him with glory and honor.

You have made him to have dominion over the works of Your hands;

And put all things under his feet.

O Eternal, our God,

How glorious is Your name in all the earth!

Psalm 8:2, 4–10

CREATING WITH
KAVANAH
Themes:
a. We praise God with our abilities.
b. It is impossible to thank God for all the gifts of life.
c. Every human being is a precious part of creation.

35

SECTION TWO

שְׁמַע

The *Sh'ma*

BAR'CHU: THE CALL TO WORSHIP

Bar'chu

בָּרְכוּ

בָּרְכוּ אֶת־יי הַמְבֹרָךְ!

Praise the One to whom our praise is due!

בָּרוּךְ יי הַמְבֹרָךְ לְעוֹלָם וָעֶד!

Praised be the One to whom our praise is due, now and for ever!

COMMENTARY

With the בָּרְכוּ (*Bar'chu*), we begin a new section of our service called the שְׁמַע (*Sh'ma*). This section includes the יוֹצֵר (*Yotzer*), "Creator of Light"; the אַהֲבָה רַבָּה (*Ahavah Rabbah*), "Deep Love"; the שְׁמַע; the וְאָהַבְתָּ (*V'ahavta*), "You Shall Love"; and the גְאוּלָה (*G'ulah*), "Redemption."

Origins of the בָּרְכוּ

The בָּרְכוּ is a very ancient Jewish call to worship. We are told that when the Jewish people returned from the Babylonian exile, sometime around 421 B.C.E., their leaders, Ezra and Nehemiah, called them together to hear the Torah and to pledge to uphold it. At that time, the people were called to prayer with these words:

קוּמוּ בָּרְכוּ אֶת־יְהֹוָה אֱלֹהֵיכֶם מִן הָעוֹלָם עַד הָעוֹלָם.

Stand and bless *Adonai* your God who is forever and ever.

וִיבָרְכוּ שֵׁם כְּבֹדֶךָ וּמְרוֹמַם עַל כָּל־בְּרָכָה וּתְהִלָּה.

And say: Praised be Your glorious name, and may it be exalted by every blessing and praise.

Nehemiah 9:5

Compare these words found in Nehemiah 9:5 with those of the בָּרְכוּ. At times you may wish to call your congregation to worship with the words in Nehemiah rather than the בָּרְכוּ.

Refer to the prayer in Nehemiah 9:6–10:1.

What do you learn from the prayer about the author's beliefs and his thoughts about the people of Israel? Are there parts of this prayer that you could use today?

After reading the prayer to the people, the leaders "set their seal" upon it. Why?

You might wish to write a prayer for your congregation, then read it and have everyone sign it.

What Is a Minyan?

Notice that the emphasis of the בָּרְכוּ, and the words found in the Book of Nehemiah, is upon *calling the congregation* together for prayer. Jewish tradition emphasizes praying with a community. The Rabbis of the Talmud teach that "the prayers of those who pray with a congregation are answered."

What is meant by "congregation" or "community" in Judaism? And why does Jewish tradition consider prayer with a congregation superior to praying alone?

According to traditional Jewish law and practice, ten men past the age of thirteen form a מִנְיָן *(minyan)*, or "quorum." In Reform, Conservative, and Reconstructionist synagogues today, women as well as men are counted in a מִנְיָן. A מִנְיָן may be ten men, ten women, or a mixture of the two.

39

We are not sure when or where this tradition of needing a מִנְיָן to pray developed. Some say that the number ten was taken from the first sentence of Psalm 82. It reads:

אֱלֹהִים נִצָּב בַּעֲדַת־אֵל.

God is present in the congregation of the Eternal One.

The word עֵדָה (eidah), "congregation," is used here in its Hebrew construct form עֲדַת (adat), "congregation of." So what does that have to do with the number ten? Well, the Rabbis point out that עֵדָה is also used by the Torah (Numbers 14:27) when it refers to the ten spies who were sent by Moses to explore the Land of Israel and then return with a report. Those ten spies were called עֵדָה.

Because עֵדָה is used in the spy story to refer to ten men and עֲדַת in the psalm to refer to "congregation [of]," Jewish tradition defined a מִנְיָן as ten adults.

Why Pray with a מִנְיָן?

There are several answers that can be given to this question. We will discuss some of them further on in *B'chol L'vavcha*. One way of answering the question, however, is to make a list of the reasons why you prefer to share experiences with friends.

Make up such a list. Then discuss it, asking what reasons you have for praying with others. If someone wants to take the other side of the argument, you may want to arrange a debate. You may also wish to develop a sermon on the question and present it at one of your services.

Another way of answering the question is to look at the answers given to us by other Jews. Here is one response written by the great Jewish poet Y'hudah HaLevi. He lived in Spain during the years 1085 to 1140 and wrote many poems that have become a part of Jewish worship. In his book, called *The Kuzari*, he tried to answer many difficult questions about Jewish tradition, history, and faith. This is what he wrote about praying with a מִנְיָן:

Praying with a congregation has many advantages. In the first place, a community will never pray for something that is harmful to the individual, while sometimes an individual will ask for things that can be harmful to others. That is why it is taught that a person should recite prayers with a congregation.

40

A person who prays only for himself is like one who goes alone into his house and refuses to help others in the work of the community. . . . It is the duty of each person to bear hardships for the sake of the common good of all.

Why does Y'hudah HaLevi make the connection between praying alone and not fulfilling one's community obligations? Would you agree with him?

Is someone more apt to be selfish in prayers while praying alone? How might the presence of others remind us that we have responsibilities to others?

The founder of Reconstructionist Judaism, Mordecai Kaplan, offers another reason for praying with a minyan:

When we worship in public we know our life is part of a larger life, a wave of an ocean of being—this first-hand experience of that larger life which is God.

What does Mordecai Kaplan believe that we learn by praying in public? Why is it important to remember that we are part of something larger than ourselves?

Mordecai Kaplan says that by praying with a group, we can feel closer to God. How might praying with a מִנְיָן help us sense God's presence?

YOTZER: CREATOR OF LIGHT

Yotzer יוֹצֵר

בָּרוּךְ אַתָּה יי, אֱלֹהֵינוּ מֶלֶךְ הָעוֹלָם, יוֹצֵר אוֹר וּבוֹרֵא חְשֶׁךְ,
עֹשֶׂה שָׁלוֹם וּבוֹרֵא אֶת־הַכֹּל. הַמֵּאִיר לָאָרֶץ וְלַדָּרִים עָלֶיהָ
בְּרַחֲמִים, וּבְטוּבוֹ מְחַדֵּשׁ בְּכָל־יוֹם תָּמִיד מַעֲשֵׂה בְרֵאשִׁית.
מָה רַבּוּ מַעֲשֶׂיךָ, יי! כֻּלָּם בְּחָכְמָה עָשִׂיתָ, מָלְאָה הָאָרֶץ
קִנְיָנֶךָ. תִּתְבָּרַךְ, יי אֱלֹהֵינוּ, עַל־שֶׁבַח מַעֲשֵׂה יָדֶיךָ, וְעַל־
מְאוֹרֵי־אוֹר שֶׁעָשִׂיתָ: יְפָאֲרוּךָ. סֶלָה. בָּרוּךְ אַתָּה יי, יוֹצֵר
הַמְּאוֹרוֹת.

We praise You, Eternal God, Sovereign of the universe. Your mercy makes light to shine over the earth and all its inhabitants, and Your goodness renews day by day the work of creation. How manifold are Your works, O God! In wisdom You have made them all. The heavens declare Your glory. The earth reveals Your creative power. You form light and darkness, bring harmony into nature, and peace to the human heart. We praise You, O God, Creator of light.

COMMENTARY

In Jewish tradition this prayer is called the יוֹצֵר, which means "Former" or "Creator," because it praises God as the Creator and Maker of heaven and earth. The title יוֹצֵר is taken from the first Hebrew word after the opening phrase: בָּרוּךְ אַתָּה יְיָ, אֱלֹהֵינוּ מֶלֶךְ הָעוֹלָם, יוֹצֵר .... Its theme is praise to God, who restores light to the earth every morning. This prayer was written over 2,000 years ago and may have been used as a part of the Temple service.

When we look at it carefully, we get a good insight into what its author had in mind.

Wonders of Nature

The wonder and order of nature have always stirred the imaginations of sensitive and poetic human beings. The Torah begins with the story of creation, and the prophets and Psalmists all wrote songs of praise to God as the Creator and Source of all nature. They believed that just as the paintings of artists reveal their talents so, too, do the beauties and wonders of nature reveal the powers of God.

The poet and philosopher Moses ibn Ezra, who lived in Spain from 1070 to 1138, wrote the following poem about God's relationship to nature:

> O God, where shall we find You?
> We see You in the starry field,
> We see You in the harvest yield,
> In every breath, in every sound,
> An echo of Your presence is found.
> The blade of grass, the simple flower,
> Bear witness to Your wonderful power.

The modern poet Ruth F. Brin praised God's creative power in this poem:

In Praise: Genesis 1, 2

> Hail the hand that scattered space with stars,
> Wrapped whirling world in bright blue blanket, air,
> Made worlds within worlds, elements in earth,
> Souls within skins, every one a teeming universe,
> Every tree a system of semantics, and pushed
> Beyond probability to place consciousness
> On this cooling crust of burning rock.
>
> Oh praise that hand, mind, heart, soul, power, or force
> That so inclosed, separated, limited planets, trees, humans
> Yet breaks all bounds and borders
> To lavish on us light, love, life
> This trembling glory.

One of the important points made in the יוֹצֵר, in Rabbi Joshua ben Karhah's statement (page 44), and in Moses ibn Ezra's and Ruth Brin's poems is that

God is not only the Creator of the huge and endless universe in which we live but that God's power extends to every star, every tree, and even the smallest blade of grass.

Today we are aware of atoms and many universes beyond ours. How might we express the ideas we find in Ibn Ezra's and Ruth Brin's poems in a modern prayer? Imagine yourself first studying a tiny particle of the world through a microscope and then looking out into space through a telescope. What words of prayer might you use to express what you have seen and felt?

Creator of All Things

The יוֹצֵר includes the phrase: "You form light and darkness."

These words, and this idea about God, were taken by the prayer's author from Isaiah. The prophet, speaking in the name of God, said:

> I am the Eternal One, and there is none else.
> I form light and create darkness,
> I make peace and create evil.
>
> Isaiah 45:6–7

Some ancient religions taught that there were two gods at war with one another for control of the universe. One was a god of light and good; the other was a god of darkness and evil. This idea is called "dualism"—belief in two gods. The followers of Zoroastrianism, a Persian religion founded about 600 B.C.E., believed that the world is a struggle between Spenta Mainya (the spirit of good) and Angra Mainya (the spirit of evil).

Judaism rejected dualism and taught that one God was the creative power responsible for everything.

Compare Isaiah's words with those found in our prayer. Notice how the author of the יוֹצֵר did not use the last phrase: "create evil." Why was this change made?

It could be that the author did not want to refer to God as a "Creator of evil" in the midst of prayer. Perhaps there is another reason. The author may have disagreed with Isaiah's belief that God creates evil and preferred to teach that nature is filled with many mysteries we may never fully understand, including the bad things that happen to good people. Can you think of any other reasons why the author of the יוֹצֵר deliberately changed Isaiah's words? Who or what do you think is responsible for the evils that we experience or encounter in life?

Light and Life

In the expression "Your mercy makes light to shine over the earth and all its inhabitants," we see the sensitivity of the prayer writer to nature and especially to the part played in nature by the power of light.

Have you ever tried to grow a seed or flower inside your house? What are the conditions you must provide for it to grow? What part does light play in the growing process?

Modern science teaches us that no living thing can exist without the immediate or, at least, indirect influence of light. It is the power of light that sets the forces of life in motion.

Creation Is Daily Renewed

In Jewish tradition, God is not thought of as a far-off machine that has nothing to do with nature and us. The author of the יוֹצֵר says that God's goodness "renews day by day the work of creation." What the poet is saying is that God is a Power, constantly at work, sustaining all the starry skies, the fields and forests, animal life, and the existence of human beings.

Can you think of examples in nature where renewal takes place? What about within the human body?

How Great Are Your Works

We have already mentioned that the Book of Psalms was one of the most important sources of prayer for Jews and Jewish poets. Often we find that the author of a prayer will borrow a line or a phrase from a psalm. Having called attention to the order and beauty of nature, the author of the יוֹצֵר quotes from one of the most lovely of all nature psalms (Psalm 104:24). Look at the whole psalm and then compare it with the יוֹצֵר prayer.

Four Prayers on the יוֹצֵר Theme

How Glorious Is Your Name

O Eternal, our God, how glorious is Your name in all the earth.

When we see the heavens, the work of Your fingers,

The moon and the stars, which You have placed there;

The gold of the sun, the silver of the moon, and the diamond sparkle of the stars;

The cool, green grass, the gentle flowers, the freshness of flowing streams,

We give thanks to You, who made them all;

And put beauty and goodness within them.

All the world sings its song to You:

The song of the trees, when the wind stirs their leaves,

The song of the sea, when the waves kiss the shore.

The song of human praise to You, O God, for all the works of creation.

Arranged by HJF

Let Us Imagine

Let us imagine a world without the grace of color, where regal red or leafy green would never more be seen.

> We give thanks for the colors of the rainbow, for eyes that see, for the gift of beauty.

Let us imagine a world in deathlike silence, never knowing the joy of sound.

> We give thanks for words that speak to our minds, for songs that lift our spirits, and for souls that know how to listen.

Let us imagine a world in which nothing can be known, where day and night, winter and summer, or the flow of the tides can never be predicted.

> We give thanks for nature's wondrous order, for the stars in the sky to the pulsebeat within us.

Let us imagine a world without love, where each person is alone and unable to share with others.

> We give thanks for the power of love within us. You, O God, have made it possible for us to know the joy of friendship and the benefit of reaching out to help those in need.

Based on a prayer by Rabbi Henry Cohen

We Praise You

We praise You
for breathing into us the breath of life.
Praised are You, Holy One, Who sculpts the moon and sprinkles
the stars above, who shapes the world, and life, and time.
Who plants wonder in our world each day.
Who wipes our brow when we are weary, and
gives us drink when we are dry.
Who lights our soul with dance and hope.
Who blows the flame upon us,
And delights in our glow.

Rabbi Vicki Hollander

The Blessed God

אֵל בָּרוּךְ גְּדוֹל דֵּעָה,
הֵכִין וּפָעַל זָהֱרֵי חַמָּה,
טוֹב יָצַר כָּבוֹד לִשְׁמוֹ,
מְאוֹרוֹת נָתַן סְבִיבוֹת עֻזּוֹ.
פִּנּוֹת צְבָאָיו קְדוֹשִׁים, רוֹמְמֵי שַׁדַּי,
תָּמִיד מְסַפְּרִים כְּבוֹד אֵל וּקְדֻשָּׁתוֹ.

The blessed God, great in knowledge,
Formed and made the suns' rays.
The Eternal One created it in goodness, a glory to God's name.
God set the lights of the skies rotating with divine power.
All the hosts of heaven praise the Almighty.
They continually declare God's glory and holiness.

אֵל בָּרוּךְ (*El Baruch*) is a poetic acrostic. An acrostic is a poem in which the author uses the letters of the alphabet to develop a theme or, in some cases, to sign his or her name. An example of an acrostic in English is: Consider And Respect Everyone.

The אֵל בָּרוּךְ was written by the eighth-century Jewish mystic who used the twenty-two letters of the Hebrew alphabet in their order from *alef* to *tav*. In doing so, the author cleverly reminds us that just as God is praised by all nature, so should God be praised with every letter and word known to the human mind. For there is no end of thanking God for the gifts of life.

AHAVAH RABBAH: DEEP LOVE

Ahavah Rabbah   אַהֲבָה רַבָּה

אַהֲבָה רַבָּה אֲהַבְתָּנוּ, יי אֱלֹהֵינוּ, חֶמְלָה גְדוֹלָה וִיתֵרָה
חָמַלְתָּ עָלֵינוּ. אָבִינוּ מַלְכֵּנוּ, בַּעֲבוּר אֲבוֹתֵינוּ וְאִמּוֹתֵינוּ
שֶׁבָּטְחוּ בְךָ וַתְּלַמְּדֵם חֻקֵּי חַיִּים, כֵּן תְּחָנֵּנוּ וּתְלַמְּדֵנוּ. אָבִינוּ,
הָאָב הָרַחֲמָן, הַמְרַחֵם, רַחֵם עָלֵינוּ וְתֵן בְּלִבֵּנוּ לְהָבִין
וּלְהַשְׂכִּיל, לִשְׁמֹעַ, לִלְמֹד וּלְלַמֵּד, לִשְׁמֹר וְלַעֲשׂוֹת וּלְקַיֵּם

אֶת־כָּל־דִּבְרֵי תַלְמוּד תּוֹרָתֶךָ בְּאַהֲבָה. וְהָאֵר עֵינֵינוּ
בְּתוֹרָתֶךָ, וְדַבֵּק לִבֵּנוּ בְּמִצְוֹתֶיךָ, וְיַחֵד לְבָבֵנוּ לְאַהֲבָה
וּלְיִרְאָה אֶת־שְׁמֶךָ. וְלֹא־נֵבוֹשׁ לְעוֹלָם וָעֶד, כִּי בְשֵׁם קָדְשְׁךָ
הַגָּדוֹל וְהַנּוֹרָא בָּטָחְנוּ. נָגִילָה וְנִשְׂמְחָה בִּישׁוּעָתֶךָ, כִּי אֵל
פּוֹעֵל יְשׁוּעוֹת אָתָּה, וּבָנוּ בָחַרְתָּ וְקֵרַבְתָּנוּ לְשִׁמְךָ הַגָּדוֹל
סֶלָה בֶּאֱמֶת, לְהוֹדוֹת לְךָ וּלְיַחֶדְךָ בְּאַהֲבָה.
בָּרוּךְ אַתָּה יְיָ, הַבּוֹחֵר בְּעַמּוֹ יִשְׂרָאֵל בְּאַהֲבָה.

Deep is Your love for us, abiding Your compassion. From of old we have put our trust in You, and You have taught us the laws of life. Be gracious now to us, that we may understand and fulfill the teachings in Your word.

Enlighten our eyes in Your Torah, that we may cling to Your mitzvot. Unite our hearts to love and revere Your name.

We trust in You and rejoice in Your saving power, for You are the Source of our help. You have called us and drawn us near to You in faithfulness.

Joyfully we lift up our voices and proclaim Your unity, O God. In love, You have called us to Your service.

COMMENTARY

The אַהֲבָה רַבָּה prayer takes its name from its first two Hebrew words. Its theme is love. It speaks of God's love for the Jewish people and of the people's devotion to God. Like the יוֹצֵר, the אַהֲבָה רַבָּה was composed during the existence of the Temple and was made a part of the Temple service by the Rabbis of the Great Assembly.

Love, God, Torah, and Israel

The highest expression of love is giving. When we give something that we prize and cherish to another person, we are giving more than an object; we are giving of ourselves and of our love.

Jewish tradition teaches that God, out of אַהֲבָה, chose to give the Torah to the people of Israel. And the people of Israel, in accepting the Torah, chose to live according to God's mitzvot. Notice that the first and last word of the אַהֲבָה רַבָּה prayer is אַהֲבָה, "love." In this way, the prayer reminds us of the loving relationship among God, Israel, and Torah.

What do you think Jewish tradition means when it speaks of God as loving and choosing Israel? Are Jews chosen for special privileges? Are they "superior" to others? Is that what being "chosen" or loved by God means?

According to the prophet Isaiah, "being chosen by God" was not a privilege but a task. The Jew was selected for special responsibilities. Speaking in the name of God, Isaiah said:

> But you, Israel, My servant...
> You whom I have taken hold of from the ends of the earth...
> And said unto you: "You are My servant;
> I have chosen you...."
> I, the Eternal One, have called you to righteousness,
> And taken you by the hand,
> And kept you; I have made you a covenant people,
> A light to the nations.
>
> Isaiah 41:8, 9; 42:6

What does Isaiah regard as Israel's task as a chosen people? What do you think it means to be a "servant" for God?

Some years ago, Zvi Kolitz discovered the story of Yossel Rakover, a Chasidic Jew who died fighting the Nazis in the Warsaw Ghetto in 1943. Kolitz was deeply moved by Rakover's fate and tried to reconstruct what the thoughts of a pious Jew might have been in the last hours of his life. His beautiful "Testament of Yossel Rakover" provides a valuable insight into what Jewish tradition teaches us about Israel's task as a chosen people or "servant" of God.

The Testament of Yossel Rakover

I am proud that I am a Jew, not in spite of the world's treatment of us, but precisely because of this treatment. I should be ashamed to belong to the people who spawned and raised the criminals who are responsible for the deeds that have been perpetuated against us.

I am proud to be a Jew because it is an art to be a Jew, because it is difficult to be a Jew. It is no art to be an Englishman, an American, or a Frenchman. It may be easier, more comfortable to be one of them, but not more honorable. Yes, it is an honor to be a Jew.

I believe that to be a Jew means to be a fighter, an everlasting swimmer against the turbulent, criminal human current. . . .

I am happy to belong to the unhappiest people of the world, whose precepts represent the loftiest and most beautiful of all morality and laws.

I believe that to be a Jew is an inborn trait. One is born a Jew exactly as one is born an artist. It is impossible to be released from being a Jew. That is our godly attribute that has made us a chosen people. Those who do not understand will never understand the higher meaning of our martyrdom. If I ever doubted that God once designated us as the chosen people, I would believe now that our tribulations have made us the chosen one.

What does Zvi Kolitz's "Testament of Yossel Rakover" reveal the task of the Jew to be? What can it teach us about the meaning of being a "chosen people"? What does the "Testament of Yossel Rakover" have in common with the prophet Isaiah's understanding of the Jewish people and its task?

Unite Our Hearts

In the אַהֲבָה רַבָּה prayer we have the words וְיַחֵד לְבָבֵנוּ (v'yacheid l'vaveinu), "and unite our hearts." What does this expression mean?

We know that in order for artists or athletes to perform with excellence, they must give total attention to their task. The same can be said about prayer or living as a Jew. It takes complete devotion, or what the Rabbis called כַּוָּנָה.

There may be another meaning for וְיַחֵד לְבָבֵנוּ. Often when we set out to do something that we believe is right, we meet obstacles. There may be people who laugh at us or call us foolish. It may be that in doing what we feel is right, we will have to stand up against many who disagree with us. At such times, we are called upon to act with added courage and determination. Perhaps that is what is meant by the prayer's words "unite our hearts to love and revere Your name."

The Purpose of the Mitzvot

The יוֹצֵר prayer praises God as the Creator of all the stars of heaven. For centuries, travelers have used the stars as guides for direction. Jewish tradition teaches us that there is another source of direction for human beings. The Torah provides us with ethical מִצְווֹת, commandments that help us to

The sage Rav once declared: "The mitzvot were given to the people Israel only in order that human beings should be purified through their fulfillment of them."

B'reishit Rabbah

51

understand the difference between good and evil, right and wrong. For instance, the Torah teaches us about how we should treat the poor and the sick, and what our responsibilities are to parents, strangers, and neighbors.

The Rabbis of the Talmud believed that "if there were no Torah, the world would not continue to exist" (BT *N'darim* 32a). What led them to such a conclusion?

Perhaps they thought it would be impossible to have a society without laws and people devoted to living by them. And, perhaps, because they loved the Torah so much for what it taught them about justice, truth, the sacredness of life, and peace, they could not conceive of a world existing without its wisdom.

The אַהֲבָה רַבָּה prayer speaks of the Jewish people's devotion to Torah. It emphasizes the special task of the Jew to study Torah and live according to its מִצְוֹת.

Five Prayers on the אַהֲבָה רַבָּה Theme

Eternal Love

אַהֲבַת עוֹלָם בֵּית יִשְׂרָאֵל עַמְּךָ אָהָבְתָּ. תּוֹרָה וּמִצְוֹת, חֻקִּים וּמִשְׁפָּטִים אוֹתָנוּ לִמַּדְתָּ. עַל־כֵּן, יי אֱלֹהֵינוּ, בְּשָׁכְבֵנוּ וּבְקוּמֵנוּ נָשִׂיחַ בְּחֻקֶּיךָ, וְנִשְׂמַח בְּדִבְרֵי תוֹרָתְךָ וּבְמִצְוֹתֶיךָ לְעוֹלָם וָעֶד. כִּי הֵם חַיֵּינוּ וְאֹרֶךְ יָמֵינוּ, וּבָהֶם נֶהְגֶּה יוֹמָם וָלָיְלָה. וְאַהֲבָתְךָ אַל־תָּסוּר מִמֶּנּוּ לְעוֹלָמִים! בָּרוּךְ אַתָּה יי, אוֹהֵב עַמּוֹ יִשְׂרָאֵל.

Unending is Your love for Your people, the House of Israel: Torah and mitzvot, laws and precepts have You taught us. Therefore, O God, when we lie down and when we rise up, we will meditate on Your laws and rejoice in Your Torah and mitzvot for ever. Day and night we will reflect on them, for they are our life and the length of our days. Then Your love shall never depart from our hearts! We praise You, O God: You love Your people Israel.

The אַהֲבַת עוֹלָם (*Ahavat Olam*) prayer is the evening version of the אַהֲבָה רַבָּה and was most likely composed by the same author or authors. Notice that its themes are parallel to those found in the אַהֲבָה רַבָּה.

CREATING WITH
KAVANAH

Themes:
a. Love of God for Israel.
b. The special tasks of the people of Israel.
c. The responsibility of being a Jew.
d. The challenge of doing מִצְוֹת with כַּוָּנָה.

You Were God

You were God
And we were Israel,
God alone
And lonely people,
Long ago.

You loved us a great love
And You taught us
How to respond to You.

Through Mitzvot
Recollections
Celebrations
Torah.

They are the light of our eyes
The uniqueness of our being.

In the joy of them
You have drawn us close to You.

In the truth of them
We have discovered You, the only One.

We are together still.

You respond to every people
In Your chosen way.
With Your love
You have chosen to respond to us.

With our love
We offer You our praise.

On Wings of Awe

We Are Loved

We are loved by an unending love.
We are embraced by arms that find us
even when we are hidden from ourselves.

We are touched by fingers that soothe us
even when we are too proud for soothing.
We are counseled by voices that guide us
even when we are too embittered to hear.
We are loved by an unending love.

We are supported by hands that uplift us
even in the midst of a fall.
We are urged on by eyes that meet us
even when we are too weak for meeting.
We are loved by an unending love.

Embraced, touched, soothed, and counseled...
ours are the arms, the fingers, the voices;
ours are the hands, the eyes, the smiles;
We are loved by an unending love.

Blessed are You, who loves Your people Israel.

Adapted from Rabbi M. Shapiro, "Unending Love"

Where Can We Find You?

O God, how can we know You? Where can we find You? We discover You in observing the beauty and order of nature. And we find You, O God, in the fulfillment of the mitzvot of Torah.

When we are moved to be loving to others, and to strive for truth, we discover You within us. When we are kind and give of what we have to those in need, we feel Your presence. And when we heal another person's hurt, or give comfort, we sense Your goodness, O God, at work in our lives.

We give thanks to You for the Torah which teaches us that we can find You in the fulfillment of Your mitzvot.

HJF

The Challenge of Torah

With love, O Eternal One our God, You have given the gift of Torah to the people of Israel. Through it our people has sought to bring human cooperation and peace to the world. Often they were called upon to sacrifice their comfort, safety, possessions, and even their lives in order to fulfill the mitzvot of Torah.

May we be worthy of the gifts of Torah and the devotion of our people. Help us to study Torah carefully and to apply its mitzvot to our lives. We praise You, O Eternal One, who in love has given us the responsibilities and challenges of Torah.

HJF

The Mitzvot of Torah

The אַהֲבָה רַבָּה and אַהֲבַת עוֹלָם, like many prayers within our prayer book and Jewish tradition, refer to the מִצְוֹת, the commandments of Torah. Just what are the מִצְוֹת?

According to the Rabbis there are 613 מִצְוֹת in the Torah. They are divided into two categories. Those that begin with the words "You shall not..." are called the "negative מִצְוֹת" because they tell us what we should not do. Those that begin with "You shall..." are called "positive מִצְוֹת," because they tell us what we ought to do. Most of the מִצְוֹת are found in Exodus, Leviticus, and Deuteronomy.

Jewish tradition also divides the מִצְוֹת into two other categories. There are the מִצְוֹת of ritual called מִצְוֹת בֵּין אָדָם לַמָּקוֹם (mitzvot bein adam lamakom), commandments between the individual and God. These מִצְוֹת deal with the Jewish holidays, Shabbat, religious practices, and what a Jew is allowed to eat. The other category is מִצְוֹת בֵּין אָדָם לְחֲבֵרוֹ (mitzvot bein adam l'chaveiro), commandments between the individual and other human beings. These are meant to help a person know the difference between right and wrong and live a just, truthful, and good life.

On the next two pages are some examples of the מִצְוֹת. You may want to compare and contrast them. After reading and discussing them, open your Bible to Leviticus, read chapter 19, and then try to distinguish which מִצְוֹת are בֵּין אָדָם לַמָּקוֹם and which are מִצְוֹת בֵּין אָדָם לְחֲבֵרוֹ.

Examples of מִצְוֹת בֵּין אָדָם לַמָּקוֹם

Shabbat

Remember the Shabbat day to keep it holy.

Exodus 20:8

Sukkot

You shall keep the Feast of Tabernacles [Sukkot] for seven days.

Deuteronomy 16:13

Pesach

Observe the month of Aviv, and keep the Passover unto the Eternal One your God.

Deuteronomy 16:1

Rosh HaShanah

In the seventh month, in the first day of the month, shall be a solemn rest unto you, a memorial proclaimed with the blast of horns, a holy convocation.

Leviticus 23:24

Yom Kippur

On the tenth day of the seventh month is the day of atonement; there shall be a holy convocation unto you, and you shall afflict your souls....

Leviticus 23:27

Food

These are the living things that you may eat among all the beasts that are on the earth. Whatever has a parted hoof, and is completely cloven-footed, and chews its cud—these you may eat.

Leviticus 11:2–3

The pig, because it has a parted hoof and is cloven-footed, but does not chew the cud—it is unclean for you. Of its flesh you may not eat.

Leviticus 11:7–8

Examples of מִצְווֹת בֵּין אָדָם לְחֲבֵרוֹ

Honor your father and your mother.

Exodus 20:12

You shall not murder.

Exodus 20:13

You shall not bear false witness.

Exodus 20:13

You shall not follow the majority to do evil.

Exodus 23:2

You shall not oppress the stranger.

Exodus 23:9

When you reap the harvest of your land, you shall not reap the corners of your field...you shall leave them for the poor and for the stranger.

Leviticus 19:9–10

You shall love your neighbor as yourself.

Leviticus 19:18

You shall have just balances and just weights.

Leviticus 19:36

You shall not force judgment; you shall not respect persons in judgment; neither shall you take a gift, for a gift blinds the eyes of the wise and perverts the words of the righteous.

Deuteronomy 16:19

You shall not remove your neighbor's landmark.

Deuteronomy 19:14

Do All This

We are teaching Torah daily by the way we solve problems, stand up for justice, take care of one another, protect the earth, put out love and kindness, persistence and forgiveness. The message is to do this as well as possible and to learn from our mistakes. That is how we make a holy Torah for today.

Rabbi Julie Greenberg

Are the מִצְווֹת Too Difficult?

Can a person live according to the מִצְווֹת, or are they too difficult or idealistic?

Someone must have asked Moses the same question, for the Torah contains his answer. Speaking to the people of Israel, he said:

> For this מִצְוָה that I command you this day is not too hard for you, neither is it far off. It is not in heaven, that you should say: "Who shall go up into heaven and bring it to us and make us hear it, that we may do it?" Neither is it beyond the sea, that you should say: "Who shall go over the sea for us and bring it to us and make us hear it, that we may do it?" But the word is very near to you; it is in your mouth and in your heart, that you may do it.
>
> Deuteronomy 30:11–14

What do you think of Moses' statement about the מִצְווֹת? Are any of the examples of מִצְווֹת too difficult or impossible to do? Are some more easy to perform than others? Why? The Rabbis of the Talmud summarize Moses' statement in the following way: "The מִצְווֹת were given that we might live by them" (*Tosefta Shabbat*). What do you think they meant by the phrase "live by them"?

Do Them Every Day with All Your Heart

The Rabbis loved to play with the meaning of numbers and words. They noticed that there were 365 negative מִצְווֹת and 248 positive מִצְווֹת. And so they taught:

> Moses was given 365 negative מִצְווֹת, which correspond to the 365 days of the year.
>
> And he was given 248 positive מִצְווֹת, which correspond to the 248 parts of the human body.
>
> This teaches that we should be doing the מִצְווֹת every day and with all our human powers.
>
> BT *Makot 23b–24a*

A Story

A man died and was brought before the Heavenly Court. His sins and good deeds (מִצְוֹת) were placed on the scales, and the sins far outweighed the good deeds. Suddenly a fur coat was piled on the scale containing the good deeds, and, this side becoming heavier, the man was sent to Paradise.

He said to the Angel who escorted him: "But I cannot understand why the fur coat was brought in."

The Angel replied: "One cold wintry night you traveled on a sled, and a poor man asked for a ride. You took him in, and, noticing his thin clothes, you placed your fur coat on him to give him warmth. This act of kindness more than offset your transgressions."

The Hasidic Anthology: Tales and Teachings of the Hasidim, ed. Louis I. Newman

A Lesson

Rabbi Y'hudah HaNasi, who was responsible for creating one of the first collections of Jewish law, the Mishnah, taught his students: "Be as careful to do an easy מִצְוָה as to do a difficult one. For you cannot know all of the consequences of doing a מִצְוָה" (*Pirkei Avot* 2:1). What are some of the small, seemingly unimportant things people have done for you that have meant much more than they might have imagined? How would you connect Rabbi Y'hudah's statement to the story above?

HANDS OF SERVICE

With the affairs of human beings, knowledge of truth must continually be renewed by ceaseless effort, if it is not to be lost.

It resembles a statue of marble which stands in the desert and is continually threatened with burial by the shifting sand.

The hands of service must ever be at work in order that the marble continue lastingly to shine in the sun.

Albert Einstein

How would you relate Albert Einstein's statement to the Jewish duty of doing mitzvot?

SH'MA: HEAR, O ISRAEL

Sh'ma   שְׁמַע

שְׁמַע יִשְׂרָאֵל: יהוה אֱלֹהֵינוּ, יהוה אֶחָד!

Hear O Israel: the Eternal One is our God, the Eternal God alone!

בָּרוּךְ שֵׁם כְּבוֹד מַלְכוּתוֹ לְעוֹלָם וָעֶד!

Blessed is God's glorious majesty for ever and ever!

59

COMMENTARY

Almost since the beginning of Jewish tradition, the שְׁמַע has been considered the most important statement of a Jew's belief in God. It was spoken daily in the prayers at the Temple, and the Rabbis included it in the morning and evening services of the synagogue. The שְׁמַע is taken from Deuteronomy 6:4.

Why has the שְׁמַע been considered so important in Jewish tradition? What meaning does it have that Jews throughout the centuries have lovingly repeated its words and have even died with them on their lips?

As God Is One, Humanity Is One

Ancient people believed in many gods. They worshiped stones, animals, stars, and, at times, their kings and queens. Because each people had its own gods, and often its own land, it considered itself separate and unrelated to the other peoples living near it.

With the birth of Judaism, a new idea of God was introduced to the world. Judaism taught that there was one God and that God was the Creator of everything—therefore, the Creator of every human being and all peoples.

This idea meant that no matter what a man or woman's language, or land, or nation was, he or she was related to all people. Since God was the Creator of all people, that meant that all were brothers and sisters.

The prophet Malachi stated the Jewish idea of one God and one interrelated humanity in the form of a question:

Have we not all one Source?
Has not one God created us?

Malachi 2:10

When we say the שְׁמַע, we affirm that just as God is one, so are all human beings united in one human family.

We Are Witnesses

שְׁמַע יִשְׂרָאֵל: יהוה אֱלֹהֵינוּ, יהוה אֶחָד!

Notice that the last letters of the first and last words of the שְׁמַע (the ע and the ד) are enlarged. It is the tradition to print them that way in the Torah and in many prayer books. When the ע and ד are brought together, they form the word עֵד (eid), which means "witness." The Rabbis teach that when we say the שְׁמַע, we remind ourselves that we are supposed to be witnesses for God.

What does it mean to be a "witness"? Witnesses give testimony in a court; that is, they tell the judge and jury what they have seen or heard. Witnesses take on a very important task because their testimony may determine what will happen to the person or matter on trial.

How can a person be a "witness for God"? In Jewish tradition, we are witnesses for God when we act according to the מִצְוֹת. For example, when we are helpful to a person in need because we know that we should "love our neighbor as ourself" (Leviticus 19:18), we are showing others the influence of God and the מִצְוֹת in our lives.

Each time we say the שְׁמַע and see the ע and ד, we should be reminded of our ethical responsibilities and of the sacred task we have to be witnesses of God.

A Danger?

What should receive our highest human loyalty? Our race? Gender? Nation? Religion? Family?

That, of course, is a difficult question. Jewish tradition would answer that we owe our highest allegiance to God. In the Ten Commandments we are told: "You shall have no other gods beside Me" (Exodus 20:3).

In ancient times human beings often worshiped a variety of gods. Among the Greeks there were gods for love, wisdom, truth, and mercy. People gave loyalty to whatever god meant the most to them. In modern times people have worshiped political leaders or given their total allegiance to the nation or to their possessions. Hitler asked for, and received, a worshipful loyalty from his people. To many of them, he became a god.

Jewish tradition has always taught that there was one God, that God was spiritual and not physical, and that human beings could experience God in a whole variety of ways. There are moments when we find God in the beauty and mystery of nature, or in the events and accomplishments of human history. There are other times when we encounter God's power in love and friendship, or when we are moved to reach out and help others.

The God of the universe, Judaism teaches, deserves the highest loyalty because God alone is the source of all that we experience in life. Allegiance to God is meant to prevent us from giving our highest loyalties to "other gods" like human beings, a nation, a political party, possessions, or the quest for fame.

WITNESSES?

You are My witnesses—declares Adonai—and I am God.

Isaiah 43:12

In the *P'sikta D'Rav Kahana*, Rabbi Shimon bar Yochai interpreted the above as follows:

When "you are My witnesses," then "I am God."

When you are not My witnesses, then I am—as it were—not God.

What could Rabbi Shimon bar Yochai have meant?

The sentence of the שְׁמַע was meant to warn Jews against the danger of worshiping "other gods" (אֱלֹהִים אֲחֵרִים). Students of Jewish tradition point out that this, too, is why the letters ע and ד were enlarged. If they were not, it would be easy to change the meaning of the שְׁמַע.

For example, the ע in the word שְׁמַע could be changed to an א, and the ד in the word אֶחָד could be changed to a ר. Instead of reading שְׁמַע (with the accent on the last syllable), "Hear, O Israel: the Eternal One is our God, the Eternal God alone [אֶחָד]," the sentence would read שֶׁמָּא (shèma, with the stress on the first syllable), "Perhaps, O Israel, the Eternal One our God is אַחֵר [acheir, 'another']." In order to make sure that such a distortion would never happen, the letters ע and ד were enlarged.

What does it mean to give (to a human being, a nation, a race, a god of mercy) total loyalty? Why is such allegiance dangerous? Look at Exodus, chapter 32. Why was the building and worship of the Golden Calf considered by the Torah to be such an evil? Look at I Samuel, chapter 8. Why does Samuel oppose the appointment of a king? What might his opposition have to do with the שְׁמַע and with the commandment "You shall have no other gods beside Me"?

A Tale of Terror

When the Crusaders reached Xanten, near the Rhine (Germany), in June 1096, the Jewish community was about to welcome Shabbat. Hearing the Crusaders approach and fearing the worst, Rabbi Moshe HaCohen called everyone in the community together.

He told them to have courage. He warned them that death was near. Together they ate the Shabbat meal and then concluded it with grace. After grace they added the following blessing:

Praised be You, O Eternal One our God, Ruler of the universe, who has made us holy with Your commandments and commanded us to make Your name sacred in public.

שְׁמַע יִשְׂרָאֵל: יהוה אֱלֹהֵינוּ, יהוה אֶחָד!

Hear, O Israel: the Eternal One is our God, the Eternal God alone!

Having concluded the שְׁמַע, they went to their synagogue, where they were murdered by the Crusaders. Their act of courage and faith was an act of קִדּוּשׁ הַשֵּׁם.

Kiddush HaShem—קִדּוּשׁ הַשֵּׁם

Kiddush HaShem means "making sacred God's name." How does a person "make sacred God's name"? Jewish tradition teaches that one who acts to bring honor, respect, or credit to the Jewish people or faith is performing an act of קִדּוּשׁ הַשֵּׁם. To give one's life in a time of persecution, as did the followers of Rabbi Moshe HaCohen, is to fulfill the highest demand of קִדּוּשׁ הַשֵּׁם.

The Talmud teaches us that קִדּוּשׁ הַשֵּׁם also extends to the Jews' relationship with non-Jews. A Jew should never do anything to a non-Jew that might provoke a false or bad impression of the moral standards of Judaism.

The following story about Rabbi Shimon ben Shetach, who was president of the Sanhedrin during the first century B.C.E., illustrates this lesson:

One day, the students of Rabbi Shimon ben Shetach joyfully announced to him that they had found a precious stone in the collar of the donkey he had just purchased from an Arab.

Rabbi Shimon said to them: "Return the precious stone to the Arab."

His students were surprised. "Why should it be returned? After all, you bought the donkey. It is yours!"

"I purchased the donkey," said Rabbi Shimon, "not the precious stone. Return it now to the Arab."

When they gave the stone to the Arab and explained to him what had happened and all that Rabbi Shimon had taught them, the Arab exclaimed: "Praised be the God of Shimon ben Shetach!"

D'varim Rabbah 3:5

Why was Rabbi Shimon's act considered by Jewish tradition as an act of קִדּוּשׁ הַשֵּׁם? Why did the Arab praise the God of Rabbi Shimon, rather than Rabbi Shimon himself?

Poem on the שְׁמַע Theme

Guardian of Israel

שׁוֹמֵר יִשְׂרָאֵל, שְׁמֹר שְׁאֵרִית יִשְׂרָאֵל,
וְאַל יֹאבַד יִשְׂרָאֵל, הָאוֹמְרִים שְׁמַע יִשְׂרָאֵל.
שׁוֹמֵר גּוֹי אֶחָד, שְׁמֹר שְׁאֵרִית עַם אֶחָד,
וְאַל יֹאבַד גּוֹי אֶחָד,
הַמְיַחֲדִים שְׁמָךְ, יְיָ אֱלֹהֵינוּ, יְיָ אֶחָד.

O Guardian of Israel, preserve the remnant of the people of Israel,
and let not Israel, the people who say "Hear, O Israel," be destroyed.
O Guardian of the one people, preserve the remnant of that one people,
and let not that one people who unify Your name with the words
"The Eternal One is our God, the Eternal God alone" be destroyed.

Many times in the history of our people, the words of the שְׁמַע were the last words spoken by those who died at the hands of cruel oppressors. The שׁוֹמֵר יִשְׂרָאֵל (Shomeir Yisrael) is a prayer and song of hope. It asks God to preserve and help Israel, the people who proclaim God's unity. Notice how the poet has incorporated the words of the שְׁמַע into the poem.

64

V'AHAVTA: YOU SHALL LOVE

V'ahavta   וְאָהַבְתָּ

וְאָהַבְתָּ אֵת יְהֹוָה אֱלֹהֶיךָ בְּכָל־לְבָבְךָ וּבְכָל־נַפְשְׁךָ
וּבְכָל־מְאֹדֶךָ: וְהָיוּ הַדְּבָרִים הָאֵלֶּה אֲשֶׁר אָנֹכִי מְצַוְּךָ הַיּוֹם
עַל־לְבָבֶךָ: וְשִׁנַּנְתָּם לְבָנֶיךָ וְדִבַּרְתָּ בָּם בְּשִׁבְתְּךָ בְּבֵיתֶךָ
וּבְלֶכְתְּךָ בַדֶּרֶךְ וּבְשָׁכְבְּךָ וּבְקוּמֶךָ: וּקְשַׁרְתָּם לְאוֹת עַל־יָדֶךָ
וְהָיוּ לְטֹטָפֹת בֵּין עֵינֶיךָ: וּכְתַבְתָּם עַל־מְזֻזוֹת בֵּיתֶךָ
וּבִשְׁעָרֶיךָ:

לְמַעַן תִּזְכְּרוּ וַעֲשִׂיתֶם אֶת־כָּל־מִצְוֹתָי וִהְיִיתֶם קְדֹשִׁים
לֵאלֹהֵיכֶם: אֲנִי יְהֹוָה אֱלֹהֵיכֶם אֲשֶׁר הוֹצֵאתִי אֶתְכֶם מֵאֶרֶץ
מִצְרַיִם לִהְיוֹת לָכֶם לֵאלֹהִים אֲנִי יְהֹוָה אֱלֹהֵיכֶם:

You shall love your Eternal God with all your heart, with all your mind, with all your being. Set these words, which I command you this day, upon your heart. Teach them faithfully to your children; speak of them in your home and on your way, when you lie down and when you rise up. Bind them as a sign upon your hand; let them be symbols before your eyes; inscribe them on the doorposts of your house, and on your gates.

Be mindful of all my mitzvot, and do them: so shall you consecrate yourselves to your God. I am your Eternal God who led you out of Egypt to be your God; I am your Eternal God.

COMMENTARY

In the Torah, the sentence of the שְׁמַע is followed by the paragraph that begins with the words: "You shall love your Eternal God...." This paragraph, Deuteronomy 6:4–9, along with Deuteronomy 11:13–21 and Numbers 15:37–41 make up the section of the service that has traditionally been known as the שְׁמַע. The words of the שְׁמַע are placed into the מְזוּזָה (mezuzah), placed upon the doorpost, and within the תְּפִלִּין (t'fillin), phylacteries, used in morning worship (except on Shabbat and holidays).

The theme of the וְאָהַבְתָּ paragraph is the love of God. What can we mean when we speak of "loving God"? How does a Jew demonstrate such love? An exploration of the וְאָהַבְתָּ paragraph can help us answer these questions.

You Shall Love

What do we mean by "love"? Love is the highest expression of the human spirit, and no explanation will ever fully define its power and meaning. When we consider what love means to each of us, we may think of sharing, giving, respecting, honoring, understanding, appreciating, and being deeply sensitive to the feelings of others.

It has been said that we cannot love another person until we love ourselves. If that is so, then perhaps it is also true that we cannot really love God until we love ourselves. After all, how can we begin to appreciate the complexities, wonders, and order of God's creation until we appreciate how complex and amazing are our bodies and our lives?

How do we achieve self-love? The great talmudic sage Rabbi Hillel once said: "If I am not for myself, who will be for me? But if I am only for myself, what am I? And if not now, when?" What do you think he meant by that statement? What does it have to do with self-love and the love of God?

With All Your Heart

We have already seen that the Rabbis enjoyed drawing lessons from the way in which words were spelled or written. In the case of the וְאָהַבְתָּ paragraph, they call attention to the word לְבָבְךָ (l'vavcha), "your heart." Usually the word לֵב (lev), "heart," is written with one ב. As we can see, it appears with two in the וְאָהַבְתָּ paragraph. Why?

Each person, the Rabbis explain, has two competing powers within. They are called יֵצֶר הַטּוֹב (yetzer hatov), "the power for goodness," and יֵצֶר הָרָע (yetzer hara), "the power for evil." Often these powers are at odds with one another. Each ב in the word לְבָבְךָ symbolizes one of these powers.

For example, when we see something we would very much like to possess and we are tempted to take it, we are feeling the יֵצֶר הָרָע. And when our conscience tells us that it is wrong to steal, that is our יֵצֶר הַטּוֹב speaking within us.

Our task, the Rabbis teach, is to let the יֵצֶר הַטּוֹב control and guide the יֵצֶר הָרָע. When we say the words "You shall love your Eternal God with all your heart," we remind ourselves that the love of God is achieved when we use all our powers for goodness to do the right thing and for the benefit of others.

With All Your Mind

The Sages who interpreted this phrase understood the word נֶפֶשׁ (nefesh), "mind" or "soul," to mean a person's life. During Roman oppression and the Middle Ages, many Jews died as martyrs rather than abandon Judaism or the Jewish people.

One of the most famous and powerful stories of loving God "with all your soul" tells about the death of Rabbi Akiva. Condemned to death by the Romans, this great Sage recited the *Sh'ma* even as he was being horribly tortured. His disciples asked, "How can you pray these words at this terrible time?" Rabbi Akiva replied: "All my life, the verse that says *'b'chol nafsh'cha'* has troubled me—it means to love God with all your soul, even if you must give up your soul. I prayed always to be able to fulfill this, and now I can!"

To die for one's faith, as we have already seen, is called קִדּוּשׁ הַשֵּׁם, "the making sacred of God's name." The words "with all your soul" recall the bravery of those who gave their נֶפֶשׁ in the name of Jewish dignity and for the cause of human freedom.

When we think about the meaning of the words "with all your soul," we are challenged with a question. Does being a Jew mean so much to us that we could love God with all our soul the way our Jewish ancestors did in the past?

With All Your Being

The Rabbis teach that "being or might" means a person's material possessions—money, property, all that one possess. What can it mean to love God with your money and property?

The *Zohar*, a book written and studied by Jewish mystics, gives us one answer to think about: "How does one love the Eternal One? By surrounding oneself with kindness on every side and by doing kind deeds for all without sparing one's strength or one's property."

Set These Words, Which I Command You This Day, upon Your Heart

By "these words" is meant not only the שְׁמַע, but the Ten Commandments and all of the מִצְוֹת of the Torah.

Teach Them Faithfully to Your Children

The love of Judaism comes from a knowledge and experience of Torah. A favorite statement of Jewish tradition is "The study of Torah equals everything else."

Judaism has always stressed the importance of education. And it has also stressed the teaching role and responsibilities of parents. The father and mother, through their words and example, have the chief influence upon a child's development. In recognition of this, Jewish tradition counsels parents: "Provide your children with a clear, and not confused or stammering, knowledge of the duties and teachings of Torah" *(Sifrei)*.

What would you consider the Jewish responsibilities of parents today? You might want to investigate this question by having some students make up a list; some others ask their parents; and, perhaps, some others question the rabbi. Afterwards, compare the different lists and discuss them.

What do you think of the following observation by Rabbi Morris Adler?

Judaism begins at home.... It begins in homes where Judaism lives in the atmosphere and is integrated in the normal pattern of daily life. It begins in homes where the Jewish words re-echo, where the Jewish book is honored, and the Jewish song is heard. It begins in homes where the child sees and participates in symbols and rites that link him to a people and culture. It begins in homes where the Jewish ceremonial object is visible. It begins in the home where into the deepest layers of a child's developing personality are woven strands of love for and devotion to the life of the Jewish community.

Modern Treasury of Jewish Thoughts

Speak of Them

One interpretation of this phrase is as follows: "Make them [the מִצְוֹת] your most important guide and not something to which you pay lip service. Make sure you apply them to all your business dealings" *(Sifrei)*.

Another interpretation reminds us that words are easily spoken—especially words of anger, criticism, flattery, and exaggeration.

The Chasidic rabbi known as the Koretzer taught that דבר serves as a root for both "speak" and "control." The phrase וְדִבַּרְתָּ בָּם (v'dibarta bam), "speak of them," teaches us that we must be careful to control the words of our mouth so that we do not speak in anger, falsehood, and flattery.

Bind Them as a Sign upon Your Hand; Let Them Be Symbols before Your Eyes

The command to wear תְּפִלִּין is based on four separate places in the Torah: Exodus 13:1–10, 11–16; Deuteronomy 6:4–9; 11:13–21. One box is placed on the weak arm facing the heart (i.e., the left arm if you are right-handed), and the other is placed on the center of the forehead.

Inscribe Them on the Doorposts of Your House, and on Your Gates

This phrase was interpreted as the command to place a מְזוּזָה, containing the first two paragraphs of the שְׁמַע, upon the doorposts. According to tradition, the מְזוּזָה is fixed on the right-hand doorpost as one enters a synagogue, house, or room.

Be Mindful of All My Mitzvot, and Be Holy to Your God (Numbers 15:40)

What can it mean to "be holy" to your God?

The word קְדוֹשִׁים (k'doshim), "holy," also means different, distinct, special, and sacred. What do these definitions have in common? The word for a marriage ceremony in Jewish tradition is קִדּוּשִׁין (kiddushin). Can you guess why the two might be related?

In Leviticus 19:2, we find the commandment קְדוֹשִׁים תִּהְיוּ (K'doshim tih'yu), "You shall be holy."

Look at chapter 19 of Leviticus and try to figure out what קְדוֹשִׁים means there.

The Rabbis interpreted the commandment to "be holy" in the following way: "God says: 'If you observe My מִצְווֹת then you will be holy.'" What do you suppose they meant?

Love of God

וְאָהַבְתָּ אֵת יְהֹוָה אֱלֹהֶיךָ

We love God when we strive for right over wrong, truth over falsehood, peace instead of quarreling.

בְּכָל־לְבָבְךָ

We love with full hearts when we learn to appreciate ourselves—our talents and abilities.

וּבְכָל־נַפְשְׁךָ

We love with our souls when we are ready to sacrifice for what we believe.

וּבְכָל־מְאֹדֶךָ

We love with our might when we are willing to share what we have with others.

לְמַעַן תִּזְכְּרוּ וַעֲשִׂיתֶם אֶת־כָּל־מִצְוֹתָי

We love God when the doing of the מִצְוֹת leads us to love others and to work for a better world.

G'ULAH: REDEMPTION

G'ulah   גְּאוּלָה

אֱמֶת וְיַצִּיב וְיָשָׁר וְקַיָּם וְטוֹב וְיָפֶה הַדָּבָר הַזֶּה עָלֵינוּ לְעוֹלָם וָעֶד.

True and enduring, correct and forever, good and beautiful is Your eternal Torah upon us.

מִמִּצְרַיִם גְּאַלְתָּנוּ, יי אֱלֹהֵינוּ, וּמִבֵּית עֲבָדִים פְּדִיתָנוּ. מֹשֶׁה וּמִרְיָם וּבְנֵי יִשְׂרָאֵל לְךָ עָנוּ שִׁירָה בְּשִׂמְחָה רַבָּה, וְאָמְרוּ כֻלָּם:

From Egypt You liberated us. From the house of bondage You freed us. Moses, Miriam, and the children of Israel responded to You with a song of great joy. Together they sang:

CREATING WITH
KAVANAH

Themes:

a. Love of God means loving oneself and other human beings.

b. Love of self means learning to let our powers for goodness and truth direct our actions.

c. Love of God for the Jew means living in such a way that we are witness to the highest in our ethical and religious traditions.

d. Love of God means giving of what we possess—sharing generously with others.

e. Love of God means doing all we can to transmit our heritage from one generation to the next.

f. Love of God means controlling our tendency to exaggerate or misuse words.

g. Love of God means seeking to make our lives sacred through the fulfillment of מִצְוֹת.

Holiness is not freely given. It is the result of devotion, striving, and effort.

When Jews seek to fulfill each מִצְוָה with love and care, they are on the way to holiness.

מִי־כָמֹכָה בָּאֵלִם, יהוה? מִי כָּמֹכָה, נֶאְדָּר בַּקֹּדֶשׁ, נוֹרָא
תְהִלֹּת, עֹשֵׂה פֶלֶא?
שִׁירָה חֲדָשָׁה שִׁבְּחוּ גְאוּלִים לְשִׁמְךָ עַל־שְׂפַת הַיָּם;
יַחַד כֻּלָּם הוֹדוּ וְהִמְלִיכוּ וְאָמְרוּ:
יהוה יִמְלֹךְ לְעֹלָם וָעֶד.

Who is like You, Eternal One, among the gods that are
worshiped? Who is like You, majestic in holiness, awesome in
splendor, doing wonders?
A new song the redeemed sang to Your name. At the shore of
the sea, saved from destruction, they proclaimed Your sovereign
power:
"The Eternal One will reign for ever and ever!"

COMMENTARY

This prayer, closing the section of the שְׁמַע, is known as גְּאוּלָה (G'ulah),
"Redemption." The word "redemption" means deliver or save. The theme of
our prayer is the redemption of Israel from Egyptian slavery.

History, as we have noted before, plays a significant role in Jewish
prayer. Jews see God as a power at work in the events of individuals and
nations. The first sentence of the Ten Commandments declares:

I am the Eternal One, your God, who brought you out of the land of
Egypt, out of the house of bondage.

Exodus 20:2

The Exodus from Egypt is one of the most important events in all of
Jewish history. After four hundred years of slavery, our ancestors experienced
God's love and God's redeeming power. The prayer *Mi Chamocha* comes
directly from the Torah. It is part of the joyful song that the Israelites sang
after God had split the Red Sea and brought them to freedom. According to
Jewish legend, God actually appeared to the Israelites at this incredible
moment. Even babies who had not yet been born were miraculously able to
look up and behold God's presence!

In Jewish tradition, the first exodus from oppression became a symbol for
freedom from all slaveries and hardships. When Jews recalled the Exodus

71

from Egypt in their prayers, they remembered all the redemptions of their past. They recalled the bitter oppressions by the Babylonians, the Greeks, the Romans, the Crusaders, and all the other nations who had cruelly persecuted them.

When they sang מִי־כָמֹכָה בָּאֵלִם (Mi chamochah ba-elim?), "Who is like You among the gods that are worshiped?" they expressed the hope for the day when all men and women would live in freedom, security, and dignity. In the Second Book of Maccabees, we find a beautiful prayer for גְּאוּלָה, written perhaps by one of those who fought for Jewish freedom during the Maccabean revolt:

> O Eternal One, gather together our scattered people. Set at liberty those who are in slavery. Look upon those who are despised and let the nations know that You are God.
>
> II Maccabees 1:27–28

All Kinds of Slavery

While the word "slavery" might make us think first of the Israelites' slavery in Egypt or the enslavement of African Americans in the South, there are all kinds of slavery. It is slavery when people are not allowed free speech or when they are denied the right to worship as they wish by oppressive governments. Poverty and horrible living conditions are forms of slavery. And we can be slaves to bad habits or to fear when it makes us afraid to say what we really feel or think.

Can you think of other examples of slavery? What about the plight of minorities, the condition of women, some relationships between husband and wife, or between children and parents? Would you consider these forms of slavery?

Moses Maimonides, the great Jewish medieval philosopher, once wrote: "We naturally like what we have become accustomed to....This is one of the causes that prevents people from finding the truth." Would you agree with Maimonides? Can you think of illustrations in your life that prove his conclusion?

A Chasidic teacher once told his students: "Habit is a thief!" What did he mean? Is habit a form of self-oppression?

There are those who would argue that the pursuit of wealth is a form of slavery. Would you agree? The Mishnah asks the question: "Who is rich?" Then it gives this answer: "Those who are happy with their portion." Is that really an answer to the question? How would you answer it?

TWO VIEWS OF SLAVERY

The person who lives by a waterfall is hardly disturbed by its roar.
Judah Moscato

The real slavery of Israel in Egypt was that they had learned to endure it.
Rabbi Simchah Bunam

How are these two views related? Is there a connection between them and the following from BT Yoma 86b: "A sin repeated seems permitted"?

Expressing Joy and Hope

As we have learned, the prayer *Mi Chamocha* is part of the song of thanksgiving sung by the Israelites after they crossed the Red Sea. The whole song can be found in Exodus 15.

After singing, Miriam took a timbrel, an instrument similar to a tambourine, and led the women in a joyful dance of celebration. In recent years, many prayers and poems have been composed to honor Miriam and her way of praising God with dance and music.

Words are not the only way to pray. Our prayers can be expressed through singing, dancing, playing an instrument, or through the silence of meditation. Why not try some of these forms with the גְּאוּלָה prayer?

CREATING WITH *KAVANAH*

Themes:
a. God works through history toward human freedom.
b. Slavery can be the result of fear, poverty, or habit.
c. Thanksgiving, hope, and the quest for freedom can be expressed in prayer through dance, song, and other creative forms.

73

Five Readings on the גְּאוּלָה Theme

At the Shores

At the shores of the Red Sea, Miriam took up her timbrel and sang her song: a song of praise to God. With confidence and love, she led our ancestors through their fear and hesitation, until all hands were joined, all voices raised in hymn and thanksgiving. May her example lead us, too; and may her song soon grow to be truly ours:

The song of women and men joined in understanding and respect.

The song of God's miracles: an earth protected and cherished; a gift for our children and generations to come.

The song of a land once ravished by war, now quiet and content; her soldiers home, to leave no more.

The song of a world redeemed: the song of peace.

Rabbi Elyse Goldstein

Help Us to Be Free

Slavery is not only a problem of the past. Modern men and women can be slaves.

When we think only of ourselves, we are slaves to selfishness.

When we are hateful to others because of their color or creed, we are slaves to prejudice.

When we always crave what others have, we are slaves to greed.

When we spread lying words about others, we are slaves to falsehood.

When we always have to be right, or the winner, we are slaves to false pride.

When we are afraid to speak out against something we know is wrong, we are slaves to fear.

O Eternal One our God, help us to be free.

HJF

THE DIVINE SPIRIT

This ancient tale of wonder underscores the sense of daily miracle in our lives: According to the midrash, the sea did not split until one Israelite, Nachshon ben Amminadav, had the courage to walk upright into the water. Perhaps it was the divine spirit in Nachshon, rather than the magic of Moses' wand, that caused the sea to split.

Arthur Green

What does this quote teach us about the partnership between God and humanity? Why is this partnership important when we ask God to end slavery and redeem the oppressed?

The Treasures of Our Faith

[According to the Torah, Moses brought Joseph's bones with the Israelites out of Egypt.]

The bones of Joseph,
Tenderly transported step by step for forty years
As our ancestors crossed the desert from slavery into freedom.
The bones were remnants of our treasured foundation.
Israel was the hope of the future.
We nurtured our roots as we carried those bones.
We grasped for the future as we stood at Sinai.
Scared
Awed
Fearful
Inspired
We learned that the treasures of our faith
Flourish when we connect our sacred traditions, the vessels we carry,
with our future aspirations, the vessels we seek.
And our bodies fill with Divine soul, today singing the words of both yesterday and of tomorrow.

Rabbi Zachary R. Shapiro

A New Translation

Let us bless the source of life,
source of faith and daring,
wellspring of new song
and the courage to mend.

Marcia Falk, "Blessing of Redemption"

Our People Has Suffered

[The צוּר יִשְׂרָאֵל (*Tzur Yisrael*) prayer below is frequently included in the גְּאוּלָה as a way of asking God and reminding Jews to rescue those who are still oppressed and yearning to be free.]

Our people has suffered from cruel hate and oppression.
> So teach us not to hate our fellow human beings.

Pharaoh, Haman, Antiochus, and Hitler—all sought to destroy us.
> So teach us to treasure our faith and live it proudly.

Even today there are people and nations who preach anti-Semitism and who are slaves to the sickness of prejudice.

צוּר יִשְׂרָאֵל, קוּמָה בְּעֶזְרַת יִשְׂרָאֵל,
וּפְדֵה כִנְאֻמֶךָ יְהוּדָה וְיִשְׂרָאֵל.
גֹּאֲלֵנוּ, יי צְבָאוֹת שְׁמוֹ, קְדוֹשׁ יִשְׂרָאֵל.
בָּרוּךְ אַתָּה יי, גָּאַל יִשְׂרָאֵל.

O Rock of Israel, come to Israel's help. Our Redeemer is God Most High, the Holy One of Israel. We praise You, O God, Redeemer of Israel.

HJF

עֲמִידָה

The *Amidah*

The Shabbat *Amidah*

On the *Amidah*

As human beings we have a variety of concerns, feelings, and problems. Some of them we like to share with those we love; others we prefer to keep private. Jewish prayer makes room for both our personal meditations and the concerns we want to share with the community. Perhaps the most beautiful example of the combination of private and community prayer is found in the section of worship known as the עֲמִידָה (Amidah).

The word עֲמִידָה means "standing," and it describes the way in which its prayers are recited. Usually, in a traditional synagogue, the congregation stands and reads the עֲמִידָה in silence. Afterwards, the חַזָּן (chazan), "cantor" or "leader," repeats the prayers. The Talmud informs us that the original reason for the repetition was for those who could not read. The Rabbis wanted everyone to feel included in the congregation.

שְׁמוֹנֶה־עֶשְׂרֵה and תְּפִלָּה

There are two other names by which the עֲמִידָה is known. It is known as the שְׁמוֹנֶה־עֶשְׂרֵה (Sh'moneh Esreih), "Eighteen," because it was originally composed of eighteen different blessings. It is also called תְּפִלָּה (T'filah), "Prayer," because it was considered the heart of Jewish worship.

After the destruction of the Second Temple (70 C.E.), the Jewish people suffered bitter persecution at the hands of the Romans. During the second century C.E., another prayer was added to the עֲמִידָה. It was called מַכְנִיעַ זֵדִים (Machnia Zeidim), "Humbling the Arrogant" (see page 90). Since that time, there have been nineteen blessings in the שְׁמוֹנֶה־עֶשְׂרֵה with a personal meditation, אֱלֹהַי נְצוֹר (Elohai N'tzor), added in the fourth century C.E.

Who Wrote the עֲמִידָה? AMIDAH

We are not sure who composed all of the prayers that make up the עֲמִידָה. According to tradition, the עֲמִידָה was written by the Rabbis of the Great Assembly and made an official part of Jewish worship by Rabban Gamliel, the head of the academy at Yavneh in about 100 C.E. For nearly 2,000 years, then, the עֲמִידָה has been recited by Jews in synagogues and in private meditation.

There are two traditional forms of the עֲמִידָה. There is the daily עֲמִידָה and the special Shabbat and holiday עֲמִידָה. The latter is called

תְּפִלַּת שֶׁבַע (T'filat Sheva) because it contains seven prayers. The תְּפִלַּת שֶׁבַע is composed of the first three prayers of the daily עֲמִידָה, a special prayer for Shabbat or a holiday called קְדוּשַׁת הַיּוֹם (K'dushat HaYom), and then the last three prayers of the daily עֲמִידָה. See the diagram below for comparison.

We are told that the Rabbis instituted the shorter תְּפִלַּת שֶׁבַע because they did not think that the middle thirteen prayers of the עֲמִידָה were appropriate to the mood and meaning of Shabbat and the holidays. The middle thirteen prayers, the Rabbis thought, reminded us of all of our needs and problems. On Shabbat and the holidays, we should be filled with joy, not the worries or problems of the weekday.

Since *B'chol L'vavcha* is meant for use on Shabbat, you will find the whole Shabbat עֲמִידָה with commentary and additional prayers starting on page 101. On the next few pages is a description of each of the middle thirteen prayers of the daily עֲמִידָה. Having studied them, you may wish to use them, or their themes, in the creation of some of your own עֲמִידָה prayers.

The Daily *Amidah* שְׁמוֹנֶה-עֶשְׂרֵה		The Shabbat and Holiday *Amidah* תְּפִלַּת שֶׁבַע	
Avot	אָבוֹת	Avot	אָבוֹת
G'vurot	גְּבוּרוֹת	G'vurot	גְּבוּרוֹת
K'dushah	קְדוּשָׁה	K'dushah	קְדוּשָׁה
Binah	בִּינָה		
T'shuvah	תְּשׁוּבָה		
S'lichah	סְלִיחָה		
G'ulah	גְּאוּלָה		
R'fuah	רְפוּאָה		
Birkat HaShanim	בִּרְכַּת הַשָּׁנִים		
Kibbutz Galuyot	קִבּוּץ גָּלֻיּוֹת	K'dushat HaYom	קְדוּשַׁת הַיּוֹם
Tzedakah Umishpat	צְדָקָה וּמִשְׁפָּט		
Machnia Zeidim	מַכְנִיעַ זֵדִים		
Al HaTzaddikim	עַל הַצַּדִּיקִים		
Boneih Y'rushalayim	בּוֹנֵה יְרוּשָׁלַיִם		
Keren Y'shuah	קֶרֶן יְשׁוּעָה		
Shomei-a T'filah	שׁוֹמֵעַ תְּפִלָּה		
Avodah	עֲבוֹדָה	Avodah	עֲבוֹדָה
Hodaah	הוֹדָאָה	Hodaah	הוֹדָאָה
Birkat Shalom	בִּרְכַּת שָׁלוֹם	Birkat Shalom	בִּרְכַּת שָׁלוֹם
*Elohai Netzor	אֱלֹהַי נְצוֹר	*Elohai Netzor	אֱלֹהַי נְצוֹר

*See Commentary, page 160.

THE DAILY *AMIDAH*
THE MIDDLE THIRTEEN PRAYERS

Binah בִּינָה Wisdom

אַתָּה חוֹנֵן לְאָדָם דַּעַת וּמְלַמֵּד לֶאֱנוֹשׁ בִּינָה. חָנֵּנוּ מֵאִתְּךָ דֵּעָה, בִּינָה וְהַשְׂכֵּל. בָּרוּךְ אַתָּה יי, חוֹנֵן הַדָּעַת.

By Your grace we have the power to gain knowledge and to learn wisdom. Favor us with knowledge, wisdom, and insight, for You are their Source. We praise You, O God, gracious Giver of knowledge.

Study and the pursuit of knowledge have always been considered extremely important within Jewish life. Achad Ha-Am, the modern Jewish essayist, once wrote: "Learning, learning, learning—that is the secret of Jewish survival."

In the complicated modern world we are often overwhelmed by the number of facts and things we must know. Yet, as some philosophers have pointed out, there is a difference between knowing many facts and possessing wisdom. What do you think that difference is? How would you define בִּינָה?

In Kohelet (Ecclesiastes), the biblical philosopher wrote: "One who increases knowledge increases sorrow." What does this mean? Would you agree or disagree?

On בִּינָה

One loves God only by virtue of knowledge, and the degree of love corresponds to the degree of knowledge.
Moses Maimonides

Acquire the habit of saying "I do not know," lest you be led to lie.
BT *B'rachot* 4a

When you do not know, do not be ashamed to admit it.
Derech Eretz 1:22

You must learn to know others in order to know yourself.
Ludwig Boerne

To know a person you must ride in the same coach with that person.
Yiddish proverb

80

T'shuvah תְּשׁוּבָה Repentance

הֲשִׁיבֵנוּ אָבִינוּ לְתוֹרָתֶךָ, וְקָרְבֵנוּ מַלְכֵּנוּ לַעֲבוֹדָתֶךָ, וְהַחֲזִירֵנוּ בִּתְשׁוּבָה שְׁלֵמָה לְפָנֶיךָ. בָּרוּךְ אַתָּה יי, הָרוֹצֶה בִּתְשׁוּבָה.

Help us, our Creator, to return to Your Teaching; draw us near, our Sovereign, to Your service; and bring us back into Your presence in perfect repentance. We praise You, O God: You delight in repentance.

All of us make mistakes and do things for which we are sorry. תְּשׁוּבָה, "repentance," is taken from the Hebrew word שׁוּב (shuv), which means "return."

When we have done something wrong and realize it, our duty is to *return* and seek to correct our mistake. That turning, in Jewish tradition, is called תְּשׁוּבָה.

The Rabbis teach that "תְּשׁוּבָה makes a person a new creature" and that תְּשׁוּבָה is great because "it brings healing into the world" (*Midrash T'hillim* 18a and BT *Yoma* 86a). What do you think the Rabbis meant by those statements? Compare them with those in the section "On תְּשׁוּבָה."

In the year 1180, Moses Maimonides writes that "תְּשׁוּבָה means that the sinner forsakes his sins, casts them out of his mind, seeks forgiveness from those he has wronged, and pledges in his heart to sin no more" (*Misheh Torah, T'shuvah,* 2.2). What do you think of this definition of תְּשׁוּבָה? Is it too difficult? If you had done something wrong, how would you make תְּשׁוּבָה?

On תְּשׁוּבָה

If one says, I will sin again and repent again, that person will have no opportunity to repent.
JT Yoma 8:9

Repentance is a fierce battle with the heart.
Orot Tzaddikim

The test of repentance is refraining from sin on two occasions when the same temptation returns.
BT Yoma 86b

Great is repentance, for it turns sins into incentives for right conduct.
BT Yoma 86b

S'lichah סְלִיחָה Forgiveness

סְלַח־לָנוּ אָבִינוּ כִּי חָטָאנוּ, מְחַל־לָנוּ מַלְכֵּנוּ כִּי פָשָׁעְנוּ, כִּי מוֹחֵל וְסוֹלֵחַ אֶתָּה. בָּרוּךְ אַתָּה יי, חַנּוּן הַמַּרְבֶּה לִסְלוֹחַ.

Forgive us, our Creator, for we have sinned; pardon us, our Sovereign, for we have transgressed; for You are One who pardons and forgives. We praise You, O God, gracious and quick to forgive.

Rabbi Eleazer ben Judah taught his students that "the most beautiful thing a person can do is to forgive." And the sage Rabah taught that "the person who forgives...will be forgiven" (BT *Yoma* 23a).

We have already noted that Jewish tradition challenges us to imitate God. Our prayers for סְלִיחָה remind us that God is "gracious and quick to forgive." They challenge us to be forgiving in our relationships with others.

סְלִיחָה is not an easy matter to achieve. It takes courage to admit that we have been wrong or have hurt another person—and then to ask him or her for forgiveness. Nor is it any easier when we have been harmed by another, or angered by someone's insensitivity, to grant forgiveness.

Why do you think סְלִיחָה is so difficult for us to achieve? In what way might this prayer help achieve סְלִיחָה more easily in our behavior with others?

What do you think the Rabbis meant by the following statement about סְלִיחָה? "Whoever, instead of forgiving, takes vengeance or bears a grudge acts like one who, having cut one's hand while handling a knife, avenges oneself by stabbing the other hand."

G'ulah גְּאוּלָה Redemption

רְאֵה בְעָנְיֵנוּ וְרִיבָה רִיבֵנוּ, וּגְאָלֵנוּ מְהֵרָה לְמַעַן שְׁמֶךָ, כִּי גוֹאֵל חָזָק אָתָּה. בָּרוּךְ אַתָּה יי, גּוֹאֵל יִשְׂרָאֵל.

Look upon our affliction and help us in our need; O mighty Redeemer, redeem us speedily for Your name's sake. We praise You, O God, Redeemer of Israel.

It is thought that this prayer was written during the time of the Maccabees, when Jews were being persecuted by Antiochus.

Notice that the next to last word is גוֹאֵל (Go-eil), "Redeemer," and that the prayer calls upon God to help us.

Do you think God can help us, in difficult times, with our problems?

In situations of distress, it is natural for us to reach out for help. At times we need courage and determination. At other moments we require renewed strength.

Sometimes that renewal can come from our knowledge of history. For example, knowing that our people has survived storms of hate and persecution may give us courage to endure the difficulties that face us. It may reaffirm our faith in God as a source of גְּאוּלָה and as a power at work in history for goodness, truth, and peace.

Can you think of examples from Jewish history that might provide you with courage in a time of difficulty? Draw up a list, and share your ideas with others in your discussion group. Are there other sources, besides human history, from which we might derive faith or strength in times of distress?

> *After escaping from Egyptian slavery, the Torah tells us that Moses, Miriam, and the Israelites sang:*
>
> Who is like You, O Eternal One,
>   among the mighty;
> Who is like You,
>   majestic in holiness....
> In Your love You lead
>   the people You redeemed;
> In Your strength You
>   guide them to Your holy abode.
>
> Exodus 15:11–13

R'fuah רְפוּאָה Healing

רְפָאֵנוּ יְיָ וְנֵרָפֵא. הוֹשִׁיעֵנוּ וְנִוָּשֵׁעָה. כִּי תְהִלָּתֵנוּ אָתָּה. וְהַעֲלֵה רְפוּאָה שְׁלֵמָה לְכָל מַכּוֹתֵינוּ. כִּי אֵל מֶלֶךְ רוֹפֵא נֶאֱמָן וְרַחֲמָן אָתָּה. בָּרוּךְ אַתָּה יְיָ, רוֹפֵא חוֹלֵי עַמּוֹ יִשְׂרָאֵל.

Heal us, Eternal God, and we shall be cured. Save us and we shall be saved. For You are worthy of our praise. Grant complete healing to all our sicknesses, for You are a faithful and merciful healer. We praise You, O God, Healer of the sick of the people Israel.

83

Sickness and disease frightens all of us. Our prayer for רְפוּאָה, "healing," is a natural expression of our human need in times of sickness and pain. Its words speak of God as a power at work in the universe for healing and health. Do you think that makes sense? In what ways might we think of God as a source of healing or health?

The healing of a wound or overcoming of a sickness is the result of marvelous powers at work in our bodies. Were it not for these healing powers, life would be impossible and filled with constant, unbearable tragedy. In what ways might the healing powers in our bodies be a part of God's power to heal?

Bikur Cholim and Healing

Often, worshipers pause at this place in the עֲמִידָה to offer a special prayer for someone who is suffering from illness.

Whoever visits the sick helps them to recover.
BT *N'darim* 40a

The sages of the Talmud considered בִּקּוּר חוֹלִים *(bikur cholim)*, "visiting of the sick," to be a מִצְוָה of great importance. Rabbi Eleazar taught: "Do not forget to visit the sick, for you will be loved for it" (BT *N'darim* 41a). And Rabbi Akiva once observed: "Whoever does not visit the sick is like a murderer!" (BT *N'darim* 40a). What do you think Rabbis Eleazar and Akiva meant? How might visiting a sick friend, a loved one, or the aged be helpful to them? In what ways might it contribute to their cure?

In some Jewish communities there are *bikur cholim* groups. Their task is to visit those who are sick and in need of friendship and concern. If your congregation does not currently sponsor such a group, they may wish to consider establishing one.

For Jews Only?

In the traditional version of this prayer, God is praised as "Healer of the sick of the people Israel." Is it possible that those who composed this prayer thought that God only took care of the needs of Jews? Why did the prayer not end "Healer of the sick," as the Reform version does?

It could be that, since the congregation was Jewish, the concern of the worshiper was turned exclusively to the Jewish people. There are many times when we limit our prayers to our immediate family or to the group in which we find ourselves. Do you think such prayers are selfish or narrow? How would you prefer to end the רְפוּאָה prayer? Can you think of any other reasons why the traditional רְפוּאָה prayer ends with the words "Healer of the sick of the people Israel" and why the Reform version ends as it does?

Birkat HaShanim בִּרְכַּת הַשָּׁנִים Blessing for the Years

בָּרֵךְ עָלֵינוּ, יי אֱלֹהֵינוּ, אֶת־הַשָּׁנָה הַזֹּאת וְאֶת־כָּל־מִינֵי תְבוּאָתָהּ לְטוֹבָה. וְתֵן בְּרָכָה עַל־פְּנֵי הָאֲדָמָה, וְשַׂבְּעֵנוּ מִטּוּבֶךָ. בָּרוּךְ אַתָּה יי, מְבָרֵךְ הַשָּׁנִים.

Bless this year for us, Eternal God: may its produce bring us well-being. Bestow Your blessing on the earth, that all Your children may share its abundance in peace. We praise You, O God, for You bless earth's seasons from year to year.

The בִּרְכַּת הַשָּׁנִים prayer praises God for the bounty of nature. It reminds us that we depend on nature for our survival. Is it really necessary for us to be reminded of such an obvious fact? What might be the connection between this prayer and the blessing said before we eat?

A Tale

The Kobriner Rebbe once turned to his followers and asked: "Do you know where God is?"

When he saw that they could not answer his question, he took a small piece of bread and showed it to them. "God," he said, "is in this piece of bread. Without God's power in all nature, this piece of bread could not exist."

How can one say: "God is in this piece of bread"? What do you suppose the Kobriner Rebbe meant? What does his observation have to do with the בִּרְכַּת הַשָּׁנִים prayer or with the blessing we say before eating?

Imitating God

We have already noted that Judaism considers it a person's task to imitate God. What does the בִּרְכַּת הַשָּׁנִים prayer teach us about our task?

In the Torah we read: "If your brother becomes poor, and his means of support fail, you must uphold him....I am the Eternal One your God" (Leviticus 25:35–38). Study the whole passage, and discuss it in light of the בִּרְכַּת הַשָּׁנִים.

Kibbutz Galuyot קִבּוּץ גָּלֻיּוֹת Gathering of the Exiles

תְּקַע בְּשׁוֹפָר גָּדוֹל לְחֵרוּתֵנוּ. וְשָׂא נֵס לְקַבֵּץ גָּלֻיּוֹתֵנוּ. וְקַבְּצֵנוּ יַחַד מֵאַרְבַּע כַּנְפוֹת הָאָרֶץ. בָּרוּךְ אַתָּה יְיָ, מְקַבֵּץ נִדְחֵי עַמּוֹ יִשְׂרָאֵל.

Blow the shofar for the freedom of our people. Lift up a banner and gather our exiled people from the four corners of the earth. We praise You, O God, who gathers the exiled of the people Israel.

An Ancient Idea

The קִבּוּץ גָּלֻיּוֹת prayer voices the hope that someday all who wish will be free to live their lives in the Land of Israel.

The idea of the Jewish people's return to the Land of Israel is nearly as old as the Jewish people itself. Moses led the people out of Egypt so that they could return to the Promised Land. And when the Babylonians destroyed Israel and took thousands of Jews away as captives, the prophets spoke of the day when all of the exiled would be returned to Israel. The words of Isaiah are typical.

And it shall come to pass in that day,
That the Eternal One will set the divine hand again the second time,
To recover the remnant of God's people...
And will assemble the exiled of Israel,
And gather together the scattered of Judah
From the four corners of the earth.

Isaiah 11:11–12

86

What Is Exile?

What does it mean to live in גָּלוּת (*galut*), "exile"? Moses ibn Ezra, the Spanish Jewish poet (1060–1138), defined exile as "a form of imprisonment...the refugees are like plants without soil and water." The Zionist leader Chaim Greenberg once wrote: "Wherever Jews live as a minority is exile."

What do Ibn Ezra and Greenberg mean by exile? What is bad about living in exile?

How does living in Israel solve the problems of "exile" for the Jew? Do you believe that there are still some Jews who are living in exile? Are there other people who might be considered exiles? How would you compare their situation to that of the Jewish people?

Someone once remarked: "It is easier to take a Jew out of exile than to take exile out of the Jew." What do you think this means? Is it possible for the Jew to live in the Land of Israel and still be in exile?

Freedom for All Peoples

Since the establishment of the State of Israel and the return to it of many oppressed Jews, the קִבּוּץ גָּלִיּוֹת prayer may appear to have less meaning today. After nearly 2,000 years, the hope this prayer expresses is being realized.

As a result, the Reform prayer book, *Gates of Prayer*, contains the following new version.

תְּקַע בְּשׁוֹפָר גָּדוֹל לְחֵרוּתֵנוּ, וְשָׂא נֵס לִפְדוֹת עֲשׁוּקֵינוּ, וְקוֹל דְּרוֹר יִשָּׁמַע בְּאַרְבַּע כַּנְפוֹת הָאָרֶץ. בָּרוּךְ אַתָּה יי, פּוֹדֶה עֲשׁוּקִים.

Sound the great shofar to proclaim freedom, raise high the banner of liberation for the oppressed, and let the song of liberty be heard in the four corners of the earth. We praise You, O God, Redeemer of the oppressed.

What do you think of this change? What peoples are still oppressed today? Is it important to include them in our prayers. Why?

Tzedakah Umishpat צְדָקָה וּמִשְׁפָּט Righteousness and Justice

עַל שׁוֹפְטֵי אֶרֶץ שְׁפוֹךְ רוּחֶךָ, וְהַדְרִיכֵם בְּמִשְׁפְּטֵי צִדְקֶךָ, וּמְלוֹךְ עָלֵינוּ אַתָּה לְבַדֶּךָ, בְּחֶסֶד וּבְרַחֲמִים. בָּרוּךְ אַתָּה יי, מֶלֶךְ אוֹהֵב צְדָקָה וּמִשְׁפָּט.

Bestow your spirit upon the rulers of all lands; guide them that they may govern justly. Thus shall love and compassion be enthroned among us. We praise You, Eternal One, the Sovereign God who loves righteous and justice.

The Psalmist once asked the question: "O Eternal One, who shall dwell in Your sanctuary?" By that question the Psalmist meant: "Who is really the religious person?"

That is a question many of us still ask. How does a religious person's behavior differ from those who are not religious? Is being "religious" only a matter of rituals and ceremonies?

The Psalmist, quoted above, tried to answer his own question. He wrote the following:

He who walks uprightly and works righteousness
And speaks truth in his heart;
Who has no slander upon his tongue,

Nor does evil to his fellow,

Nor takes up a reproach against his neighbor;

In whose eyes an evil person is despised,

But who honors them who fear the Lord;

He who keeps his word even if it brings him pain,

He who does not put out his money on interest,

Nor take a bribe against the innocent.

Psalm 15

How does the author of Psalm 15 define a "religious" person? Would you agree or disagree with this definition? Why? Are there important aspects of being religious that this psalm fails to mention? What part do rituals and prayer play in helping a person become truly religious? What is the relationship of the צְדָקָה וּמִשְׁפָּט prayer to being a "religious" person?

Machnia Zeidim מַכְנִיעַ זֵדִים Humbling the Arrogant

וְלַמַּלְשִׁינִים אַל תְּהִי תִקְוָה. וּמַלְכוּת זָדוֹן מְהֵרָה תְעַקֵּר וּתְשַׁבֵּר וּתְמַגֵּר
וְתַכְנִיעַ בִּמְהֵרָה בְיָמֵינוּ. בָּרוּךְ אַתָּה יְיָ, שֹׁבֵר אוֹיְבִים וּמַכְנִיעַ זֵדִים.

Let there be no hope for those who slander others. May arrogant governments be quickly uprooted, destroyed, and humbled. We praise You, O God, who destroys the wicked and humbles the arrogant.

The Jewish people has often suffered from unjust and selfish leaders who blamed Jews for their own mistakes. Throughout history, Jews have been tortured and even killed for remaining faithful to their Judaism and to the Jewish people.

The prayer מַכְנִיעַ זֵדִים was written by Shmuel HaKatan at the request of Rabban Gamliel during the second century C.E. At the time Jews suffered from the brutal persecution of the Romans. Rabbi Shmuel HaKatan's prayer voices the hope that all evil governments and arrogant leaders—all men and women who are enemies of freedom and human dignity—will be humbled and destroyed.

Slanderers

When Rabbi Shmuel HaKatan wrote the מַכְנִיעַ זֵדִים prayer, he had in mind not only those governments that persecuted Jews, but also Jews who had become informers and slanderers against the Jewish community. Why would a Jew become an informer or slanderer against other Jews? Can you think of any other examples where Jews have become informers for anti-Semites? What motivated them?

On Evil

If you were given the task of composing such a prayer today, what might you write? What are the "enemies of freedom and human dignity" today? What might it mean when we ask God to uproot, destroy, or humble those who are responsible for evil?

The following prayer is the new version of מַכְנִיעַ זֵדִים that appears in the Reform prayer book, *Gates of Prayer.* What do you think the author of the new version of this ancient prayer had in mind? Which characteristics does it single out as leading to evil?

וְלָרִשְׁעָה אַל־תְּהִי תִקְוָה, וְהַתּוֹעִים אֵלֶיךָ יָשׁוּבוּ, וּמַלְכוּת זָדוֹן מְהֵרָה תְשַׁבֵּר. תַּקֵּן מַלְכוּתְךָ בְּתוֹכֵנוּ, בְּקָרוֹב בְּיָמֵינוּ לְעוֹלָם וָעֶד. בָּרוּךְ אַתָּה יי, הַמַּשְׁבִּית רֶשַׁע מִן־הָאָרֶץ.

Let the reign of evil afflict us no more. May every errant heart find its way back to you. O help us to shatter the dominion of arrogance, to raise up a better world where virtue will ennoble the life of your children. We praise You, O God, whose will it is that evil may vanish from the earth.

Al HaTzaddikim עַל הַצַּדִּיקִים The Righteous

עַל־הַצַּדִּיקִים וְעַל־הַחֲסִידִים וְעַל גֵּרֵי הַצֶּדֶק וְעָלֵינוּ יֶהֱמוּ רַחֲמֶיךָ, יי אֱלֹהֵינוּ, וְתֵן שָׂכָר טוֹב לְכָל הַבּוֹטְחִים בְּשִׁמְךָ בֶּאֱמֶת, וְשִׂים חֶלְקֵנוּ עִמָּהֶם לְעוֹלָם. בָּרוּךְ אַתָּה יי, מִשְׁעָן וּמִבְטָח לַצַּדִּיקִים.

For the righteous and faithful of all humankind, for all who join their lives to ours, for all who put their trust in You, and for all honest men and women, we ask Your favor, Eternal God. Grant that we may always be numbered among them. We praise You, O God, Staff and Support of the righteous.

The word צַדִּיקִים (tzaddikim) is the plural of צַדִּיק (tzaddik), which means "righteous." Who is a צַדִּיק, a "righteous person"?

The Talmud tells us that a צַדִּיק is "good to God and good to people" (BT Kiddushin 40a). Does being "good to people" necessarily make one "good to God"? What does our relationship to people have to do with our relationship to God? You may wish to arrange a debate on these questions. If you do, be sure to look at Exodus 20–23 and Deuteronomy 22–26. Compare the commandments of Torah with the talmudic statement that a צַדִּיק is one who is "good to God and good to people."

The Talmud also teaches that a צַדִּיק "says little and does much" (BT Bava M'tzia 87a). Would you agree with the Talmud that "saying little and doing much" is an important quality of a צַדִּיק? Why? What other qualities of character would you consider important in making a person a צַדִּיק?

According to the Rabbis, there are different levels of righteousness. For instance, they claim that Noah, whom the Torah calls righteous, was not a true צַדִּיק. Why? Because when he heard that the world was going to be destroyed, he did not pray for those who were doomed. On the other hand, Abraham is considered by the Sages to have been a true צַדִּיק. Why? Because

STATEMENTS ABOUT THE RIGHTEOUS

The following are some statements from Jewish tradition about the "righteous." Try to understand what they mean and how they might apply to being a צַדִּיק today.

The righteous are superior to angels.

BT *Sanhedrin* 93a

Righteous persons do not take what is not theirs.

BT *Sanhedrin* 99b

The righteous protect a city more than sand holds back the sea.

BT *Bava Batra* 7b

The righteous are called God's friends.

Seder Eliyahu Rabbah

When the righteous depart, blessing departs.

Eliezer ben Shimon

The righteous cast out hatred.

Apocrypha

when he heard that the inhabitants of Sodom were about to be destroyed, he argued with God and prayed for the people of Sodom (*Zohar* I, 82a). What is it about Noah that disqualified him from being a צַדִּיק? Look at Exodus 32:1–14. Would Moses rate as a צַדִּיק? Why?

Which people in our time would you consider צַדִּיקִים? You may wish to draw up a list and discuss your opinions with those in your study group.

Hearing and Seeing

Chasidism teaches that the צַדִּיק is a person who is capable of experiencing God's power in all earthly things. The צַדִּיק hears and sees God everywhere. The Koretzer Rebbe taught that the צַדִּיק "is always able to see without eyes and to hear without ears." What do you think the Koretzer meant by that? Can we really see without eyes or hear without ears? Can a blind person see and a deaf person hear? What can a צַדִּיק see and hear without eyes and ears?

We have already noted that the authors of our prayer book often borrowed phrases and ideas from the Hebrew Bible. Look at Psalm 37:39–40, and compare what you find there with the עַל הַצַדִּיקִים prayer.

Boneih Y'rushalayim בּוֹנֵה יְרוּשָׁלַיִם Rebuilding Jerusalem

וְלִירוּשָׁלַיִם עִירְךָ בְּרַחֲמִים תָּשׁוּב. וּבְנֵה אוֹתָהּ בְּקָרוֹב בְּיָמֵינוּ בִּנְיַן עוֹלָם. וְכִסֵּא דָוִד מְהֵרָה לְתוֹכָהּ תָּכִין. בָּרוּךְ אַתָּה יְיָ, בּוֹנֵה יְרוּשָׁלָיִם.

Return, O God, to Jerusalem, Your city, in mercy. May it be rebuilt and established in our days as an eternal symbol. May the seat of David be there. We praise You, O God, who gives us faith to rebuild Jerusalem.

When King Solomon dedicated the first Temple in Jerusalem, he prayed: "O Eternal One, hear the prayers...of your people Israel when they pray toward this place" (I Kings 8:30). Since that time, Jews have always faced toward Jerusalem when they prayed. The Rabbis give us the following directions:

> If a Jew is east of Jerusalem, he should turn his face to the west; if in the west, toward the east; if in the south, toward the north; if in the north, toward the south. In this way all of Israel will be turning their hearts toward one place.
>
> BT *B'rachot* 30a

92

What do the Rabbis mean by their explanation: "In this way all of Israel will be turning their hearts toward one place"? What meaning do you think has been added to Jewish history and prayer by all Jews facing toward Jerusalem when they pray? In most synagogues today, the ark is situated so that the congregation prays facing Jerusalem. In the city of Jerusalem, synagogues are built so that worshipers face the place where the Temple once stood. What does this mean to you as a Jew?

Two Jerusalems!

The talmudic sage Rabbi Yochanan bar Napacha, once declared:

> The Holy One, blessed be God, said: "I will not enter the heavenly Jerusalem until I can enter the earthly Jerusalem."
>
> BT *Taanit* 5a

What do you think Rabbi Yochanan bar Napacha meant?

Perhaps he believed that there were two Jerusalems. That may seem a strange idea at first. But many Jews throughout the centuries have believed it with all their hearts. And there are Jews today who still teach that there are two Jerusalems.

The first is the city where people live and where the modern State of Israel has its busy capital. This is the Jerusalem that devoted Jews have longed to visit or to live in throughout the centuries.

The other Jerusalem is what might be called a symbol. It is the perfect city of peace, a city where justice, mercy, love, and goodness are to be found. This is the "heavenly Jerusalem" to which Rabbi Yochanan bar Napacha referred, and according to tradition, this is the city that the Messiah will establish. This "heavenly Jerusalem" is an ideal and a great human hope.

How are the two Jerusalems interrelated? How might the ideal of the "heavenly Jerusalem" be applied to all cities in the world? How does such an idea relate to the בּוֹנֶה יְרוּשָׁלַיִם prayer?

Jerusalem is a sacred city not only for the Jewish people, who built it three thousand years ago, but also for Christians and Moslems, who attach special religious events to it. The following prayer for Jerusalem appears in the Reform prayer book, *Gates of Prayer.*

שְׁכוֹן, יי אֱלֹהֵינוּ, בְּתוֹךְ יְרוּשָׁלַיִם עִירֶךָ, וִיהִי שָׁלוֹם בִּשְׁעָרֶיהָ, וְשַׁלְוָה בְּלֵב יוֹשְׁבֶיהָ, וְתוֹרָתְךָ מִצִּיּוֹן תֵּצֵא, וּדְבָרְךָ מִירוּשָׁלָיִם. בָּרוּךְ אַתָּה יי, בּוֹנֵה יְרוּשָׁלָיִם.

Let your presence be manifest in Jerusalem, Your city. Establish peace in her gates and quietness in the hearts of all who dwell there. Let Your Torah go forth from Zion, Your word from Jerusalem. We praise You, O God, Builder of Jerusalem.

Compare the traditional prayer and the contemporary version. What differentiates them? Which do you prefer and why? If you were writing your own prayer for Jerusalem, what would it be?

THE HOPE

Israel's national anthem is called "Hatikvah," which means "The Hope." Based on a poem by Naphtali Imber, its first section is as follows:

כָּל עוֹד בַּלֵּבָב פְּנִימָה
נֶפֶשׁ יְהוּדִי הוֹמִיָּה
וּלְפַאֲתֵי מִזְרָח קָדִימָה
עַיִן לְצִיּוֹן צוֹפִיָּה.
עוֹד לֹא אָבְדָה תִקְוָתֵנוּ,
הַתִּקְוָה שְׁנוֹת אַלְפַּיִם,
לִהְיוֹת עַם חָפְשִׁי בְּאַרְצֵנוּ,
בְּאֶרֶץ צִיּוֹן וִירוּשָׁלָיִם.

So long as still within the heart a Jewish spirit sings,
so long as the eye looks eastward, gazing toward Zion,
our hope is not lost—
that hope of two thousand years,
to be a free people in our land,
the land of Zion and Jerusalem.

Do you think that this hope has been completely fulfilled? How might we apply Rabbi Yochanan's belief in two Jerusalems to our understanding of the words of "Hatikvah"?

94

Remembering Jerusalem

Why do you suppose Jews have remembered Jerusalem in their prayers throughout the centuries? David Ben-Gurion, the first prime minister of the State of Israel, once said: "Jerusalem...has been and will remain forever the capital of the Jewish people." What did he mean? Would you agree with him?

Keren Y'shuah קֶרֶן יְשׁוּעָה The Messianic Hope

אֶת צֶמַח דָּוִד עַבְדְּךָ מְהֵרָה תַצְמִיחַ. וְקַרְנוֹ תָּרוּם בִּישׁוּעָתֶךָ. כִּי לִישׁוּעָתְךָ קִוִּינוּ כָּל הַיּוֹם. בָּרוּךְ אַתָּה יְיָ, מַצְמִיחַ קֶרֶן יְשׁוּעָה.

May the Messiah, a descendant of David, come speedily, for we long each day for Your salvation. We praise You, O God, who brings forth salvation.

Perhaps one of the most important visions that the prophets of Israel gave to the Jewish people, and to all people, was the hope for a time when human beings would live in justice, peace, and mutual understanding—and war would be no more. That vision is known within Jewish tradition as the "messianic hope." Why? What does the establishment of a day of peace and justice for all have to do with the coming of the Messiah?

Who Is the Messiah?

The traditional version of the קֶרֶן יְשׁוּעָה prayer begins by calling the Messiah צֶמַח דָּוִד (tzemach David), a descendant of David. For those who composed our prayer, who was the "descendant of David" supposed to be?

In the Book of Isaiah, the prophet tells us:

> And there shall come forth a descendant out of the stock of Jesse [David]
> And the spirit of the Eternal One shall rest upon him,
> The spirit of wisdom and understanding,
> The spirit of counsel and might,
> The spirit of knowledge and fear of God.

> Isaiah 11:1–2

The prophet Isaiah then goes on to explain how this descendant of David will bring about a new day of peace not only for human beings but for the animal kingdom as well. (Look at chapter 11 in the Book of Isaiah.) In another place Isaiah proclaims:

> [The descendant of David will sit]
> Upon the throne of David, and upon his kingdom,
> To establish it and uphold it
> Through justice and through righteousness.
>
> Isaiah 9:6

According to the prophet Isaiah, the צֶמַח דָוִד, descendant of David, is to occupy the ancient king's throne. This helps us understand why the descendant of David is called the Messiah. In Hebrew, the word for messiah is מָשִׁיחַ (mashiach), which means "the anointed one." In ancient Israel, the king was anointed upon assuming the throne.

The Messiah and a New Day of Peace

The prophet Isaiah, who wrote the words we find in chapters 9 and 11, lived during the Babylonian exile. Like many Jews of his day, he longed to return to the Land of Israel and to rebuild Jewish national life. His hope was that a new descendant of David would be placed on the throne; that the Temple would be rebuilt; and that Jewish life would see an end to the cruel Babylonian exile. Eventually, his hope became a great vision not only for Jews but for all people. It is expressed with beauty in the following words:

> And it shall come to pass in the end of days,
> That the mountain of God's house
> Shall be established as the top of the mountains
> And shall be exalted above the hills;
> And all nations shall flow unto it.
> And many peoples shall go and say:
> "Come, let us go up to God's mountain
> To the House of the God of Jacob;
> And He will teach us of His ways,
> And we will walk in His paths."
> For out of Zion shall go forth the law,
> And the word of the Eternal One from Jerusalem.
> And He shall judge between the nations,

And shall decide for many peoples;

And they shall beat their swords into plowshares,

And their spears into pruning-hooks;

Nation shall not lift up sword against nation,

Neither shall they learn war any more.

Isaiah 2:2–4

Often our ideals are not realized. This, however, does not mean that they are either false or unimportant. Isaiah's vision, for instance, has continued to live in the hearts of human beings for centuries. Our קֶרֶן יְשׁוּעָה prayer is an excellent example of the power of Isaiah's hope. It was added to the original *Amidah* as the nineteenth benediction. This was done in about the third century C.E., after the destruction of the Second Temple and another dispersion of the Jewish people. The קֶרֶן יְשׁוּעָה prayer was an expression of the Jewish people's hope for a re-establishment of their Jewish state and the fulfillment of the messianic vision.

Christianity and the Messiah

According to the Christian Scriptures, the followers of Jesus believed that he was the צֶמַח דָוִד, descendant of David, and the Messiah. They called him *Christos*, which in Greek means "messiah" or "anointed one." The Romans, who put Jesus to death, placed a sign over his head that read: "Jesus, king of the Jews." They were mocking him for claiming to be the Messiah.

Jews rejected Jesus as the Messiah because he did not bring about the realization of the messianic vision. The Christian Church holds that Jesus will return and in the "Second Coming" will bring about the promised messianic times.

The Messiah and Us

What can the קֶרֶן יְשׁוּעָה prayer possibly mean to us Jews? Can we still believe that one human being—the Messiah—will be able to bring about Isaiah's vision of a world of justice, human love, and peace?

We are told that Rabbi Eliezer Lippmann constantly asked Rabbi Mendel of Kossov: "Why has the Messiah not come?" One day Rabbi Mendel answered: "He has not come because we are today just the same as we were yesterday" (*Hasidic Anthology*). What do you think Rabbi Mendel meant? According to him, upon what does the coming of the Messiah depend?

Another Chasidic leader, the Stretiner Rebbe, taught his students: "All Jews have within them something of the Messiah. And the Messiah will not arrive to heal the world until Jews develop and perfect the Messiah within them." Are the Stretiner Rebbe and Rabbi Mendel saying the same thing? What can it mean for Jews to "develop and perfect the Messiah within them"? How does this idea relate to the Reform version of the קֶרֶן יְשׁוּעָה prayer below?

Reform Version of קֶרֶן יְשׁוּעָה

אֶת־צֶמַח צְדָקָה מְהֵרָה תַצְמִיחַ, וְקֶרֶן יְשׁוּעָה תָּרוּם כִּנְאָמֶךָ, כִּי לִישׁוּעָתְךָ קִוִּינוּ כָּל־הַיּוֹם. בָּרוּךְ אַתָּה יי, מַצְמִיחַ קֶרֶן יְשׁוּעָה.

Let the plant of righteousness blossom and flourish, and let the light of deliverance shine forth according to Your word: we await Your deliverance all the day. We praise You, O God: You will cause the light of deliverance to dawn for all the world.

Orthodox and Conservative Jews continue to pray for the arrival of the Messiah, who will lead humanity into an era of justice and peace. However Reform Jews ask for the inspiration to let *tzedakah*, or "righteousness," deliver them and all people from cruelty and evil. Reform Jews believe that they have the responsibility to "cause the light of deliverance to dawn for all the world" through their mitzvah deeds. The messianic hope for a time of justice and truth, love and peace will be realized through us.

The following two prayers express the Reform Jewish views of the קֶרֶן יְשׁוּעָה prayer:

And so
When we do a mitzvah with food or plants or paper or another human being,
When we thank the Creator for having formed this beautiful and strong and fragrant thing,
We awaken the spark of light within,
And suddenly its fire starts to grow,
And it rises, flaming higher and higher and higher,
Soon to be reunited with its source.

As we have the power, through each mitzvah we do,
To redeem the sparks of light from the tyranny of matter,
In just such a way
God redeems us.

Alfred Jospe and Richard N. Levy, Bridges to a Holy Time

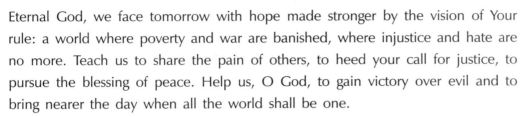

Eternal God, we face tomorrow with hope made stronger by the vision of Your rule: a world where poverty and war are banished, where injustice and hate are no more. Teach us to share the pain of others, to heed your call for justice, to pursue the blessing of peace. Help us, O God, to gain victory over evil and to bring nearer the day when all the world shall be one.

HJF

Compare the traditional and Reform versions of the קֶרֶן יְשׁוּעָה prayers. Which for you contains a more powerful meaning? Why? How do the above prayers deal with the idea of the Messiah? Compose your own version of the קֶרֶן יְשׁוּעָה prayer. What hopes have you emphasized, and who is responsible for bringing them about?

Shomei-a T'filah שׁוֹמֵעַ תְּפִלָּה

שְׁמַע קוֹלֵנוּ, יי אֱלֹהֵינוּ, חוּס וְרַחֵם עָלֵינוּ, וְקַבֵּל בְּרַחֲמִים וּבְרָצוֹן
אֶת־תְּפִלָּתֵנוּ, כִּי אֵל שׁוֹמֵעַ תְּפִלּוֹת וְתַחֲנוּנִים אָתָּה. בָּרוּךְ אַתָּה יי, שׁוֹמֵעַ
תְּפִלָּה.

Hear our voice, Eternal God; have compassion upon us, and accept our prayer with favor and mercy, for You are a God who hears prayer and supplication. We praise You, O God: You hearken to prayer.

This prayer raises an interesting and important question. Does God hear and answer our prayers?

Some Jews believe that God does actually hear and respond to our prayers. They argue that if God did not hear prayer, then what would be the use of praying? They also hold that the belief that God hears prayer is a matter of faith.

Other Jews have difficulty believing that God hears and answers prayer. They point out that if God responds to prayer, then why did God not save the sick little child whose parents prayed for it to live?

Other Ways

There are no easy or simple answers to such questions. There may, however, be other ways of thinking about whether or not God hears our prayers.

Judaism teaches that each person is created in the image of God and has within a "spark of the Divine." Some call that spark our conscience. Others refer to it as our נֶפֶשׁ (nefesh), or soul. When we pray, it is possible to say that the "spark of the Divine" within us hears our prayer. In that sense, many Jews believe that God hears prayer.

There is another way of looking at this prayer. Jewish tradition teaches that through prayer, we follow the Torah's command to serve God with all of our heart. This means that even when we may doubt that God will answer our prayer exactly as we would like, prayer is still an important mitzvah. In reaching out to God and sharing with God our hopes, fears, and feelings, we demonstrate our desire to serve God with a whole heart.

Finally, we might understand this prayer as referring to more than the words we offer in synagogue. The modern writer Rachel Levin Varnhagen taught: "Holy, true, and honest purposes are prayer." Prayer is more than what we say to God; it is the way we conduct ourselves when we try to do what is right. When we say that God hears our prayer, then, we might mean that God notices when we behave in ways that are holy, true, and honest.

Discuss these explanations with your study group. Do you hold any of these ideals for yourself? Can you think of other ways to understand this prayer?

Does God Answer?

It is one thing to say that "God hears our prayers," but quite another to hold that God answers them. What about the answer? Can we say, in any way, that God answers our prayers?

The answer offered earlier by Rabbi Morris Adler may be helpful. He wrote:

> Our prayers are answered not when we are given what we ask but when we are challenged to be what we can be.
>
> *Modern Treasury of Jewish Thoughts*

What do you think Rabbi Adler means? What is he trying to teach us about prayer and its place in our lives?

Perhaps the deepest meaning and benefit of prayer is that it allows us to think about our lives and all that we experience. It provides us with the opportunity to judge ourselves and to deepen our appreciation of our abilities. It leads us to be more sensitive, aware, and concerned human beings.

Rav Kook, one of the outstanding leaders of Orthodox Jewry in the Land of Israel during the early twentieth century (1864–1935), wrote that "through prayer we lift ourselves to a world of perfection." What did he mean by his statement? Is Rav Kook's observation close to that of Rabbi Adler? How do you suppose Rav Kook might answer the question "Does God hear and answer our prayers?"

Once we have an understanding of the traditional עֲמִידָה, we can create our own. We might begin by making use of some of the middle thirteen prayers. Choose and develop your prayer or prayers on the basis of the commentaries.

One of the important lessons we have learned from our study of the עֲמִידָה is that the Rabbis developed prayers in response to the needs of their people and times. In creating our own עֲמִידָה prayers, we should do the same. Our age and our problems present us with new challenges. In the creation of our עֲמִידָה, we can use the traditional prayers, and we can develop new ones that will speak of the hopes, joys, doubts, and fears that we feel in our hearts.

THE SHABBAT *AMIDAH*

AVOT: ANCESTORS

Avot

אָבוֹת

בָּרוּךְ אַתָּה יי, אֱלֹהֵינוּ וֵאלֹהֵי אֲבוֹתֵינוּ וְאִמּוֹתֵינוּ: אֱלֹהֵי אַבְרָהָם, אֱלֹהֵי יִצְחָק, וֵאלֹהֵי יַעֲקֹב. אֱלֹהֵי שָׂרָה, אֱלֹהֵי רִבְקָה, אֱלֹהֵי לֵאָה וֵאלֹהֵי רָחֵל. הָאֵל הַגָּדוֹל הַגִּבּוֹר וְהַנּוֹרָא, אֵל עֶלְיוֹן, גּוֹמֵל חֲסָדִים טוֹבִים וְקוֹנֵה הַכֹּל, וְזוֹכֵר חַסְדֵי אָבוֹת וְאִמָּהוֹת, וּמֵבִיא גְאֻלָּה לִבְנֵי בְנֵיהֶם, לְמַעַן שְׁמוֹ בְּאַהֲבָה. בָּרוּךְ אַתָּה יי, מָגֵן אַבְרָהָם וְעֶזְרַת שָׂרָה.

> Praised be our God, the God of our fathers and our mothers: God of Abraham, God of Isaac, and God of Jacob; God of Sarah, God of Rebekah, God of Leah, and God of Rachel; great, mighty, and awesome, God supreme. Ruler of all the living, Your ways are ways of love. You remember the faithfulness of our ancestors, and in love bring redemption to their children's children for the sake of Your name. You are our Sovereign and our Help, our Redeemer and our Shield. We praise You, Eternal One, Shield of Abraham, Protector of Sarah.

COMMENTARY

This is the first prayer of the עֲמִידָה. It is called the אָבוֹת because its opening phrase refers to God as אֱלֹהֵי אֲבוֹתֵינוּ (*Elohei avoteinu*), "God of our ancestors." The ancestors mentioned here are the patriarchs and the matriarchs of Jewish tradition—Abraham, Isaac, Jacob, Sarah, Rebekah, Rachel, and Leah.

Why is such a formula used? Would it not be sufficient to say simply אֱלֹהֵינוּ (*Eloheinu*), "our God"? Why use such a long introduction mentioning Abraham, Isaac, and Jacob, Sarah, Rebekah, Rachel, and Leah?

An Ancient Formula

Actually, the use of the formula "God of Abraham, God of Isaac, and God of Jacob" is a very ancient one in the Jewish tradition.

In the biblical story of the Exodus, Moses asks God: "What should I say when the people want to know who sent me to take them out of Egyptian slavery?" The Torah tells us that God replied to Moses with the words: "Tell them that the Eternal One, the God of your ancestors, the God of Abraham, the God of Isaac, the God of Jacob, sent me to you. And that is My name for all generations" (Exodus 3:15).

At a very early period in Jewish history, the Torah designated the phrase אֱלֹהֵי אֲבֹתֵיכֶם אֱלֹהֵי אַבְרָהָם אֱלֹהֵי יִצְחָק וֵאלֹהֵי יַעֲקֹב, God of our ancestors, God of Abraham, God of Isaac, and God of Jacob, as the way in which God should be addressed. This may explain why the formula is used so frequently in Jewish prayer.

Sexist Language

The אָבוֹת prayer raises a difficult question for modern prayer book translators. The word אָבוֹת literally means "fathers." Yet, what about the important women in Jewish tradition? Are they not as important as Abraham, Isaac, and Jacob?

For many Jews, this has been a difficult issue to resolve. The traditional version of the אָבוֹת, which has been used for centuries, echoes the ancient formula in the Book of Exodus and mentions only the patriarchs of Judaism—Abraham, Isaac, and Jacob. However, Reform Jews have developed a new version of the אָבוֹת. This Reform prayer includes the names of Judaism's matriarchs—Sarah, Rebekah, Rachel, and Leah—and celebrates these women's relationships with God as well as their important place in Jewish history.

Why have Reform Jews felt the need to mention specifically the matriarchs of Judaism in the אָבוֹת? There are several reasons. Although countless women have helped shape Jewish history—from biblical times to the present day—they are often overshadowed by their male contemporaries. When we learn about Judaism and study important Jews, we frequently forget the contributions of Jewish heroines. Unless we make an effort to rediscover and reclaim the experiences of Jewish women, we might think that only men play an important role in Judaism. By specifically mentioning Sarah, Rebekah, Rachel, and Leah, the Reform version of the אָבוֹת reminds us that women have an equally important role to play in Jewish life. And when we call upon God as the God not only of the fathers but also of the mothers, we are reminded that God responds to women with the same love and compassion God gives to men.

Compare some translations of prayers from traditional prayer books to those in Gates of Prayer. *Are they male-centered? How do you feel about a prayer that speaks of "God of our fathers"? If you were composing or translating a prayer book today, what rules would you follow regarding its language? What about descriptions of God? Do you favor using masculine or feminine pronouns to refer to God? What are some alternatives to talking about God as "He" or "She"?*

What about Today?

We may now understand why it is important to call upon God as the God of our ancestors, but what can this prayer mean for us today? Those who have interpreted the אָבוֹת prayer point out at least three important meanings.

I. Remembering Our History

There are those who believe that the phrase "God of our ancestors" is meant to call our attention to the long history of our people.

Certainly, when we say the formula "God of our ancestors..." we are immediately reminded that we are part of a people and heritage that reaches back over 4,000 years. As descendants of Abraham, Isaac, Jacob, Sarah, Rebekah, Leah, and Rachel, we are related to the Maccabees, the Sages of the Talmud, those who suffered in the Crusades, the great Chasidic leaders, those who perished in the Holocaust, and those who have built the modern State of Israel. In other words when we say אֲבוֹתֵינוּ, "God of our ancestors," we identify ourselves as a part of the Jewish people.

Have you ever looked at an old family album? What kind of feelings did you have? Would you have experienced different feelings had the album belonged to a friend rather than to your family? Why? How can saying the אָבוֹת prayer be compared to looking into a family album? How do both experiences connect us to our past? How can saying the אָבוֹת prayer help us to identify with our tradition and people in all ages and places?

The modern rabbi Samuel E. Karff teaches that the prayer book is "designed to evoke, express, confirm that we individuals—with all the personal agendas and histories which distinguish us from each other—share a common story that is key to our life's meaning." Do you agree? How does this statement relate to our understanding of the אָבוֹת?

II. The Changing Idea of God

The Sages of Jewish tradition offer us another interpretation of the phrase "our God and God of our ancestors." It is what we might call a "theological" explanation. The word "theological" means the study of what we mean by God. What does the אָבוֹת prayer teach us about God?

Some teachers of Judaism believe that the concept or idea of God has developed and changed over the centuries. They argue that just as each of us has a different idea of God, so too did our matriarchs and patriarchs. Those who hold this view point out that the formula "our God and God of our ancestors" is meant to teach us that just as Abraham's idea of God was different than Isaac's, and Sarah's different from Rebekah's, so too it is permissible, and even natural, for Jews today to have varying ideas of God.

Perhaps an analogy will help us understand this idea better. When two people look at a beautiful picture, they each have their own unique

104

conception of what they see and what the artist meant to portray. The picture that is seen by both is the same picture, but there are two different ideas or views of it.

> *You need a room, five chairs, some paper, and some pencils. Take a number of objects and place them together in the middle of the room. Place the chairs about six feet away from the collage of objects. Invite five people to be seated. Give them thirty seconds to look and one minute to write what they see. Then compare the varying views. What does this teach us about the different ways people understand God?*

You may wish to ask some members of your congregation to write out their ideas about God. Compare and contrast them. How do they differ? How are they alike? What relationship do they have to ideas of God in Jewish tradition? Do you think the idea of God will continue to change? In what ways?

III. Two Kinds of Faith and People

There is still another explanation of our phrase "God of our ancestors." It comes from the wisdom of Chasidism.

Why, the Rabbis ask, do we say "our God and God of our ancestors"? We do so because there are two kinds of people who believe in God.

Some people believe in God because they have taken on the faith of their ancestors, and their beliefs are strong because they have the support of tradition. Others have come to their beliefs on their own, through much thinking and studying.

What are the advantages and disadvantages of each of each of these beliefs in God?

The advantage of the first is that, no matter what arguments others may bring up against their idea of God, their faith cannot be shaken because it was taken from their ancestors and is based on a tradition. But this has a disadvantage as well. Because they have not arrived at their beliefs on their own, through study and thinking, they are accepting blindly what others have told them.

The advantage of the second is that they have come to their beliefs on their own. The disadvantage is that, because their idea of God is based only upon their own study and thinking, it may easily be contradicted by someone with a good argument.

The Chasidim point out that when we say אֱלֹהֵינוּ, "our God," we realize that every person must reach for his or her own conclusions and idea of God. And when we say אֱלֹהֵי אֲבוֹתֵינוּ, "God of our ancestors," we recognize that we can gain many helpful insights from the views of Jews throughout the ages.

Can you name some ideas of God from the past that are helpful to you in formulating your own view? What does the אָבוֹת prayer tell us about God? How do its ideas affect yours?

The Devotion of Our Ancestors

In the אָבוֹת, we have the statement "You remember the faithfulness of our ancestors." What can such a statement mean?

Jewish tradition teaches that the deeds of loving-kindness performed by Abraham, Isaac, and Jacob, Sarah, Rebekah, Leah, and Rachel are remembered by God from generation to generation and that they confer merit and benefit upon all the Jewish people. This idea is known as זְכוּת אָבוֹת (z'chut avot), "the merit of the ancestors." The Rabbis of the Talmud teach that "זְכוּת אָבוֹת will aid the people of Israel in reaching the messianic age" (B'reishit Rabbah 70:8). What did the Rabbis mean by that? Did they really think that Jews are somehow given credit or special merit by God for the good deeds of our matriarchs and patriarchs?

In a way, that is precisely what the Rabbis believed. They reasoned that just as the generosity, kindness, or contributions of a father or mother can confer the credit or merit of a respected name upon their children, so too did the good deeds of Abraham, Isaac, Jacob, Sarah, Rebekah, Leah, and Rachel confer merit upon the Jewish people.

106

How do you react to such an idea? What might it teach us about our responsibilities to our families and our people? What are the ways we might earn credit or merit for Jews in the next generation?

Prayers on the אָבוֹת Theme

God Remembers, We Remember

Our God and God of our ancestors,

As You remember the faithfulness of Abraham, Isaac, and Jacob,
    let us remember to be loyal to You and to our people Israel.

As You remember the love of Sarah, Rebekah, Rachel, and Leah,
    let us remember to give unconditional love to our families.

As You remember the gentleness of Ruth and the nurturing love of Naomi,
    let us remember to be gentle in love and friendship,
    to nurture others by our love and compassion.

As You remember the warm hospitality of Abraham and Sarah,
    let us remember to be open and kind to those whom our lives touch.

As You remember the devotion of Your prophets, Amos and Micah, to the poor, the widow, the orphan,
    let us remember those around us who need help.

As You remember Jeremiah and Isaiah's summons to do justice,
    let us remember to work to make our own society more just.

As you remember the courage of our ancestors who suffered for their faithfulness to You,
    let us remember to have the courage to be our true selves,
    to live up to our ideals despite the scoffing or indifference of others.

Rabbi Barton G. Lee

CREATING WITH KAVANAH

Themes:

a. Our history and identity as Jews.

b. The idea of God is constantly changing and developing.

c. Each Jew should develop his or her idea of God based on study and tradition.

d. We benefit from the acts of our ancestors and should live so that future Jews will benefit from us.

107

In Each Age

In each age
we receive and transmit
Torah.
At each moment
we are addressed by the
Word.
In each age
we are challenged
by our ancient teaching.
At each moment
we stand face to Face with
Truth.
In each age
we add our wisdom
to that which has gone before.
At each moment
the knowing heart
is filled with wonder.
In each age
the children of Torah
become its builders
and seek to set the world firm
on a foundation of Truth.

Rabbi Rami M. Shapiro

God of Our Ancestors

The Eternal One of the universe is our God, even as God was the God of our ancestors. Our own experience and the historic wisdom of our people unite to teach us of God's redeeming love.

An unbroken chain of tradition links us with the earliest teachers of our faith. May we be reverent in our study of their words and find in them the inspiration to live in obedience to God's will.

Let us learn to enrich the teaching of our heritage with the knowledge of our own time. So shall we, by our lives and our labors, bring nearer to its realization the great hope, inherited from our ages past, for the redemption of all humanity in a world transformed by liberty, justice, and peace.

Adapted from Service of the Heart

From My Mother's House

My mother's mother died in the spring
of her days. And her daughter did not
remember her face. Her image,
engraved upon my grandfather's heart,
was erased from the world of figures
after his death.

Only her mirror remained in the house,
grown deeper with age within its silver
frame. And I, her pale granddaughter,
who do not resemble her, look into it
today as if into a lake that hides its
treasures beneath the water.

Deep down, behind my face, I see a
young woman, pink-cheeked, smiling.
She is wearing a wig. Now she is
hanging a long earring from her ear
lobe, threading it through the tiny
opening in the dainty flesh of her ear.

Deep down, behind my face, glows the
clear golden speck of her eyes. And the
mirror carries on the family tradition:
that she was very beautiful.

Lea Goldberg, translated by T. Carmi

Your Children Shall Be a Blessing

Our Fathers prayed, each through his own experience of God, each through his
own private vision that his people came to share. And each of our Mothers had
her own vision.

Abraham, who knew the fervor of the morning prayer, pleaded the cause of
cities.

Sarah, who knew the pain of waiting, hoped for new life.

Isaac, meditating in the afternoon, lifted his eyes to find love. Rebekah left home
and kin to answer God's call, to share the hope of those who came before her.

And Jacob, when the sun had set, offered up his night prayer as a ladder reaching into heaven. Rachel and Leah, sisters, became rivals, then friends. They are the Mothers of this people Israel.

To all their prayers came the response: Your children shall be a blessing. Their striving has come down to us as a command: Act, that others may find blessing through your lives!

O God, You are the Source of blessing. Your presence was the Shield of our Fathers, the Help of our Mothers. Your promise is our hope.

Adapted from Gates of Prayer (1975)

Give Us Jews

O Eternal One, give us Jews of inspiration! Jews who lead with willing hands and hearts.

Jews who, like Abraham and Esther, are devoted to their people.

O Eternal One, give us righteous Jews! Jews who are just and free.

Jews who work together and respond to their people's needs.

O Eternal One, give us Jews of courage! Jews of faith and vision.

Jews who, like our ancestors, dare to do the right.

O Eternal One, give us Jews of truth! Jews who stand up for what they believe.

Jews who strive after knowledge and seek a future of peace for all.

HJF

Moving in the Spaces

Standing here in Abraham's desert
Affirming: one God.

Moving in the old spaces
Warmed by our ancestors' embrace.

Standing here in Sarah's tent
Laughing: new life.

110

Moving in the old spaces
Renewed by our ancestors' hope.

Standing here in my place
Listening to our voices: yearning.

Moving in my own spaces
Translating the silence.

Sandy Eisenberg Sasso, "Standing Here"

G'VUROT: GOD'S POWER

The Traditional *G'vurot*

גְּבוּרוֹת

אַתָּה גִּבּוֹר לְעוֹלָם, אֲדֹנָי. מְחַיֵּה מֵתִים אַתָּה, רַב לְהוֹשִׁיעַ.
מְכַלְכֵּל חַיִּים בְּחֶסֶד, מְחַיֵּה מֵתִים בְּרַחֲמִים רַבִּים. סוֹמֵךְ
נוֹפְלִים, וְרוֹפֵא חוֹלִים, וּמַתִּיר אֲסוּרִים, וּמְקַיֵּם אֱמוּנָתוֹ
לִישֵׁנֵי עָפָר. מִי כָמוֹךָ, בַּעַל גְּבוּרוֹת, וּמִי דּוֹמֶה לָּךְ, מֶלֶךְ
מֵמִית וּמְחַיֶּה, וּמַצְמִיחַ יְשׁוּעָה? וְנֶאֱמָן אַתָּה לְהַחֲיוֹת מֵתִים.
בָּרוּךְ אַתָּה יְיָ, מְחַיֵּה הַמֵּתִים.

Eternal is Your power, O God. You revive the dead, and You are mighty to save. In loving-kindness You sustain the living. With abundant mercy You revive the dead. You uphold the falling, heal the sick, free the captives, and keep faith with those who sleep in the earth. Who is like You, almighty God, and who can be compared to You, the Author of life and death, and the Source of salvation? You are faithful to revive the dead. We praise You, O God, who revives the dead.

The Reform *G'vurot*   גְּבוּרוֹת

אַתָּה גִּבּוֹר לְעוֹלָם, אֲדֹנָי, מְחַיֵּה הַכֹּל אַתָּה, רַב לְהוֹשִׁיעַ.
מְכַלְכֵּל חַיִּים בְּחֶסֶד, מְחַיֵּה הַכֹּל בְּרַחֲמִים רַבִּים. סוֹמֵךְ
נוֹפְלִים, וְרוֹפֵא חוֹלִים, וּמַתִּיר אֲסוּרִים, וּמְקַיֵּם אֱמוּנָתוֹ
לִישֵׁנֵי עָפָר. מִי כָמְוֹךָ בַּעַל גְּבוּרוֹת, וּמִי דּוֹמֶה לָּךְ, מֶלֶךְ
מֵמִית וּמְחַיֵּה וּמַצְמִיחַ יְשׁוּעָה? וְנֶאֱמָן אַתָּה לְהַחֲיוֹת הַכֹּל.
בָּרוּךְ אַתָּה יי, מְחַיֵּה הַכֹּל.

Eternal is Your might, O God; all life is Your gift; great is Your power to save! With love You sustain the living, with great compassion give life to all. You send help to the falling and healing to the sick; You bring freedom to the captive and keep faith with those who sleep in the dust. Who is like You, Mighty One, Author of life and death, Source of salvation? We praise You, O God, the Source of life.

COMMENTARY

While the first prayer of the עֲמִידָה, the אָבוֹת, speaks of God at work in history, the גְּבוּרוֹת praises God as the Power that sustains all nature.

Compare the two versions of the גְּבוּרוֹת. Their language is similar and different in very important ways. First, let us discuss what the two versions have in common.

Eternal Is Your Power

Some of the most beautiful poetry of the Hebrew Bible is found in the Book of Psalms, סֵפֶר תְּהִלִּים (*Sefer T'hillim*). Many of the psalms were composed for use by the people when they worshiped at the Temple in Jerusalem. A favorite subject of the Psalmists was nature. They wrote about the wonders of the heavens, the stars, the winds, and the earth with its valleys, mountains, running streams, and the fruits of the fields. Like many great poets over the centuries, the Psalmists saw God's power at work in nature. Here are some examples of what they wrote:

112

The heavens declare the glory of God,
And the skies show God's handiwork.

Psalm 19:2

The earth is the Eternal One's and all its fullness;
The world and all that dwell there.

Psalm 24:1

Eternal One, You have have been our dwelling place in all generations.
Before the mountains were brought forth,
Or ever you had formed the earth and the world.
Even from everlasting to everlasting, You are God.

Psalm 90:1–2

How great are Your works, O Eternal One!
In wisdom you have made all of them....
You send forth Your spirit and they are created;
And You renew the face of the earth.

Psalm 104:24, 30

Who can express the mighty acts of the Eternal One,
Or make all God's praise to be heard?

Psalm 106:2

What do these expressions from the Psalmists have in common? How do these Psalmists understand God? Open your Bible to Psalm 104. What is God's relationship to nature as described in Psalm 104?

The author of the גְבוּרוֹת prayer, like the Psalmists, saw the wonderful power of God at work in all nature. He called God מְכַלְכֵּל חַיִּים בְּחֶסֶד (m'chalkeil chayim b'chesed), the Power "who in loving-kindness sustains the living." What do you think is meant by that expression? Which of the psalms quoted above comes close to expressing the same idea? If you were to compose a prayer or poem about God's power in the universe, what are some of the examples you might use? What about those mentioned in the גְבוּרוֹת prayer?

113

You Uphold the Falling, Heal the Sick, Free the Captives

A Sage of Jewish tradition once taught that "God shares in the affliction of the community and of the individual" (*M'chilta*, Exodus 12:41). What do you believe the Sage had in mind? How is it possible to think of God as sharing the pain, hurt, or problems of a community or an individual?

Perhaps a few analogies will help us. When a child is injured in an accident, the parents and grandparents participate in the child's pain. When a great leader is killed by an assassin's bullet, the pain is not only felt by the family but by all of those who relied upon that person for leadership. When one parent is sick, the entire family is affected and may suffer.

What do these examples have in common? What do they teach us about our relationships with others? If each of us is made in "the image of God," and we feel pain or suffer, is it possible to say that God suffers as well?

In Jewish tradition we are taught that God's power is found not only in the far-off heavens or in the realm of nature, but also in human life—in each of us.

The phrase "You uphold the falling, heal the sick, free the captives..." means that God, somehow, gives support to those who suffer, healing to those who are ill, and freedom to those who are prisoners. Is this really true? How is it possible to say that God heals the sick or frees the captives? (See discussion on "*R'fuah*, Healing," pages 83–84).

Some people might respond by saying that the way God helps us in times of trouble is a mystery. It cannot be understood by the human mind any more than we can understand why we were born to live in the twenty-first century instead of the fifteenth century. God's ways are not ours, and God is beyond our knowledge. All we can do is feel God's power in our lives and understand small fragments of vast and mighty acts.

What do you think of such a view? Does it make sense to you? Would you agree or disagree with it?

The Berditschever Rebbe, a leader of Chasidism, offers us another way of looking at God's power at work in our lives. He once explained to his followers that "those who seek God in prayer and in the deeds of their lives will receive in return the strength to serve God further."

In other words, God may help those suffering by inspiring them to find new strength and determination. God may aid the sick by enabling them to discover new hope and courage. And God's influence may be at work in the prisoner who finds within himself or herself the power to stand up to oppression and strive for freedom.

What do you think of the Berditschever's statement? How might the doing of charity give "strength" to a person in pain? How might the knowledge that there are powers of healing in the world, and in us, help a person overcome sickness? A prisoner of war, who was captive for over two years, was asked how he had managed to live through his ordeal. He answered: "It was a matter of faith and hope. I had faith that God would not allow me to be forgotten and hope that I would live to be free once again." What did the prisoner mean by "God would not allow me to be forgotten"? How would you relate the Berditschever's and the prisoner's statements to the גְבוּרוֹת prayer?

Who Revives the Dead

We now come to the difference between the two versions of the גְבוּרוֹת prayer. In Orthodox and Conservative prayer books, the גְבוּרוֹת contains the words מְחַיֶּה מֵתִים (m'chayeih meitim), "who revives the dead," and לְהַחֲיוֹת מֵתִים (l'hachayot meitim), "to revive the dead."

In *Gates of Prayer*, the Reform prayer book, the words מְחַיֶּה הַכֹּל (m'chayeih hakol), "who sustains all life," are substituted for מְחַיֶּה מֵתִים. In the *Union Prayer Book*, used for many years by Reform Jews, the words נוֹטֵעַ בְּתוֹכֵינוּ חַיֵּי עוֹלָם (notei-a b'tocheinu chayei olam), "who has implanted within us eternal life," were used in place of מְחַיֶּה מֵתִים in the final blessing.

What did those who composed the original גְבוּרוֹת prayer mean by the words מְחַיֶּה מֵתִים? What can it mean to praise God for "reviving the dead"? Can those who have died live again?

The concept of the dead coming to life again is called "resurrection." There is no explicit mention of resurrection in the Hebrew Bible. Some scholars believe that the idea of life after death became popular among some Jews during the Babylonian exile. Others think that the idea spread among Jews after the coming of Alexander the Great and Greek culture to the Land of Israel.

We do know that the subject of resurrection was a source of disagreement in the Jewish community over 2,000 years ago. The Talmud records that the Sadducees did not believe in resurrection, while the Pharisees did. The Sadducees argued that resurrection was not mentioned in the Bible and therefore could not be accepted as a legitimate Jewish belief. The Pharisees, on the other hand, sought to prove that resurrection was indeed mentioned in the Bible and held that belief in life after death was a central teaching of Judaism. Here are two examples of how our ancient Rabbis sought to prove that resurrection is mentioned in the Bible:

(continued on the next page)

Rabbi Joshua ben Levi said: How can we prove resurrection from the Bible? We can do so from the Bible verse, "Happy are those who dwell in Your house; they shall ever praise You" (Psalm 84:5). Note that the verse does not say "they praised You" but rather, "they *shall* ever praise You." From this (the future tense) we learn that resurrection is taught in the Bible.

Rabbi Chiya ben Aba said in Rabbi Yochanan's name: How can we prove resurrection from the Bible? We can do so from the Bible verse, "Your watchmen shall lift up the voice, and with the voice they will sing together" (Isaiah 52:8). Note that the verse does not say "sang together" but, rather, they *will* sing together." From this (the future tense) we learn that resurrection is taught in the Bible.

BT *Sanhedrin* 91b

By resurrection the Pharisees meant that, at sometime in the future history of the world, all those who had ever lived would be brought back to life by God. This idea of resurrection became popular and accepted by most Jews. It was included in the גְּבוּרוֹת prayer because it seemed to reflect the greatness of God's power. If God could create life, it seemed logical to assume that God could also revive it after death.

What do you think of the argument of the Pharisees? Would you agree that they prove that resurrection is taught in the Bible? Do you believe that God gives us life after death?

Who Sustains All Life

When Reform Judaism came into existence in the early nineteenth century, it rejected the concept of resurrection and substituted the belief in the "immortality of the soul." The Reformers argued that once a person died, that person was dead and the body could not be revived. They did, however, agree with the traditional Jewish belief that each person is given a נֶפֶשׁ. This נֶפֶשׁ is not physical but spiritual. It is a spark of God, and it is eternal just as God is eternal. Rather than using the phrase מְחַיֶּה מֵתִים, which speaks of reviving the dead, the rabbis of Reform Judaism chose instead the phrase נוֹטֵעַ בְּתוֹכֵינוּ חַיֵּי עוֹלָם, "who has implanted within us eternal life." In making that change, they meant to call attention to their belief that the נֶפֶשׁ, which God gives to each person, will live on forever.

One of the early leaders of Reform Judaism, Rabbi Abraham Geiger, argued for the change in the following way: "From now on, the hope for an afterlife should not be expressed in terms which suggest a future revival, a resurrection of the body; rather, they must stress the immortality of the human soul."

Within *Gates of Prayer*, Reform rabbis have made another change in the גְּבוּרוֹת prayer. Now, instead of נוֹטֵעַ בְּתוֹכֵינוּ חַיֵּי עוֹלָם, they have chosen the words מְחַיֵּי הַכֹּל, "who sustains all life."

What do you think of these changes by Reform Jews? Does it make more sense to you to speak of a soul that lives forever rather than the resurrection of the dead? Which of the versions do you prefer? If you were composing a new גְּבוּרוֹת prayer, how would you express the idea of immortality?

Another Possibility

Some Jews have trouble believing that people have an eternal soul or that there can be any kind of resurrection of the dead. They argue that our ideas and what we share with others make up our immortality. Rabbi Roland Gittelsohn expresses this thought in the book *Man's Best Hope*. He writes:

It is my ideas which are important—ideas which have come to me largely from many who died long ago, which are now being filtered through my own mind and which, if they are at all valid, will influence the lives of others after I myself am gone. If this is the truly significant part of me, and if there is every reason to believe that this will endure forever, what more do I need by way of immortality?

In short, my immortality consists of my contribution to the ongoing process of evolution. This is the purpose of my life, hence the only eternally valid meaning in my death.

When I die, there will be little or much remaining, dependent upon how I shall have conducted myself prior to that moment.

Another way of stating this possibility of immortality is to compare our life to a beautiful flower. After the flower has faded and been thrown away, we still have the memory of it in our minds. That memory can bring us much joy and satisfaction. In this sense, our immortality is in the memory of those who knew us, loved us, and were influenced by us.

into the beyond of dying, to anticipate psychically what death alone can reveal existentially, seems to me a lack of faith disguised as faith. Genuine faith says: I know nothing about death, but I do know that God is eternity, and I also know that God is my God.

Martin Buber

To celebrate life is to acknowledge the ongoing dying, and ultimately to embrace death. For although all life travels towards its death, death is not a destination: it too is a journey to beginnings: all death leads to life again. From peelings to mulch to new potatoes, the world is ever-renewing, ever-renewed.

Marcia Falk, *The Book of Blessings*

117

Themes:
a. God's power sustains all life.
b. God's power renews life, thereby allowing for growth and evolution.
c. God's power is felt in our hearts—it can strengthen the sick and give hope to the needy.
d. God's power makes it possible for us to achieve immortality.

Have each person in your study group write an essay on "My Immortality." Include in it a consideration of the ideas of immortality that mean the most to you. Then share your essays in a group discussion.

Prayers on the גְּבוּרוֹת Theme

The Creative Flame

God is the oneness
That spans the deeps of space.
> Adonai is the unity of all that is,
> The rhythm of all things.
God is the creative flame
That fires lifeless matter
With living drive and purpose.
> Adonai forms mountains and creates winds,
> Implants in each person the spark of the Divine.
God is in the hope
By which we overcome
Unhappiness, helplessness, and failure.
> Adonai is in the love by which we create
> The beginnings of a new and better world.

Based upon a poem from the *Reconstructionist Prayer Book*, Mordecai M. Kaplan

Who?

Who stretched out the heavens like a curtain?
Who made the clouds?
Who sends the winds like messengers?
Who appoints the moon for seasons?
Who created the depths of the sea?

Who established the earth upon its foundations?
Who sends springs bubbling into valleys?
Who caps the mountains with flakes of snow?
Who causes the grass to shoot forth for cattle?
Who brings forth bread from the earth?

How many are Your works, *Adonai*?
In wisdom you have made them all.
Be praised, whose power
Creates and renews the face of the earth.

Based upon Psalm 104, adapted by HJF

Dialogues

The waving blue arms of the elm
and the agitated answer of the green fig,

the fat globes of yellow sugarmum
where bees suck love,

and you, in the morning's shade,
sipping hot coffee—

the darkbrown taste of the beans
and the milky froth—

say:

Indulge: the world
is abundant,
and ceaselessly dying—

This loving, dying world
to which we are given,
out of which we have come—

O body of the world,
eat with joy
the body of the world!

Marcia Falk, "The Feast"

For Being Alive

Beautiful flowers,
Blue and red and yellow and white,
Soft with the dew of the morn,

Freshly cut grass,
Cold and green....
And the rain
As it dribbles off the end of my nose.
As I lift my head to catch glimpses
Of all things—
Powdering snow
On the brown bare limbs sparkling
And on the rocks and earth—
Oh yes, oh yes, oh yes,
Halleluyah.
My eyes are dreaming,
My voice is calling out
To the sheep running in the meadow
And together
We thank God
For being alive.

> Based upon Psalm 148 from
> *A Contemporary High Holiday Service,*
> Greenberg and Sugarman

Where Shall I Find You?

Lord, where shall I find You?
Your glory fills the world.

. . . .

Behold, I find You
In the wealth of joys that quickly fade,
In the pulse of the life that comes from eternity and dances in my own blood,
In birth, which renews the generations continually,
And in death, knocking on the doors of life.

O my God,
Give me the strength never to cast off one in need,
Never to bend the knee before a haughty tyrant,
Give me strength to lift my spirit above the trivial,
To bear lightly my joys and my sorrows,
And in love to surrender all my strength to Your will.

For great are the gifts You have given me;
The sky and the light. This is my flesh.
Life and soul—
Treaures invaluable, treasures of life and love.

Rabindranath Tagore, "Where Shall I Find You?"

A Sacred Pilgrimage

Birth is a beginning
And death a destination
And life is a journey:
From childhood to maturity
And youth to age,
From innocence to awareness
And ignorance to knowing;
From foolishness to discretion
    And then, perhaps, to wisdom;
From weakness to strength
Or strength to weakness—
    And, often, back again;
From health to sickness
    And back, we pray, to health again;
From offense to forgiveness,
From loneliness to love,
From joy to gratitude,
From pain to compassion,
And grief to understanding—
    From fear to faith;
From defeat to defeat to defeat—
Until, looking backward or ahead,
We see that victory lies
Not at some high place along the way,
But in having made the journey, stage by stage,
    A sacred pilgrimage.
Birth is a beginning
And death a destination
And life is a journey,
A sacred pilgrimage—
    To life everlasting.

Rabbi Alvin Fine, "Birth is a Beginning"

K'DUSHAH: SANCTIFICATION

K'dushah   קְדוּשָׁה

נְקַדֵּשׁ אֶת־שִׁמְךָ בָּעוֹלָם, כְּשֵׁם שֶׁמַּקְדִּישִׁים אוֹתוֹ בִּשְׁמֵי
מָרוֹם, כַּכָּתוּב עַל־יַד נְבִיאֶךָ: וְקָרָא זֶה אֶל־זֶה וְאָמַר:

We sanctify Your name on earth, even as all things, to the ends
of time and space, proclaim Your holiness, and in the words of
the prophet we say:

קָדוֹשׁ, קָדוֹשׁ, קָדוֹשׁ יהוה צְבָאוֹת, מְלֹא כָל־הָאָרֶץ כְּבוֹדוֹ.

Holy, Holy, Holy is the God of all being! The whole earth is
filled with Your glory!

אַדִּיר אַדִּירֵנוּ, יהוה אֲדֹנֵינוּ, מָה־אַדִּיר שִׁמְךָ בְּכָל־הָאָרֶץ!

Source of our strength, Sovereign God, how majestic is Your
name in all the earth!

בָּרוּךְ כְּבוֹד־יהוה מִמְּקוֹמוֹ.

Praised be the glory of God in heaven and earth.

אֶחָד הוּא אֱלֹהֵינוּ, הוּא אָבִינוּ, הוּא מַלְכֵּנוּ, הוּא מוֹשִׁיעֵנוּ;
וְהוּא יַשְׁמִיעֵנוּ בְּרַחֲמָיו לְעֵינֵי כָּל־חָי:

You alone are our God and our Creator; You are our Ruler and
our Helper; and in Your mercy You reveal Yourself in the sight
of all the living:

"אֲנִי יהוה אֱלֹהֵיכֶם!"

"I am Your Eternal God!"

יִמְלֹךְ יהוה לְעוֹלָם, אֱלֹהַיִךְ צִיּוֹן, לְדֹר וָדֹר. הַלְלוּיָהּ!

The Eternal One shall reign for ever; your God, O Zion, from
generation to generation. Hallelujah!

לְדוֹר וָדוֹר נַגִּיד גָּדְלֶךָ, וּלְנֵצַח נְצָחִים קְדֻשָּׁתְךָ נַקְדִּישׁ.
וְשִׁבְחֲךָ, אֱלֹהֵינוּ, מִפִּינוּ לֹא יָמוּשׁ לְעוֹלָם וָעֶד.
בָּרוּךְ אַתָּה יְיָ, הָאֵל הַקָּדוֹשׁ.

To all generations we will make known Your greatness, and to all eternity proclaim Your holiness. Your praise, O God, shall never depart from our lips.
We praise You, Eternal One, the holy God.

COMMENTARY

In the Book of Isaiah, we are told of a strange and wonderful vision that the prophet had one day in the Temple of Jeruasalem.

Isaiah tells us that he was praying, and in the midst of his prayers he had a vision. In it he was surrounded by angels. They were moving their wings and singing the words:

קָדוֹשׁ קָדוֹשׁ קָדוֹשׁ יְיָ צְבָאוֹת, מְלֹא כָל־הָאָרֶץ כְּבוֹדוֹ.

Holy, Holy, Holy is the God of all being! The whole earth is filled with Your glory!

Isaiah 6:3

Turn to chapter 6 of Isaiah and try to imagine what Isaiah saw in his vision. What do you think is the meaning of the angels' words?

Mystery?

Isaiah's extraordinary vision, like many of our own experiences and dreams, is hard if not impossible to understand. The fact that we may not be able to comprehend something, however, does not necessarily mean that it is without significance. At times, the experiences we understand the least are the most important. Can you think of any experiences in your life that have been very important but difficult, if not impossible, to understand?

What about deep feelings of love we have for parents or that parents have for their children? What about the excitement or thrill we may experience when we hear beautiful music, or the mystery of our birth and life on earth at this time and not at another? What about the survival of the Jewish people?

Mystery is something that fills our lives. No matter how much we may know, there is still so much that we will never know. It is this mystery of life that the קְדוּשָׁה section seeks to express.

Holiness

The word קְדוּשָׁה is taken from the Hebrew קָדוֹשׁ *(kadosh)*, which means "different," "unique," "special," "sacred," "unlike anything else." What is the opposite of different or special? As we have already seen on page 69, a marriage ceremony is called קִדּוּשִׁין. What do two people do at a wedding ceremony that makes it קָדוֹשׁ? On Shabbat and on the holidays, when we make the blessing over the wine, we are "making the קִדּוּשׁ [*Kiddush*]." What makes that moment קָדוֹשׁ?

In Isaiah's vision, the angels express feelings of קְדוּשָׁה about God. The people who composed the קְדוּשָׁה took the angels' words and used them as their own. Perhaps they did so because they expressed the wonder and mystery men and women feel in moments of sensitivity and beauty. Perhaps they used Isaiah's words because they best articulated the idea of God's uniqueness and the wonder of divine power that fills all the earth.

We Sanctify Your Name

How do we "sanctify" God's name on earth? The Jewish philosopher Philo, who lived in Alexandria from about 20 B.C.E. to 40 C.E., wrote that "holiness toward God and justice toward human beings usually go together." What do you suppose Philo meant? How is "holiness" connected with "justice" toward our fellow human beings?

Moses Maimonides, in his book סֵפֶר הַמִּצְוֹת *(Sefer HaMitzvot)*, "The Book of Commandments," teaches the following:

> When the Torah says, "Be holy" (Leviticus 19:2), it means the same as if it said, "Do My commandments."

Why does Maimonides connect the doing of מִצְוֹת with קְדוּשָׁה? Are Maimonides and Philo saying the same thing?

The Baal Shem Tov, founder of Chasidism, once said to his pupils: "No two persons have the same talents. Each should strive to serve God according to his own abilities. If you imitate another, you may lose yourself. Therefore, always serve God through your own unique capacities."

According to the Baal Shem Tov, how can and should a person sanctify God's name?

What is unique about your own talents? What might the Baal Shem Tov define as קָדוֹשׁ within each person? Why is imitation dangerous? Who, among the people you have known or about whom you have read, would you consider to have achieved the expression of what is קָדוֹשׁ within them?

You may wish to have a discussion on how your congregation could help its members express their abilities and capacities.

A Person's Deeds

The Chasidic teacher known as the Sudilkover once remarked: "If a person's action is worthy, its influence makes for holiness." What kinds of actions are worthy and make for holiness?

Perhaps an example will help us understand what the Sudilkover Rebbe had in mind. We all know that there are many ways to help others. Suppose, for instance, a friend is having difficulty with a math problem. We can call him stupid and show him our paper. We can quickly tell him what to do and leave him alone to work it out by himself. We can explain the problem patiently and then stay with him so that if he needs us we will be able to offer further assistance.

What are the differences in the kinds of "help" suggested above? What makes one more worthy than the others? Which one would have an "influence making for holiness"? Why?

The great rabbi Leo Baeck, who survived a Nazi concentration camp, devoted his life to honoring God and helping his fellow Jews. He taught that not only do our good deeds bring holiness into the world—they also bring holiness to God. He wrote: "Every ethical deed and every decision for the good is a sanctification of God's name; such deeds and decisions are a realization of the divine, and through them is established a sanctuary of good upon earth, a place prepared for the dominion of God." Rabbi Baeck believes that we can draw nearer to God by doing good deeds and holy actions. Do you agree? How can our good deeds help establish "a sanctuary of good upon earth"? How does Rabbi Baeck's statement relate to the Sudilkover Rebbe's teaching about holiness?

CREATING WITH
KAVANAH
Themes:
a. The world in which we live is filled with mystery and wonder.
b. Men and women experience wonder when trying to understand their lives, abilities, and feelings.
c. Human beings achieve "holiness" through doing the מִצְווֹת.
d. Human beings achieve "holiness" through expressing their unique abilities and talents.

Prayers on the קְדוּשָׁה Theme

What Is Holiness?

The Torah commands us: "You shall be holy, for I the Eternal One, your God, am holy" (Leviticus 19:2). What is holiness?

There is holiness when we strive to be true to ourselves.

There is holiness when we bring friendship into lonely lives.

There is holiness when we reach out to help those who are in want.

There is holiness when we forget petty anger and make up with those we love.

There is holiness when we care for our environment and make it a safer to live in.

There is holiness when we praise the Eternal One who gave us the power to pray.

Holy, Holy, Holy is the Eternal God.

All life can be filled with God's glory!

Based upon *Where Can Holiness Be Found?* by Sidney Greenberg

Fill Us with the Awe of Your Holiness

Among the many appetites of man
There is a craving after God.
Among the many attributes of man
There is a talent for worshiping God.
Jews who wandered in deserts beneath the stars
Knew their hearts were hungry for God.
Jews who studied in candle-lit ghetto rooms
Thirsted longingly after God.
But we who are smothered with comfort
Sometimes forget to listen to God.
Help us, O Lord, to recognize our need,
To hear the yearning whisper of our hearts.
Help us to seek the silence of the desert
And the thoughtfulness of the house of study.
Bless us, like our ancestors in ancient days,
With that most precious gift: a sense of Thy presence.
Brush us with the wind of the wings of Thy being.
Fill us with the awe of Thy holiness.
We, too, will praise, glorify, and exalt Thy name.

Ruth F. Brin, "A Sense of Your Presense"

126

We Should Mark "Holy"

We thank You, God, that You let us see a portion of
Your goodness in each person.

You gave us the ability to reason, to plan, to teach.

You gave us the heart to love,
The strength to build.

But, in addition to wisdom, understanding, and power,

We need a sense of sacredness of daily life.
Upon our hands we should mark "Holy."
Between our eyes "Holy."
Upon our gates "Holy."

Rabbi William Sajowitz

The World's Beginning

You are the world's beginning: this world
bears witness to
You—alone, apart,
the Only God,
the Mind we glimpse in all—
Hills wrenched from earth
and skies spread out before our humbled eyes.

Inexhaustible God: You flow, burst out,
overflow: You have poured Yourself
into universes beyond thought
and they cannot contain You.
You fill the endless worlds.
Deep beyond our guess, the Deep itself
hidden, hiding, abyss, shadow, friend, 'Illusion':
What shall we call You whom we do not know?
How shall we speak to You?
We are lonely, afraid to hope:
Is the ground firm under our feet?
Or do they tremble upon a precipice?
Are You the bridge across that fearful fall?

In this dark world we search for You,
with anxious lines about our eyes,
and even for the pure the light is dim.
Our ears hear sounds from afar—
music is it? Lifeless noise?

Is there—surely there is?—an echo of love?
We look, and listen, and struggle
to gaze upon Your world
in joy in awe in love in praise:

holy, holy, holy:
the hidden God
the One who speaks—
and there is light!

Rabbi Chaim Stern

K'DUSHAT HAYOM: SANCTIFICATION OF THE DAY

K'dushat HaYom   קְדוּשַׁת הַיּוֹם

אֱלֹהֵֽינוּ וֵאלֹהֵי אֲבוֹתֵֽינוּ וְאִמּוֹתֵֽינוּ, רְצֵה בִמְנוּחָתֵֽנוּ. קַדְּשֵֽׁנוּ
בְּמִצְוֹתֶֽיךָ וְתֵן חֶלְקֵֽנוּ בְּתוֹרָתֶֽךָ. שַׂבְּעֵֽנוּ מִטּוּבֶֽךָ, וְשַׂמְּחֵֽנוּ
בִּישׁוּעָתֶֽךָ, וְטַהֵר לִבֵּֽנוּ לְעָבְדְּךָ בֶּאֱמֶת. וְהַנְחִילֵֽנוּ, יי אֱלֹהֵֽינוּ,
בְּאַהֲבָה וּבְרָצוֹן שַׁבַּת קָדְשֶֽׁךָ, וְיָנֽוּחוּ בָהּ יִשְׂרָאֵל מְקַדְּשֵׁי
שְׁמֶֽךָ. בָּרוּךְ אַתָּה יי, מְקַדֵּשׁ הַשַּׁבָּת.

Our God, God of our fathers and our mothers, may our rest on this day be pleasing in Your sight. Sanctify us with Your mitzvot, and let Your Torah be our way of life. Satisfy us with Your goodness, gladden us with Your salvation, and purify our hearts to serve You in Truth. In Your gracious love, Eternal God, let Your holy Sabbath remain our heritage, that all Israel, hallowing Your name, may find rest and peace. We praise You, O God, for the Sabbath and its holiness.

COMMENTARY

On Shabbat or on a holiday, one special prayer takes the place of the middle thirteen prayers of the daily עֲמִידָה. It is known by the name of קְדוּשַׁת הַיּוֹם (K'dushat HaYom), "the Sanctification of the Day."

The Sages who composed the עֲמִידָה for Shabbat and the holidays excluded all mention of sorrow, suffering, sin, repentance, and any other human problems from the קְדוּשַׁת הַיּוֹם and from the עֲמִידָה. Why? Why not use Shabbat or the holidays to ask God for help or for forgiveness? Why aren't such requests permitted by Jewish tradition on Shabbat?

According to the Rabbis, nothing should be mentioned in Shabbat worship that might deprive a person of the full enjoyment of Shabbat or the holiday. Even mourners must stop their mourning on Shabbat. Shabbat was to be a day of celebration and joy. The sage Rabbi Chanina, who lived in Israel in about 350 C.E., taught that "a joyous spirit should be a rule on Shabbat" (BT *Shabbat* 12a–b).

The concept of Shabbat as a day of celebration and joy is an ancient one in Jewish tradition. It is mentioned by the prophet Isaiah. Here is what he told the people of his times:

> If you will turn away your foot because of Shabbat,
> From pursuing business on My holy day;
> And call the Shabbat a delight,
> And the holy of the Eternal One honorable;
> And will honor it, not doing anything you wish,
> Nor pursuing your business, nor speaking about it;
> Then shall you delight in the Eternal One....
>
> Isaiah 58:13–14

What do you think Isaiah had in mind when he mentioned "business"? What sort of work should be forbidden on Shabbat? According to the Sages, there are thirty-nine categories of "work" that are forbidden on Shabbat. These include plowing, reaping, carrying loads, kindling a fire, writing, sewing, and buying or selling. Why might such "work" detract from the joy and celebration of Shabbat?

How Can We Celebrate Shabbat?

How can we fulfill Rabbi Chanina's teaching that "a joyous spirit should be a rule on Shabbat"? How is it possible for us and our families to develop a Shabbat celebration that brings us happiness? Perhaps some ideas from our tradition will help us formulate some practices of our own.

Our Shabbat Meal

We are told that the Sages would do everything possible to make sure that the Shabbat meal was very special. As a matter of fact, Rabbi Chiya ben Aba, who lived in Israel during the third century C.E., proclaimed that Jews should "sanctify Shabbat with food, drink, clean garments, and pleasure" (*D'varim Rabbah* 3:1).

In keeping with Rabbi Chiya ben Aba's statement, Jews throughout the centuries have sought to make the Shabbat meal a special and beautiful celebration. They would save money each week to purchase the finest foods and wine. And they would set their Shabbat tables with beautifully decorated coverings and their best dishes.

When it came time, the meal was celebrated with the lighting of Shabbat candles, the singing of the *Kiddush*, blessings of children by parents, and Shabbat songs. The Shabbat meal was a time of sharing with family and friends. If strangers happened to be passing through the town, they were invited to join in the Shabbat celebration. Thus was a unique atmosphere of joy and happiness created at the Shabbat meal.

131

Why do you think that the Shabbat meal became such an important part of the Shabbat celebration of Jews? What do eating and celebrating have to do with one another? How does singing help make an occasion joyful? Are there other holidays, not connected with Jewish tradition, where eating and celebrating go together? What does your family do for the Shabbat meal? What new ideas might you have to help make your Shabbat meal even more special?

Your congregation or study group may want to set up a Shabbat meal. Prepare the food, invite your families, and have a model Shabbat celebration.

Dressing Up!

Rabbi Chiya ben Aba mentioned that one can "sanctify Shabbat with...clean garments." Other Sages suggested that "a person's Shabbat clothes should not be like the weekday clothes." Some Jews put aside special garments that they wear only on Shabbat and on holidays. Why? In what way do clothes play a part in human celebrations?

What we choose to wear often expresses how we feel. We call it "dressing up" when we put on special clothing or a costume for an important event. What difference do you think it would make if you "dressed up" in a special garment (even a costume!) for Shabbat? How would it help make Shabbat different from all other days of the week? (You may wish to refer back to our discussion, on page 3, of the use of the *tallit* as a form of "special dress" for prayer.)

Shabbat Rest

The קְדוּשַׁת הַיּוֹם prayer begins with the phrase "Our God, God of our fathers and our mothers, may our rest on this day be pleasing in Your sight." What is meant by the word מְנוּחָתֵנוּ (m'nuchateinu), "our rest"? Is it just physical relaxation, or does Jewish tradition have much more in mind?

Rabbi Mordecai Kaplan interprets מְנוּחָתֵנוּ in the following way:

An artist cannot be continually wielding his brush. He must stop at times in his painting to freshen his vision of the object, the meaning of which he wishes to express on his canvas. Living is also an art....

The Shabbat represents those moments when we pause in our brushwork to renew our vision of the object.

STATEMENTS ON SHABBAT

Shabbat...prevents us from reducing our life to the level of a machine.
Moses Montefiore

The Jewish tradition, with its love of home life and its devotion to study, has shown how the Shabbat can be made not only a day of rest from work but a positive factor in human development and well-being.
Leon Roth

The Shabbat is the day of peace between man and nature....By not working—by not participating in the process of natural and social change—man is free from the chains of nature and from the chains of time....
Erich Fromm

How does Rabbi Kaplan define "Shabbat rest"? Why does he believe it is important for a person to "pause" in the midst of work? Would you agree with him that "living is an art"?

Our Shabbat rest can and should involve the expression of our spirits—our appreciation of music, art, and literature. It can mean the deepening of relationships with our family and friends through sharing Shabbat experiences and activities. According to Rabbi Shimon ben Lakish, "God lends to each Jew a נְשָׁמָה יְתֵרָה (n'shamah y'teirah), an extra portion of soul, on the eve of the Shabbat and takes it away at the close of the Shabbat" (BT *Beitzah* 16a).

What do you think Rabbi Shimon ben Lakish meant by his observation? What might we do on Shabbat that would enable us to express our spirits and enlarge our appreciation of the world in which we live?

To Serve You in Truth

One of the most beautiful phrases in the קְדוּשַׁת הַיּוֹם prayer is "purify our hearts to serve You in Truth." The words have been set to a number of melodies, but what do they mean? And how do they relate to our observance of Shabbat?

As we have already mentioned, the Torah forbids work on Shabbat. Some of the Sages even went so far as to forbid thinking about one's weekday or business responsibilities, since that could interfere with the full enjoyment of Shabbat. We are told, however, that "to plan for a מִצְוָה or for charity is permitted on Shabbat" (BT *Shabbat* 15a). Why do you suppose such planning was permitted?

It might be because both the performance of a מִצְוָה and the celebration of Shabbat are meant to help a person recognize how precious life is.

When, for instance, we do the מִצְוָה of caring for the sick by helping a member of our family or a friend who is ill, we may realize how important friendship and the help of others can be. We may even understand how very fortunate we are to enjoy good health. In doing the מִצְוָה then, we not only aid another person, but we also heighten our appreciation of the opportunity we have been given for life.

Themes:
a. Shabbat is a day of joy
   and celebration.
b. Work is forbidden on
   Shabbat; we are
   commanded to rest.
c. Shabbat should be
   celebrated with special
   meals, dress, and the
   study of Torah.
d. Shabbat is meant to
   increase our
   appreciation of life and
   its opportunities.
e. One may do מִצְווֹת on
   Shabbat (visit the sick,
   help a friend, and plan
   for charity).
f. Shabbat has contributed
   to the survival of the
   Jewish people and
   Judaism.
g. Keeping Shabbat holy
   is part of our covenant
   with God.

The commandment in the Torah for the observance of Shabbat is זָכוֹר אֶת יוֹם הַשַּׁבָּת לְקַדְּשׁוֹ (*Zachor et Yom HaShabbat l'kadsho*), "Remember the Shabbat day to keep it holy" (Exodus 20:8; Deuteronomy 5:12).

What can the Torah mean by asking us to keep a day קָדוֹשׁ? What might be the relationship between the doing of מִצְווֹת on Shabbat (visiting the sick, helping a friend, planning for charity) and making the day קָדוֹשׁ? What might such activities have to do with the phrase "purify our hearts to serve You in Truth" in the קְדוּשַׁת הַיּוֹם prayer?

A Complaint

The Rabbis loved to teach with legends. One of their favorites was about a complaint that the Torah once brought before God.

The Torah asked: "O Eternal One, what will happen to me when all the people of Israel are busy at work each day of the week?" God replied: "I am giving them Shabbat, and they will devote themselves to you on that day."

The point of the legend is clear. Shabbat, in Jewish tradition, is meant for study and the sharing of thoughts. That is why each Shabbat has been assigned a Torah portion for reading and discussion.

Rabbi Leo Baeck once said: "There is no Judaism without Shabbat." What do you think he meant by this observation? What is the importance of studying the Torah each Shabbat? How does such a practice help preserve the Jewish people?

The Shabbat Has Kept Israel

The Hebrew essayist Achad Ha-Am once wrote: "More than Israel has kept the Shabbat, the Shabbat has kept Israel." In what way is Achad Ha-Am's observation true? How would you relate it to the various areas and ideas discussed in this section of our commentary?

A Shabbat Prayer from Exodus

וְשָׁמְרוּ בְנֵי־יִשְׂרָאֵל אֶת־הַשַּׁבָּת, לַעֲשׂוֹת אֶת־הַשַּׁבָּת לְדֹרֹתָם בְּרִית עוֹלָם.
בֵּינִי וּבֵין בְּנֵי יִשְׂרָאֵל אוֹת הִיא לְעֹלָם. כִּי־שֵׁשֶׁת יָמִים עָשָׂה יהוה
אֶת־הַשָּׁמַיִם וְאֶת־הָאָרֶץ, וּבַיּוֹם הַשְּׁבִיעִי שָׁבַת וַיִּנָּפַשׁ.

The people of Israel shall keep the Sabbath, observing the Sabbath in every generation as a covenant for all time. It is a sign forever between Me and the people of Israel. For in six days the Eternal One made heaven and earth, but on the seventh day, God rested and was refreshed.

One of the best known commandments of Torah regarding Shabbat is known as וְשָׁמְרוּ (V'shamru), and it is recited or sung just before the קְדוּשַׁת הַיּוֹם. It is also the first paragraph of *Kiddush L'Yom Shabbat*, which is recited at the conclusion of the שַׁבָּת morning service. (For the complete קִדּוּשׁ, see page 238.) It calls Shabbat an אוֹת (ot), "sign," between God and the Jewish people. What do you think the Torah meant by such a description of Shabbat? How can a day be a "sign" between God and the Jewish people?

A Sage once taught: "To observe Shabbat is to bear witness to the Creator" (M'chilta). How does this statement help us understand the commandment (Exodus 31:16–17) to observe Shabbat? What does it mean to "bear witness to the Creator"?

Modern rabbi Arthur Green writes: "In keeping Shabbat, Israel bears witness to the fact that ours is a created world. For us this means that divinity fills the universe. Our task is to treat all living things with respect, and so enhance the divine light in them. Only by this way of living is the testimony of Shabbat made real." According to Rabbi Green, what is the relationship between treating others properly and keeping Shabbat? How does this statement relate to the Sage's teaching about observing Shabbat? What might these ideas have to do with the Creation story in the first chapters of Genesis?

Prayers on the קְדוּשַׁת הַיּוֹם Theme

Remember the Shabbat

Remember to keep the Shabbat and make it a special day.

Shabbat is special when it is the day on which we study Torah.

Shabbat is special when we join with other Jews to celebrate it.

Shabbat is special when we think of the beauty of nature and of our duty to make the world a safer and more peaceful place to live.

Shabbat is special when we share with others its joy and its song.

Remember to keep the Shabbat and make it a special day.

HJF

A New Shabbat

Lord, help us now to make this a new Shabbat.

After noise, we seek quiet;

After crowds of indifferent strangers,

We seek to touch those we love;

After concentration on work and responsibility,

We seek freedom to meditate, to listen to our inward selves.

We open our eyes to the hidden beauties

    and the infinite possibilities in the world You are creating;

We break open the gates of the reservoirs

    of goodness and kindness in ourselves and in others;

We reach toward one holy perfect moment of Shabbat.

Ruth F. Brin, "Sabbath Prayer"

Light a Candle

Light a candle.
Drink wine.
Softly the Sabbath has plucked
the sinking sun.
Slowly the Sabbath descends,
the rose of heaven in her hand.

How can the Sabbath
plant a huge and shining flower
in a blind and narrow heart?
How can the Sabbath
plant the bud of angels
in a heart of raving flesh?
Can the rose of eternity grow
in an age enslaved
to destruction,
an age enslaved
to death?

Light a candle!
Drink wine!
Slowly the Sabbath descends
and in her hand
the flower,
and in her hand
the sinking sun.

Zelda, "Light a Candle," translated by Marcia Falk

May Each Shabbat...

O Eternal One our God, may each new Shabbat strengthen our love of Torah. Let our actions toward others reflect honor upon our faith and people. Teach us to be more sensitive to the pains and feelings of our friends and family. May we always realize that we are an important link in the chain of our tradition. On this Shabbat, let us rededicate ourselves to being truthful and loving in all that we do. We praise You, O God, for the holiness and joy of this Shabbat day.

HJF

AVODAH: WORSHIP

The Traditional Avodah עֲבוֹדָה

רְצֵה, יְיָ אֱלֹהֵינוּ, בְּעַמְּךָ יִשְׂרָאֵל וּבִתְפִלָּתָם. וְהָשֵׁב אֶת הָעֲבוֹדָה לִדְבִיר בֵּיתֶךָ, (וְאִשֵּׁי יִשְׂרָאֵל) וּתְפִלָּתָם בְּאַהֲבָה תְקַבֵּל בְּרָצוֹן. וּתְהִי לְרָצוֹן תָּמִיד עֲבוֹדַת יִשְׂרָאֵל עַמֶּךָ.

Be gracious, Eternal God, to Your people Israel and their prayers. Restore the worship service of Your Temple, and receive in love and favor (the offerings and) the prayers of Israel. O may our worship always be acceptable to You.

וְתֶחֱזֶינָה עֵינֵינוּ בְּשׁוּבְךָ לְצִיּוֹן בְּרַחֲמִים. בָּרוּךְ אַתָּה יְיָ, הַמַּחֲזִיר שְׁכִינָתוֹ לְצִיּוֹן.

Let our eyes behold Your presence in our midst and in the midst of our people in Zion. We praise You, O God, who restores Your presence to Zion.

The Reform *Avodah*   עֲבוֹדָה

רְצֵה, יי אֱלֹהֵינוּ, בְּעַמְּךָ יִשְׂרָאֵל, וּתְפִלָּתָם בְּאַהֲבָה תְקַבֵּל,
וּתְהִי לְרָצוֹן תָּמִיד עֲבוֹדַת יִשְׂרָאֵל עַמֶּךָ. אֵל קָרוֹב
לְכָל־קֹרְאָיו, פְּנֵה אֶל עֲבָדֶיךָ וְחָנֵּנוּ; שְׁפוֹךְ רוּחֲךָ עָלֵינוּ,
וְתֶחֱזֶינָה עֵינֵינוּ בְּשׁוּבְךָ לְצִיּוֹן בְּרַחֲמִים. בָּרוּךְ אַתָּה יי,
הַמַּחֲזִיר שְׁכִינָתוֹ לְצִיּוֹן.

Be gracious, Eternal God, to Your people Israel, and receive our prayers with love. O may our worship always be acceptable to You. Fill us with the knowledge that You are near to all who seek You in truth. Let our eyes behold Your presence in our midst and in the midst of our people in Zion. We praise You, O God, whose presence gives life to Zion and all Israel.

COMMENTARY

There are two versions of the עֲבוֹדָה. The commentary will explore their differences.

According to the Rabbis of the Talmud, the עֲבוֹדָה prayer was said by the priests in the Temple just after they had offered the sacrifices (*Mishnah Tamid* 5:1). We are not absolutely sure what the words of the original עֲבוֹדָה prayer were. In his commentary on the Talmud, the medieval scholar Rashi (1040–1105) gives us the following version (BT *B'rachot* 11b).

The Original Temple עֲבוֹדָה Prayer

רְצֵה יְהֹוָה אֱלֹהֵינוּ עֲבוֹדַת עַמְּךָ יִשְׂרָאֵל, וְאִשֵּׁי יִשְׂרָאֵל וּתְפִלָּתָם תְּקַבֵּל
בְּרָצוֹן. בָּרוּךְ הַמְקַבֵּל עֲבוֹדַת עַמּוֹ יִשְׂרָאֵל בְּרָצוֹן.

Be gracious, O Eternal One our God, with the sacrifices of your people Israel. Accept with favor the offerings of Israel and their prayers. Praised be God, who accepts the sacrifices of the people Israel with favor.

In the Jerusalem Talmud, we are told that the final blessing used by the Temple priests was:

בָּרוּךְ אַתָּה יְהֹוָה, שֶׁאוֹתְךָ לְבַדְּךָ בְּיִרְאָה נַעֲבוֹד.

Praised be You, O Eternal One, whom alone we serve in reverence.

Later in our discussion of the עֲבוֹדָה prayer, we will compare and contrast the many changes it has undergone through the ages.

Why Sacrifices?

The word עֲבוֹדָה, when used in the context of worship at the Temple in Jerusalem, meant "sacrificial service." When the Second Temple was destroyed by the Romans in 70 C.E., prayer (תְּפִלָּה) in the synagogue took the place of sacrifices.

If we trace the history of humanity to its most primitive beginnings, we find that sacrifice played a very important part in humanity's relationship with nature and the Divine. Sacrifices were offered to express thanksgiving or praise. At times they were made as a present to the gods for rain, or sun, or the birth of new life. Sometimes, in preparation for a battle, sacrifices were offered in order to guarantee favor from the gods.

The Jewish people, like many of the ancient peoples about them, used sacrifice as the chief form of their worship. A glance at the final chapters of Exodus and at the Book of Leviticus will give you an idea of the variety of different sacrifices that ancient Jews offered at the Temple in Jerusalem. There were sin offerings, peace offerings, special Shabbat and holiday offerings, guilt offerings, meal offerings, and so on. All these offerings were ways in which early Jews celebrated life and gave thanks to God. The sin offerings and guilt offerings were means through which a person asked God for forgiveness of wrongdoings. In a sense, sacrifice played the same role for our ancient ancestors as prayer plays in our lives.

The Prophets Speak Out

One of the problems of the sacrificial offerings was that when people gave their sacrifices they often thought that they had satisfied their obligations to God. As a matter of fact, there were many people who came to believe that they could act unjustly, cheat, lie, and take advantage of the poor so long as they gave their sacrifice at the Temple. Many of these people came to think that all that God wanted from them was a sweet-smelling offering.

The prophets of Israel challenged this idea. They believed that, above all, God wanted justice, righteousness, and the pursuit of truth. For instance, the prophet Micah condemned the people of his day for their corruption and evil behavior, and he questioned their belief that God only wanted sacrifices from them. This is what he told them:

Hear now what the Eternal One says to you:
...That you may know the righteous acts of God.
Wherewith shall I come before the Eternal One
And bow myself before God on high?
Shall I come before Him with burnt offerings,
With calves of a year old?
Will the Eternal One be pleased with thousands of rams
With tens of thousands of rivers of oil?
Shall I give my first-born for my sin,
The fruit of my body for the sin of my soul?
It has been told you, O man, what is good,
And what the Eternal One requires of you:
Only to do justly, and to love mercy, and to walk humbly with
    your God.

Micah 6:1, 5–8

The prophet Amos joined Micah in condemning those who piously brought their sacrifices to the Temple and then practiced corruption in their dealings with others. Speaking in the name of God, Amos told his people who were gathered at the Temple:

Therefore, says the Eternal One....
I hate, I despise your feasts,
And I will take no delight in your solemn assemblies.
Yea, though you offer me burnt offerings and your meal offerings,
I will not accept them;
Neither will I regard the peace offerings of your fat beasts.
Take away from Me the noise of your songs;
And let Me not hear the melody of your psalteries.
But let justice well up as waters,
And righteousness as a mighty stream.

Amos 5:16, 21–24

What are both Micah and Amos saying about sacrifices? Why do they object to them? What do they believe God wants from human beings? What might Micah and Amos criticize in our society today?

Sacrifice versus Prayer

With the destruction of the Second Temple by the Romans, the עֲבוֹדָה sacrifices ceased. In their place were the prayers of the synagogue. Actually, we do not know when the synagogue came into existence. It is possible that it developed around the fourth century B.C.E., during the time that Alexander the Great conquered the Middle East. He brought with him the development of cities, and with them most likely came the building of synagogues. By the time the Second Temple was destroyed in 70 C.E., there were hundreds of synagogues throughout the Land of Israel. In fact, there was a synagogue in the Temple itself, and there were over 480 others in the city of Jerusalem. Within these synagogues, the practice of תְּפִלָּה, "prayer," was refined by our people. And when the Second Temple fell before the Romans, prayer replaced sacrifice in Jewish life.

Two Opinions

As time went by, two different opinions developed regarding the restoration of the Temple and its sacrifices.

There were those who felt that nothing could replace the old sacrificial ceremonies. Some of these people became אֲבֵלֵי צִיוֹן *(Aveilei Tziyon),* "Mourners of Zion." They refused to eat meat or drink wine. For them there "was no עֲבוֹדָה as precious to God as the עֲבוֹדָה of the Temple."

There were others, however, who felt differently. They taught that "words of learning are more valuable than burnt offerings and peace offerings" *(Avot D'Rabbi Natan).* Others who held similar views taught that "prayer is greater than sacrifices" and that "prayer is dearer to God than all good works and all good sacrifices" (Rabbi Eliezer and Rabbi Abahu).

These teachers of Judaism may have been troubled by the sacrifices of the Temple and even pleased when they ceased to be a part of Jewish practice. Why might they have been troubled by the sacrifices of the Temple? Why would they have considered prayer superior to sacrifice?

Some of the Sages realized that, if the Jewish people was to survive, it would have to overcome the loss of the Temple and sacrifices and replace

During the Six-Day War in 1967, the Israelis regained the old city of Jerusalem. Thousands rushed to the כֹּתֶל מַעֲרָבִי (Kotel Maaravi), Western Wall, and there offered prayers of thanks-giving. The Western Wall is the remaining part of that wall which sur-rounded the Temple that was destroyed by the Ro-mans in 70 C.E. It has be-come a national shrine for Jews throughout the world. Why? Why have Jews, religious and nonreligious, wept without shame upon seeing and visiting the Western Wall? A popular song about the Wall says: "There are men with hearts of stone, and there are stones with hearts of men." What do those words mean when applied to the Western Wall in Jewish tradition?

them with the synagogue and prayer. How did the successful replacement of sacrifices with prayer and the Temple with the synagogue enable Judaism to survive? Today, there are some ultra-Orthodox Jews who study the laws of the Talmud about sacrifices and who pray and prepare themselves for the rebuilding of the Jerusalem Temple and the reintroduction of animal sacrifices. Would you favor or oppose such a practice, and why?

Changing the עֲבוֹדָה Prayer

We have already noted several times that many of our prayers reflect the feelings and history of our people. The destruction of the Second Temple was a terrible moment in our national history. For some it may have seemed that Judaism and the Jewish people were destined for death. Yet for the vast majority of Jews, there was hope that someday the Temple would be rebuilt and that the Jewish people would return to their land.

In order to voice that hope, the Rabbis, after the destruction of the Second Temple, changed the words of the עֲבוֹדָה prayer. In their new version they voiced the yearning that the Temple would be rebuilt and the sacrifices restored. Their version of the עֲבוֹדָה prayer is the traditional one found on page 137 and in the prayer books of Conservative and Orthodox Jews.

The עֲבוֹדָה Prayer and Reform Jews

The founders of Reform Judaism rejected the hope for rebuilding the Temple and the restoration of sacrifices. They believed that prayer and ethical actions were higher forms of worshiping God than sacrificing animals. Since they were opposed to the reconstruction of the Temple and the reintroduction of sacrifices, they changed the words of the עֲבוֹדָה prayer.

The following is an adapted version of the prayer they included in the *Union Prayer Book*, which was used by Reform Jews until the publication of *Gates of Prayer*:

רְצֵה יְיָ אֱלֹהֵינוּ בְּעַמְּךָ יִשְׂרָאֵל וּתְפִלָּתָם בְּאַהֲבָה תְקַבֵּל וּתְהִי לְרָצוֹן תָּמִיד
עֲבֹדַת יִשְׂרָאֵל עַמֶּךָ. בָּרוּךְ אַתָּה יְיָ, שֶׁאוֹתְךָ לְבַדְּךָ בְּיִרְאָה נַעֲבוֹד.

Look with favor, O Eternal One, upon us, and may our service be acceptable to You. Praised be You, O God, whom alone we serve in reverence.

142

Compare the various versions of the עֲבוֹדָה prayer in the following order: (1) the Temple version used before the destruction; (2) the traditional version; (3) the version from the *Union Prayer Book;* and (4) the new Reform version in *Gates of Prayer* and *B'chol L'vavcha.*

What do you think of the Reformers' changes? Would it bother you to pray for the restoration of the Temple and sacrifices? Why do you think the new Reform version is different from that which appeared in the *Union Prayer Book?* If you were writing a new עֲבוֹדָה prayer, what would you include in it?

Acceptable to You

What makes a person's prayer acceptable to God? Is it the tone of voice, the bowing of the body, the pain or joy out of which the person says the prayer?

There are no easy answers to those questions. Jewish tradition, however, offers us some insights to consider.

The Rabbis teach that "prayer requires כַּוָּנָה." What is *kavanah?* Maimonides defines it as "the clearing of the mind of all private or selfish thoughts" (*T'filah* 4:16). What do you think Maimonides meant? How would "clearing the mind of all selfish thoughts" aid a person in prayer?

Some Rabbis have defined כַּוָּנָה as the total involvement and attention of a person in whatever act he or she is engaged. "To pray with כַּוָּנָה means to concentrate completely upon your prayer so that your heart is not divided" (*P'sikta Zutarta,* Deuteronomy 11:13). Rabbi Ami had something like this in his mind when he said: "A person's prayer is not acceptable unless he put his heart in his hands" (BT *Taanit* 8a). What do you think it means to "put your heart in your hands"? What is a "heart divided"?

A Sage once remarked that "prayer without כַּוָּנָה is like a body without a soul." What do you think was meant by that?

Intentions and Moods

The talmudic sage Rav, who lived in Babylonia during the third century C.E., once taught his followers that "whoever can pray for a neighbor and does not is called a sinner" (BT *B'rachot* 12b). Jewish prayer is meant to turn our attentions to the needs, problems, and concerns of others, the Jewish community, and the human community. Our prayers are "acceptable" when they express our responsibilities and relationships to others. Rabbi Isaac Luria, a mystic who lived during the sixteenth century, taught that before men or women entered into prayer, they should remember the מִצְוָה "Love your neighbor as yourself" (Leviticus 19:18). Why did Rabbi Luria make such a suggestion? What does "Love your neighbor as yourself" have to do with prayer?

Mood also plays a significant role in worship. We are told by the Rabbis: "Neither foolishness nor laziness, nor excessive piety, nor overconcern with material things ought to be the mood of worship." What is wrong with each of the things mentioned? How do they hamper prayer?

Earlier, on page 9, we included a thought from Rabbi Eliezer in which he commented that "if a person prays according to the exact text of the prayer book and adds nothing from his own mind and heart, his prayer is not proper" (BT *B'rachot* 28a). Why not? What is wrong with just saying the words? What did he mean by adding something from one's own mind? How do you add from your mind to the words written in the prayer book?

Another Rabbi taught: "Do not pray for the impossible" (*Tosefta, B'rachot* 7a). Why isn't a prayer for the impossible permissible? What is wrong about it? An example from tradition may help explain.

We are told that if you should be on your way home and see a fire in the distance, do not pray: "O God, please let the fire not be in my house!" What is wrong with that prayer? Can you think of other examples of "praying for the impossible"? Why are they not acceptable in Jewish tradition?

Prayer, an Art?

From all this it should be clear that "acceptable" prayer is an art. It requires skill, understanding, and a willingness to express our innermost feelings and selves. Just as artists cannot be successful unless they give themselves completely to the task, so too our prayers call upon us to be totally open to the world in which we live and involved in the spirit of worship.

Prayers on the עֲבוֹדָה Theme

A Prayer That Our Prayers Be Acceptable

Our God, look with pleasure on Your people Israel—female, male, child, parent, old, and young. Let our prayers renew our bond with You.

Accept in Your love our love, our prayers, and our deeds, in forms ancient and new, as the offerings of our hearts.

144

Compassionate One, hear and respond to our prayers and the prayers of Your people Israel with graciousness, compassion, and favor.

Rabbi Barton G. Lee

Accept Our Prayers

O God, hear our prayers
When they are for peace.
O God, hear our prayers
When they are for human cooperation.
O God, hear our prayers
When they are for the freedom of our people.
O God, hear our prayers
When they are for the healing of those who are sick.
O God, hear our prayers
When they remind us to be honest with ourselves and others.
O God, hear our prayers
When we offer them from our hearts.

HJF

Prayer Invites God

Prayer invites God to let His presence suffuse our spirits, to let His will prevail in our lives. Prayer cannot bring water to parched fields, nor mend a broken bridge, nor rebuild a ruined city; but prayer can water an arid soul, mend a broken heart, and rebuild a weakened will.

Rabbi Ferdinand M. Isserman, *Gates of Prayer*

We Cannot Merely Pray

We cannot merely pray to You, O God, to end war;
For we know that You have made the world in a way
That man must find his own path to peace
Within himself and with his neighbor.

We cannot merely pray to You, O God,
To end starvation;
For You have already given us the resources
With which to feed the entire world,
If we would only use them wisely.

We cannot merely pray to You, O God,
To root out prejudice;
For You have already given us eyes
With which to see the good in all men,
If we would only use them rightly.

We cannot merely pray to You, O God,
To end despair;
For You have already given us the power
To clear away slums and to give hope,
If we would only use our power justly.

We cannot merely pray to You, O God, to end disease;
For You have already given us great minds
With which to search out cures and healings,
If we would only use them constructively.

Therefore, we pray to You instead, O God,
For strength, determination, and willpower,
To *do* instead of just to pray,
To *become* instead of merely to wish.

For Your sake and for ours, speedily and soon,
That our land may be safe,
And that our lives may be blessed.

May the words that we pray, and the deeds that we do
Be acceptable before You, O Lord,
Our Rock and our Redeemer.

Rabbi Jack Riemer, "We Cannot Merely Pray to You"

Let Us Restore

Let us restore Shekhinah [God's Presence] to her place
in Israel and throughout the world,
and let us infuse all places
with her presence.

Marcia Falk, "Restoring Shekhinah, Reclaiming Home"

CREATING WITH KAVANAH

Themes:
a. The עֲבוֹדָה prayer was used in the Temple at the time of offering the sacrifices. What sort of sacrifices do we offer today?
b. Prayer and ethical behavior are interrelated in Jewish tradition.
c. The Jewish people expressed the longing for a return to the Land of Israel and a rebuilding of the Temple within their prayers.
d. Reform Jews rejected the idea of rebuilding the Temple and reintroducing sacrifices.
e. Prayer is a sacred opportunity to communicate with God.
f. Prayer demands כַּוָּנָה.
g. Prayer can turn our attention to the needs, problems, and concerns of others—the people of Israel and all peoples—and to our own inmost thoughts and needs.
h. Prayer is an art. It must be practiced and perfected.

HODAAH: THANKSGIVING

Hodaah　　　　　　　　　　　　　הוֹדָאָה

מוֹדִים אֲנַחְנוּ לָךְ, שָׁאַתָּה הוּא יי אֱלֹהֵינוּ וֵאלֹהֵי אֲבוֹתֵינוּ
וְאִמּוֹתֵינוּ לְעוֹלָם וָעֶד. צוּר חַיֵּינוּ, מָגֵן יִשְׁעֵנוּ, אַתָּה הוּא
לְדוֹר וָדוֹר. נוֹדֶה לְּךָ וּנְסַפֵּר תְּהִלָּתֶךָ, עַל־חַיֵּינוּ הַמְּסוּרִים
בְּיָדֶךָ, וְעַל־נִשְׁמוֹתֵינוּ הַפְּקוּדוֹת לָךְ, וְעַל־נִסֶּיךָ שֶׁבְּכָל־יוֹם
עִמָּנוּ, וְעַל־נִפְלְאוֹתֶיךָ וְטוֹבוֹתֶיךָ שֶׁבְּכָל־עֵת, עֶרֶב וָבֹקֶר
וְצָהֳרָיִם. הַטּוֹב: כִּי לֹא־כָלוּ רַחֲמֶיךָ, וְהַמְרַחֵם: כִּי־לֹא תַמּוּ
חֲסָדֶיךָ, מֵעוֹלָם קִוִּינוּ לָךְ.
וְעַל כֻּלָּם יִתְבָּרַךְ וְיִתְרוֹמַם שִׁמְךָ, מַלְכֵּנוּ, תָּמִיד לְעוֹלָם וָעֶד.
וְכֹל הַחַיִּים יוֹדוּךָ סֶּלָה, וִיהַלְלוּ אֶת־שִׁמְךָ בֶּאֱמֶת, הָאֵל
יְשׁוּעָתֵנוּ וְעֶזְרָתֵנוּ סֶלָה.
בָּרוּךְ אַתָּה יי, הַטּוֹב שִׁמְךָ וּלְךָ נָאֶה לְהוֹדוֹת.

We gratefully acknowledge that You are our God and the God of our people, the God of all generations. You are the Rock of our life, the Power that shields us in every age. We thank You and sing Your praises: for our lives, which are in Your hand; for our souls, which are in Your keeping; for the signs of Your presence we encounter every day; and for Your wondrous gifts at all times, morning, noon, and night. You are Goodness: Your mercies never end; You are compassion: Your love will never fail. You have always been our hope.

For all these things, O Sovereign God, let Your name be forever exalted and blessed.

O God our Redeemer and Helper, let all who live affirm You and praise Your name in truth. Eternal God, whose nature is Goodness, we give You thanks and praise.

COMMENTARY

The הוֹדָאָה (Hodaah) or מוֹדִים (Modim) prayer (as it is more commonly known) is the eighteenth prayer of the daily עֲמִידָה and the sixth of the תְּפִלַּת שֶׁבַע. Some Jewish scholars believed that the מוֹדִים prayer was recited by the priests in the Temple in Jerusalem. After the Temple was destroyed, or perhaps before, this prayer became part of the synagogue service.

Thanksgiving

The major theme of the מוֹדִים prayer is הוֹדָאָה, "thanksgiving." The word מוֹדִים, "we offer thanks," is taken from מוֹדָה and means "grateful," "thankful," or "appreciative."

The theme of thanksgiving is one of the oldest in the history of prayer. It is likely that the first sacrifices of ancient peoples were given to the gods out of gratitude for new crops, rain, or warm sun.

The Psalmists of Israel expressed thanksgiving throughout many of their poems. In Psalm 92, for instance, the poet writes:

> It is good to give thanks to the Eternal One,
> And to sing praises unto Your name, O Most High;
> To declare Your loving-kindness in the morning,
> And Your faithfulness in the night seasons....
> For You, O Eternal One, have made me glad through your work;
> I will exult in the works of Your hands.
>
> Psalm 92:2–5

Another example of thanksgiving is found in Psalm 106:1–3:

> O give thanks to God, for God is good;
> God's mercy endures forever.
> Who can express the mighty acts of the Eternal One,
> Or make all God's praise to be heard?
> Happy are they that keep justice,
> That do righteousness at all times.

Why Give Thanks

What are the Psalmists trying to say by their words of thanksgiving? Why do you suppose parents try to teach their children to say thank you? Is it simply a matter of being polite, or is it something more involved?

A Chasid was once asked: "What is stealing?" He thought for a moment and then replied: "People steal when they enjoy the benefits of the earth without giving thanks to God."

Is that really stealing? What happens inside you when you thank another person, or God, for a favor or gift? When you see a magnificent scene in nature, and you pause and are filled with wonder, have you ever felt like giving thanks to God for being alive in that moment? Would the words of the מוֹדִים prayer fit such a moment? What about the expression in Psalm 92?

In Pleasure and Pain

Rabbi Akiva, who died a martyr's death at the hands of the Romans, taught his students the following:

> Be not like those who honor their gods in prosperity and curse them in adversity. In pleasure and pain, give thanks!
>
> *M'chilta*, Exodus 20:20

What do you think he meant by that? How is it possible to give God thanks in times of pain or sorrow? Helen Keller, who lived her life in blindness and deafness, once wrote: "I have often thought it would be a blessing if each human being were stricken blind and deaf for a few days at some time during his early adult life. Darkness would make him more appreciative of sight; silence would teach him the joys of sound." What is Helen Keller trying to tell us? Would she agree with Rabbi Akiva that a person should give thanks in pleasure or in pain? Why? What are the things singled out in the מוֹדִים prayer for which we give thanks?

Within Us

When we thank another person for a gift, for helping us, or for sharing with us, more is involved than the expression of courtesy. Something happens within us as well. We not only express our gratefulness, but we become aware of how much we depend upon others for our happiness and our

---

AN ENDURING GIFT

When we recognize how everything issues from God, then that divine kindness will be ours, not only in the valleys, when times are easy, but also on the mountains, even when life is difficult—all the time. The experience then of gratitude—and subsequent expression of thanksgiving—transforms everything into an enduring gift.

Rabbi Lawrence Kushner and Dr. Nehemia Polen, *My People's Prayer Book*, vol. 2, *The Amidah*

YIDDISH PROVERB

If a Jew breaks a leg, he thanks God he did not break both legs; if he breaks both, he thanks God he did not break his neck!

What can the above mean?

Themes:
a. Thanksgiving is one of
   the oldest forms of
   prayer.
b. The מוֹדִים expresses our
   gratefulness for God's
   work in nature and in
   our lives.
c. To give thanks is to
   open ourselves to the
   wonders and joys of life.
d. Thanksgiving can and
   should include both our
   pains and pleasures.
e. Thanksgiving should
   lead us beyond our-
   selves to מִצְווֹת for
   others.
f. Thanksgiving can lead
   us to a deeper
   appreciation of what it
   means to be a Jew.

security. When we express our thanksgiving at a beautiful sight or sound, we acknowledge our relationship to all nature and life. Prayers of thanksgiving deepen our awareness and sensitivity to others, to the wonders of life, and to the joys of living.

Beyond Thanksgiving

An anonymous author once wrote: "The test of thankfulness is, not what you have to be thankful for, but whether anyone else has reason to be thankful that you are here." What do you think is meant by that observation?

The Chasidic leader known as the Alexander Rebbe once remarked: "A Jew who is not always full of joy because he or she is a Jew is ungrateful to God." Would you agree? Why should we be grateful that we are Jews?

Prayers on the הוֹדָאָה Theme

Everything That Lives
וְכֹל הַחַיִּים יוֹדוּךָ סֶּלָה

Everything that lives thanks You, O God.

The trees with lifted branches,
Flowers with budding blooms.

Birds with chirping melodies,
Animals with howling sounds.

Seas with crashing waves,
Skies with roaring thunder.

And human beings?
How do we thank You?

It has been told you what is good,
And what the Eternal One requires of you:
To do justly with others,
To be merciful in all your acts,
And to walk humbly with your God.

150

Be praised, O God of truth. It is pleasant to thank You for the gift of life.

בָּרוּךְ אַתָּה יְיָ, הַטּוֹב שִׁמְךָ וּלְךָ נָאֶה לְהוֹדוֹת.

HJF

Accept Our Gratitude

For the blessings which You lavish upon us in forest and sea, in mountain and meadow, in rain and sun, we thank You.

For the blessings You implant within us, joy and peace, meditation and laughter, we are grateful to You.

For the blessings of friendship and love, of family and community;

For the blessings we ask of You and those we cannot ask;

For the blessings You bestow upon us openly and those You give us in secret;

For all these blessings, O Lord of the universe, we thank You and are grateful to You.

For the blessings we recognize and those we fail to recognize;

For the blessings of our tradition and of our holy days;

For the blessings of return and forgiveness, of memory, of vision, and of hope,

For all these blessings which surround us on every side, O Lord, hear our thanks and accept our gratitude.

Ruth F. Brin, "For the Blessings"

I Thank You

I thank You God for this most amazing day
for the leaping greenly spirits of trees and a blue dream of sky;
and for everything which is natural, which is infinite, and which is yes.

I who have died am alive again today, and this is the sun's birthday;
this is the birthday of life and of love and wings;
and of the gay happening illimitably earth.

Now the ears of my ears awake
And now the eyes of my eyes are opened.

Author Unknown

Co-Workers with God

Behold how good and how pleasant it is for brothers and sisters to live together in peace.

We give thanks, O God, for all that is done for us by our fellow human beings. Some dig far away from the sun that we may be warm. Others serve in distant outposts that we may be secure. And still others search for cures to disease or brave the terrors of unknown skies or waters in order to help and benefit all life. Many blessings have been provided for us.

Let us then, O God, be just and generous in our relationships with others. Let us share with others what we are lucky enough to possess. Help us to give to those who are hungry and be friends to those who are lonely.

May we so live that we may be co-workers with You in building a world of cooperation and peace.

Adapted by HJF, from the *Union Prayer Book*

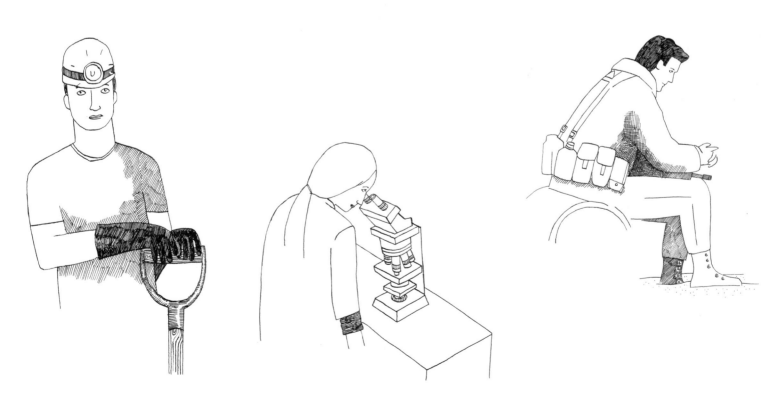

BIRKAT SHALOM: BLESSING OF PEACE

Birkat Shalom   בְּרְכַּת שָׁלוֹם

שִׂים שָׁלוֹם, טוֹבָה, וּבְרָכָה, חֵן וָחֶסֶד, וְרַחֲמִים עָלֵינוּ וְעַל־
כָּל־יִשְׂרָאֵל שְׁמֶךָ.

Grant peace, goodness, blessing, loving-kindness, and mercy to
us and to all who worship You.

בָּרְכֵנוּ אָבִינוּ כֻּלָּנוּ כְּאֶחָד בְּאוֹר פָּנֶיךָ. כִּי בְאוֹר פָּנֶיךָ נָתַתָּ
לָנוּ יְיָ אֱלֹהֵינוּ תּוֹרַת חַיִּים וְאַהֲבַת חֶסֶד וּצְדָקָה וּבְרָכָה
וְרַחֲמִים וְחַיִּים וְשָׁלוֹם.

Bless us and unite us in the light of Your presence. For in the
light of Your presence, Eternal our God, You have given us a
Torah to live by, and the power for loving-kindness, charity,
blessing, mercy, life, and peace.

וְטוֹב בְּעֵינֶיךָ לְבָרֵךְ אֶת־עַמְּךָ יִשְׂרָאֵל וְאֶת־כָּל־הָעַמִּים בְּרֹב
עֹז וְשָׁלוֹם.
בָּרוּךְ אַתָּה יְיָ, עֹשֵׂה הַשָּׁלוֹם.

May it be Your will to bless Your people Israel and all humanity
with great strength and peace.
We praise You, O God, Source of peace.

COMMENTARY

The שָׁלוֹם בְּרְכַּת (*Birkat Shalom*), "Blessing of Peace," or שָׁלוֹם שִׂים (*Sim Shalom*), as it is popularly known, is the concluding prayer of the daily and Shabbat עֲמִידָה. The talmudic sage Elazar HaKapar, who lived during the second century C.E., taught his students that the "שָׁלוֹם is the climax of all blessings." Another teacher, who lived at the same time as Elazar HaKapar, once said: "Our prayers will not help us unless we include a prayer for peace among them" (*B'midbar Rabbah* 11:17).

What do you think those two Sages meant by their statements? Why might the שָׁלוֹם שִׂים prayer have been chosen as the last prayer of the עֲמִידָה?

What Is שָׁלוֹם?

The dictionary defines "peace" as: (1) a state of quiet; (2) freedom from civil disturbance; (3) a state of security or order within a community provided for by law and custom; (4) freedom from disturbing thoughts and feelings; (5) harmony in personal relations; (6) a state of concord between governments.

The Hebrew word שָׁלוֹם means "security," "contentment," "good health," "prosperity," "friendship," and "peace of mind." How do these definitions match those given for the English word "peace"?

שָׁלוֹם is derived from the Hebrew root שלם, which means "complete," "whole," "perfect," "accomplished," or "total." שָׁלוֹם, as understood in Jewish tradition, is the highest human goal. Why is the word שָׁלוֹם used as a greeting or as a word of farewell? What is meant when we wish another person שָׁלוֹם?

Seek Peace and Pursue It

The theme of peace occupies an important place in Jewish tradition and prayer. In the Book of Psalms, סֵפֶר תְּהִלִּים, we find many statements that remind us to make the pursuit of peace our chief goal. One of the most important of these statements is found in Psalm 34:14–15:

Keep your tongue from evil,
And your lips from speaking falsehood.
Turn away from evil and do good.
Seek peace and pursue it.

We are told that once a group of students were studying the Psalmist's words. They had difficulty understanding the last sentence, so they turned to their teacher and inquired: "Why are we told both to *seek* and to *pursue* peace? Wouldn't it have been enough to say either 'seek peace' or 'pursue peace'?"

The teacher thought a moment and then responded: "The Psalmist reminds us that it is not enough to seek peace in your own place. You must also pursue it everywhere."

What is the difference between "seeking peace in your own place" and "pursuing it everywhere"? Where should one begin in seeking or pursuing peace? How important is it to find inner peace before you go out to make peace in the world? How do you find inner peace? What does the poet of Psalm 34 think is the way to personal "inner" peace? The Chasidic leader

Simchah Bunam once said: "You cannot find peace anywhere save in your own self." What do you suppose he meant by that?

War No More!

The prophets of Israel were among the first to dream of the day when all would live in peace. We have already made mention of the messianic days. In them, the prophets believed, humanity would be blessed with peace.

Many of the words and visions of the prophets have become part of our prayers. In many cases, their thoughts about peace express our feelings and aspirations in a beautiful and powerful way. Below are some selections taken from the words of the prophets. As you read them, ask yourself some of the following questions: What does the prophet define as שָׁלוֹם? How is it to be achieved? What needs to be done in our time to help make the prophet's hope for שָׁלוֹם a reality?

And they shall beat their swords into plowshares
And their spears into pruning-hooks;
Nation shall not lift up sword against nation.
Neither shall they learn war any more.

Micah 4:3 and Isaiah 2:4

The work of righteousness will be peace;
And the effect of righteousness, quietness and confidence forever.

Isaiah 32:17

Violence shall no longer be heard in your land,
Desolation nor destruction within your borders.

Isaiah 60:18

All your children shall be taught of the Eternal One;
And great shall be the peace of your children.

Isaiah 54:13

These are the things that you should do:
Let every man speak the truth with his neighbor; and make peaceful settlements within your gates.

Zechariah 8:16

The Reform prayer book, *Gates of Prayer,* contains a creative translation of the שִׂים שָׁלוֹם prayer. It reads as follows:

Grant us peace, Your most precious gift, O Eternal Source of peace, and give us the will to proclaim its message to all the peoples of the earth.

Bless our country, that it may always be a stronghold of peace, and its advocate among the nations.

May contentment reign within its borders, health and happiness within its homes.

Strengthen the bonds of friendship among the inhabitants of all lands, and may the love of Your name hallow every home and every heart. We praise You, O God, the Source of peace.

What is the message of the *Gates of Prayer* version above? Does it reflect the emphasis of the prophets? Which version of the prayer for peace do you prefer? Compare these two versions with the afternoon and evening prayer for peace found on page 157.

The Torah and שָׁלוֹם

In the שִׂים שָׁלוֹם prayer we find the words: "You have given us a Torah to live by." What is the relationship of the Torah to the pursuit and achievement of peace? As we shall see further on, when the Torah is returned to the ark we say the words:

It is a tree of life to those who hold it fast,
And all who cling to it find happiness.
Its ways are ways of pleasantness,
And all its paths are peace.

Proverbs 3:18, 17

Why is the Torah considered a "tree of life" whose paths are "peace"?

The Rabbis taught that all of the מִצְווֹת of Torah have as their chief goal the achievement of שָׁלוֹם. They taught that "the whole Torah exists for the purpose of promoting שָׁלוֹם" (BT *Gittin* 59b). How do you think the מִצְווֹת help us achieve שָׁלוֹם?

Rabbi Chanina ben Chama declared that "the students of the wise [who study Torah] increase peace in the world" (BT *B'rachot* 64a). Dr. Albert

Einstein once wrote: "Peace cannot be kept by force. It can only be achieved by understanding." Are Rabbi Chanina and Dr. Einstein saying the same thing?

The Chasidic leader Menachem Mendel of Kotzk once said: "Peace without truth is a false peace." Can there be peace with falsehood or lying? The talmudic sage Rabbi Bar Kapara offers a different view in his commentary on the story of Abraham and Sarah. When God tells the ninety-year-old Sarah that she will bear a child, she laughs, saying that her husband is too old to become a father. When God relates Sarah's reaction to Abraham, however, God reports that Sarah believed herself—not Abraham—to be too old to have a baby. According to Rabbi Bar Kapara, God told this "white lie" in order to preserve peace between husband and wife; it seems permitted, therefore, to tell small untruths for the sake of peace (*Vayikra Rabbah* 9:9). Do you agree? Do you think that, "for the sake of peace," lying or falsehood ought to be allowed in a marriage or within a family? Have the members of your study group discuss this last question with their parents and then report and discuss their findings the next time you gather together. You may also wish to invite parents to such a discussion.

Afternoon and Evening Prayer for Peace

שָׁלוֹם רָב עַל־יִשְׂרָאֵל עַמְּךָ תָּשִׂים לְעוֹלָם, כִּי אַתָּה הוּא מֶלֶךְ אָדוֹן לְכָל־הַשָּׁלוֹם. וְטוֹב בְּעֵינֶיךָ לְבָרֵךְ אֶת־עַמְּךָ יִשְׂרָאֵל וְאֶת־כָּל־הָעַמִּים בְּכָל־עֵת וּבְכָל־שָׁעָה בִּשְׁלוֹמֶךָ. בָּרוּךְ אַתָּה יי, הַמְבָרֵךְ אֶת־עַמּוֹ יִשְׂרָאֵל בַּשָּׁלוֹם.

O Sovereign Source of peace, let Israel Your people know enduring peace, for it is good in Your sight to bless Israel and all peoples continually with Your peace. We praise You, O God, for You bless Israel with peace.

The prayer שָׁלוֹם רָב (*Shalom Rav*), "Abundant Peace," is a shorter version of שִׂים שָׁלוֹם. It is used in the traditional afternoon and evening worship service as a substitute for שִׂים שָׁלוֹם. Some scholars believe that שָׁלוֹם רָב was written in the eleventh century by Jews who were suffering persecution and death during the Crusades.

The שָׁלוֹם רָב prayer is particularly appropriate for those occasions when we want to express our concern for the safety and welfare of the Jewish people.

Prayers on the בִּרְכַּת שָׁלוֹם Theme

Let All These Be Possible

Let all these be possible:
Peace
Goodness
Lives that are a blessing
Gracious acts
The love of sharing
The love of creating
Light unbound
Torah alive
Sustenance for all
Abounding life.

They're there.
Help us find them here.

On Wings of Awe

Grant peace to our world, goodness and blessing, mercy and compassion, life and love. Inspire us to banish forever hatred, war, and bloodshed. Help us to establish forever one human family doing Your will in love and peace. O God of peace, bless us with peace.

HJF

The Longing for Peace

Eternal wellspring of peace—
may we be drenched with the longing for peace
that we may give ourselves over
as the earth to the rain, to the dew,
until peace overflows our lives
as living waters overflow the seas.

Marcia Falk, "Blessing of Peace"

An Appendix to the Vision of Peace

Don't stop after beating the swords
into ploughshares, don't stop! Go on beating
and make musical instruments out of them.

Whoever wants to make war again
Will have to turn them into ploughshares first.

Yehuda Amichai

ELOHAI N'TZOR

Elohai N'tzor

אֱלֹהַי נְצוֹר

אֱלֹהַי, נְצֹר לְשׁוֹנִי מֵרָע, וּשְׂפָתַי מִדַּבֵּר מִרְמָה. וְלִמְקַלְלַי נַפְשִׁי
תִדּוֹם וְנַפְשִׁי כֶּעָפָר לַכֹּל תִּהְיֶה. פְּתַח לִבִּי בְּתוֹרָתֶךָ,
וּבְמִצְוֹתֶיךָ תִּרְדֹּף נַפְשִׁי. וְכָל־הַחוֹשְׁבִים עָלַי רָעָה, מְהֵרָה
הָפֵר עֲצָתָם וְקַלְקֵל מַחֲשַׁבְתָּם. עֲשֵׂה לְמַעַן שְׁמֶךָ, עֲשֵׂה
לְמַעַן יְמִינֶךָ, עֲשֵׂה לְמַעַן קְדֻשָּׁתֶךָ, עֲשֵׂה לְמַעַן תּוֹרָתֶךָ;
לְמַעַן יֵחָלְצוּן יְדִידֶיךָ, הוֹשִׁיעָה יְמִינְךָ וַעֲנֵנִי.

O God, keep my tongue from evil and my lips from deceit.
Help me to be silent in the face of derision, humble in the
presence of all. Open my heart to Your Torah, that I may hasten
to do Your mitzvot. Save me with Your power; in time of
trouble be my answer, that those who love You may rejoice.

יִהְיוּ לְרָצוֹן אִמְרֵי־פִי וְהֶגְיוֹן לִבִּי לְפָנֶיךָ, יהוה, צוּרִי וְגֹאֲלִי.

May the words of my mouth and the mediations of my heart be
acceptable to You, O God, my Rock and my Redeemer.

עֹשֶׂה שָׁלוֹם בִּמְרוֹמָיו, הוּא יַעֲשֶׂה שָׁלוֹם עָלֵינוּ וְעַל־כָּל־
יִשְׂרָאֵל, וְאִמְרוּ: אָמֵן.

May the one who causes peace to reign in the high heavens
cause peace to reign among us, all Israel, and all the world.

COMMENTARY

The אֱלֹהַי נְצוֹר (*Elohai N'tzor*) was composed by Mar bar Ravina, who lived in the fourth century C.E. Because of its popularity, it was later chosen to be placed at the end of the עֲמִידָה. "O God, keep [my tongue from evil]..." is the opening phrase of the prayer. The original prayer most likely concluded with the words "Save me with Your power; in time of trouble be my answer, that those who love You may rejoice." The sentence "May the words...," taken from Psalm 19, was added later to Mar's prayer. The words "May the One who causes peace..." recall the final prayer of the עֲמִידָה, the prayer for שָׁלוֹם.

Personal Prayers

Notice that the אֱלֹהַי נְצוֹר prayer is written in the singular, not the plural. All the other prayers we have studied address God as אֱלֹהֵינוּ (*Eloheinu*), "our God." Why does this prayer, at this point in our worship service (just after the עֲמִידָה), address God as אֱלֹהַי, "my God"?

A part of the answer is found in the Rabbis' understanding of prayer. They believed that there should be a balance between the expression of congregational needs and individual needs. So they created a place within the synagogue service for personal prayers. That place came just after the שִׂים שָׁלוֹם prayer of the עֲמִידָה. At that time, according to tradition, the individual could express whatever might be in his or her heart.

Mar's prayer was one of many written for this place in our service. On the next page, you will find a brief selection of some others, composed by our ancient Rabbis:

May it be Your will, O Eternal One our God, to cause love and cooperation, peace and friendship to abide in our midst; to enlarge the number of our students; to prosper our goal with happy ends and the fulfillment of our hopes. May we be among those who have a portion in the world to come. Strengthen us with good friends and with the use of our powers for goodness in this life so that reverence for Your name will always be the longing of our hearts.

Rabbi Elazar

May it be Your will, O Eternal One our God, that we may turn to You in perfect repentance so that we may not be ashamed to meet our ancestors in the world-to-come.

Rabbi Zera

May it be Your will, O Eternal One our God, to place us in light and not darkness.... Sovereign of the universe! You know that our desire is to do as You wish, but what stands in the way? It is the power of evil in us and the persecution of nations. May it be Your will to deliver us from both so we may again perform Your laws with a perfect heart.

Rabbi Alexander

What do these personal prayers have in common? How are they similar in style and theme to the אֱלֹהַי נְצוֹר? How are they different? What do you think Rabbi Zera meant by his request that we may not be ashamed to meet our ancestors in the world-to-come? What is living a life so that our ancestors will not be ashamed of us? What does that mean to you as a Jew?

Rabbi Alexander indicates that there are two things that keep a person from the pursuit of goodness. They are the power of "evil in us [יֵצֶר הָרָע] and the persecution of nations." How do each of these prevent us from doing good and pursuing justice or peace? Do you think that there are other things that keep us from the ethical life? What are they?

Just as our ancient Sages composed personal prayers that reflected their circumstances, concerns, and ideas, so have Jews throughout the ages been inspired to write their own unique prayers. On the next page is a sampling of some personal prayers from modern times:

Adonai!

Help me to understand that I am not alone.

When I feel that I am so very small

And the world is so very huge,

When I feel that the problems around me are very great

And I am very little,

When I hear of wars that I cannot stop,

Of hungry people I cannot feed,

When I see people doing wrong and I cannot help them,

When I hear of people hurting other people,

Help me to remember that You are with me—

Help me to choose You, Adonai, again and again,

To choose that way of life You have taught us to live,

that my world may be just a little better,

Just a little brighter,

because I was in it.

Siddur of I. Weiner Jewish Secondary School, Houston, Texas

We reach for You, our God
from our quiet places.
    May we stand still,
for a brief moment, and
listen to the rain—
    Stand still, for a brief
moment, and watch the
play of sunlight and
shadow on the leaves.
    For a brief moment—
listen to the world.

    Let us stop the wheels
of every day to be aware of
Shabbat. Find the stillness
of the sanctuary
which the soul cherishes.
    Renew the Covenant
of an ancient people.

We need a quiet
space to test the balance
of our days. The weight
of our own needs
against the heaviness
of the world's demands.
    The balance is
precarious—steady
us with faith.

    Quiet places and
stillness—where we will
hear our own best
impulses speak.
    Quiet places and
stillness—from which
we will reach out to
each other.

    We will find
strength in silence
and with this
strength we will
turn again to Your
service.
                    Priscilla Stern

God help us
not to tolerate and be tolerated
but to accept and be accepted
not to hide or be hidden
but to open and be opened
to extend our hands in
love, and not be afraid of rejection
or indifference or both
and to reach out to take another's hand
in love and grasp it in reception
and presence.

God help us not to judge or be judged
but to listen
and hear,
to understand and be understood.

God help us
to see past fear and uncertainty
and be seen for who we are
and who we will be.

Rabbi David Burstein

O God,
we all stood at the mountain's base
and swore ourselves to Your commands.
Though Moses stuttered horribly,
we all listened with utmost care
to every Torah-word.
It was so good to be gone from Egypt!
But now we are slaves again,
and Mitzvot are slow to be done.
Be patient with our outward hesitation.
We have not forgotten our Agreement.
You are not alone.

Danny Siegel

Dear God,

I am writing this letter because I often find it difficult to communicate with You in other, more traditional ways. You do not spring easily out of the pages of my prayer-book, nor do You float ethereally among the arched ceilings in my Temple. When I call Your name, I hear no voice responding to my own.

Would our relationship be different if I knew You on a daily basis? As it is, I seem to think of You only in times of crisis or joy. Would I feel closer to You if I turned to You at other times than when I am afraid and pleading for Your help? I do praise You in my head in rare moments of euphoria when I am especially touched by the miracle of the world You have created. Yet, this is not enough. I know there can be much more between us.

I am seeking renewal. Fill my soul with the breath of Your magnificence. Surround me with Your goodness and love. Rejuvenate me so that I may have the strength to reach out to others and revitalize them. This is my prayer, now and forevermore.

Sincerely Yours,
Randee Friedman

What themes do you find in these personal prayers? How are they similar to those written by our ancient Rabbis? How are they different? Do you feel that these modern prayers reflect some of your own hopes, fears, and dreams? If you were composing your own personal prayer, do you think it would sound more like the ancient or modern prayers? What would you like to say to God in your prayer?

We have already noted that one of the important purposes of Jewish prayer is "judging oneself." How do these personal prayers, and the אֱלֹהַי נְצוֹר prayer, lead us to "judging ourselves"? How, and with what, do they challenge us?

The Chasidic leader known as the Lizensker used to offer the following prayer:

O Eternal One! Guard us from selfish motives and from pride when we do Your מִצְוֹת. Guard us from anger and sadness, from tale-bearing and from other evil traits. May no jealousy of our friends enter our heart and no jealousy of us enter the hearts of others. Grant us the ability to appreciate only the virtues of our fellow human beings.

What are the concerns voiced by the Lizensker rabbi? Are any of them "problems" that you face or things of which you are sometimes guilty? How is the Lizensker's prayer a prayer for self-improvement?

Perhaps one of the best ways to prepare for the writing of your own אֱלֹהַי נְצוֹר *prayer is to make a list of those things that you wish to improve about yourself and life and those things that need improving for the sake of the world and humanity.*

Once you have made up such a list, compare it with those things mentioned in the prayers quoted above. Then, write your own personal meditation.

Keep My Tongue from Evil

What is meant by Mar's statement "keep my tongue from evil..."? An insight into an answer may be found in the Bratzlaver Rebbe's comment on the talmudic command "Judge not your neighbor until you stand in his place" (*Pirkei Avot* 2:5). The Bratzlaver explained that a person "should never completely criticize another, since no person can possibly know when he will stand in another's position." What did the Bratzlaver mean by his interpretation? Does this mean that we should not evaluate the words or actions of others?

What is the danger of words? The poet Heinrich Heine once observed: "When the arrow has left the bow-string it no longer belongs to the archer and, when the word has left the lips, it is no longer controlled by the speaker." What do you think he meant by that? Would you agree with Heine? Rabbi Shimon bar Yochai taught that "verbal wrong is worse than monetary wrong" (BT *Bava M'tzia* 58b). Is that true? How do Heine and Shimon bar Yochai's observations compare with one another?

Help Me to Be Silent

Does this mean that Mar believed that a person should "turn the other cheek" or let others say whatever they want without answering back in self-defense? Does Judaism teach that people should sit silently by while others curse or oppress them?

The Rabbis of the Talmud teach the following:

> Whoever suffers persecutions without striking back, whoever takes an offense in silence, whoever does good because of evil, whoever is cheerful under sufferings—is a lover of God.
>
> BT *Shabbat* 88b

How does such an expression compare with Mar's אֱלֹהַי נְצוֹר prayer? Would you agree that whoever is cheerful under sufferings is a lover of God? What is the strength and power in keeping silent before those who would persecute or say nasty things about us? Can you give examples of those who have used silence in the face of oppression, and nonviolence in the face of brutality during the last centuries? How successful were they?

Two Sides to the Issue

There are those who would argue that "silence in the face of derision or slander" or the use of nonviolence when you are attacked is wrong and even foolish. Tragically, Jews have been the recipients of hate and hostility for over 2,000 years. We have suffered at the brutal hands of the Romans, the Crusaders, and the Cossacks. During the Second World War, Hitler sought to eliminate the Jewish people from the face of the earth. Most recently, the Jews of Russia have endured bitter persecution, and Arab armies have sought to destroy the State of Israel. What do you think is the best way to meet and deal with such hostility?

According to the Talmud, "if someone comes to kill you, rise up and kill him first" (BT *B'rachot* 58b). In another place we are told: "Whoever defends Israel is exalted by God" *(P'sikta D'Rav Kahana)*. What kind of action should one take in "self-defense"? Is speaking out against those who slander Jews or other minorities justified? What other action do you think we are permitted to take?

One American Jewish organization suggests that "the best defense against hostile attitudes directed toward Jews is a firm identification with Judaism, coupled with full participation in the broad community life of America." Would you agree with that position? How does it compare with the thought expressed in the אֱלֹהַי נְצוֹר or with the statement "Whoever defends Israel is exalted by God"?

Within Jewish literature there are several suggestions about how one should treat an enemy. In Proverbs we are told: "If your enemy is hungry, give him bread to eat" (25:21). In another place we are told: "If your enemy greets you with evil, meet him with wisdom" (Apocrypha). Within the Talmud we are counseled: "Who is a hero? The person who turns an enemy into a friend" (*Avot D'Rabbi Natan* 23).

How do these suggestions about treating an enemy compare with the others already mentioned in this section? Are they more or less realistic? Which do you prefer?

Perhaps another position, between those who advocate answering violence with violence and those who believe in nonviolence, might be found in Hillel's famous statement: "If I am not for myself, who will be for me? If I am only for myself, what am I? And, if not now, when?" (*Pirkei Avot* 2:4). What do you think he meant by that? Does Hillel offer us a third alternative? What is it?

The prayer just after the עֲמִידָה is a personal one. It ought to express, in our own way, our feelings, hopes, and desires. As we have seen, it is also used as a moment of self-judgment.

Arrange a debate among two or four people in your study group on the question: How should we treat an enemy? A Jewish question-and-answer! Those participating should try to answer the question by taking examples from Jewish history and experience. Some excellent examples may be found in the history of the Maccabees, the Jews of Masada, the Jews in Christian medieval Europe, the Jews during Hitler's time, the building of the State of Israel, the Jews of Russia, the Jews of Ethiopia, and Jewish immigrants working in the garment industry at the beginning of the twentieth century.

קְרִיאַת הַתּוֹרָה

The Reading of Torah

K'riat HaTorah

קְרִיאַת הַתּוֹרָה—K'RIAT HaTorah

When and where did the custom of the reading of Torah originate? Why is the Torah divided into sections or weekly portions? What is the פָּרָשָׁה (parashah)? These are some of the questions with which we wish to deal in this section.

In Deuteronomy 31, we are told that Moses wrote the Torah and then "delivered it to the priests, the sons of Levi, who carried the Ark of the Covenant of God, and to all of the elders of Israel" (Deuteronomy 31:9). Moses commanded them to read the Torah to the people of Israel every seven years, on the Sabbatical year, during the Festival of Sukkot. Why did Moses want the people to hear the Torah?

The Book of Deuteronomy answers our questions with these words of Moses:

> Assemble the people, the men and women and the little ones, and the stranger that is within your gates, that they may hear, and learn, and fear *Adonai* your God, and observe to do all the words of this Torah; and that their children, who have not known, may hear and learn to fear *Adonai* your God....
>
> Deuteronomy 31:12–13

What, according to the above passage from Deuteronomy, is the purpose of hearing the Torah? How did the *reading* of Torah play a part in transmitting Jewish tradition from one generation to the next?

Ezra the Scribe

About the year 421 B.C.E., many Jews, under the leadership of Ezra and Nehemiah, returned from Babylonia to the Land of Israel. Their hope was to rebuild their land and to reestablish their nation. The Babylonians, who had taken them into exile in 586 B.C.E., had been defeated by the Persians, led by Cyrus. The Jewish people, who had vowed never to forget Jerusalem or "the Land," applied to Cyrus for the opportunity to return to their land. In response to their plea, the Persian leaders issued the following declaration:

> All the kingdoms of the earth, *Adonai*, the God of the heavens, has given to me, charging me to build God a house in Jerusalem, which is in Judah. Whoever there is among you of all God's people—may your God be with you—go up to Jerusalem, which is in Judah, and build the House of *Adonai*, the God of Israel, the God who is in Jerusalem. And whoever is left, in any place where you live, let the people of your place help you with silver, and with gold, and with goods, and with beasts, beside the freewill offering for the House of God that is in Jerusalem.
>
> Ezra 1:2–4

With those words, and that proclamation, Cyrus made it possible for Jews to return to the Land of Israel and to begin the long process of rebuilding the Temple. We are told that the Persian leader gave the Jews all of the precious vessels that the Babylonians had removed from the Temple, so that they could be restored to their proper place. In all, the Book of Ezra reports, over 5,400 vessels were returned to the Jewish people.

Upon their return to the Land of Israel, the Jews prepared themselves for the celebration of Rosh HaShanah and the holidays that were to follow. We learn that on Rosh HaShanah the people gathered and asked Ezra the Scribe to read the Torah to them. The Book of Nehemiah gives us the following description:

> And Ezra the priest brought the Torah before the congregation, both men and women, and all that could hear with understanding, upon the first day of the seventh month.... Also Jeshua, and Bani, and Sherebiah, Jamin, Akkub, Shabbethai, Hodiah, Maaseiah, Kelita, Azariah, Jozabad, Hanan, Pelaiah, even the Levites caused the people to understand the Torah. And the people stood in their place. And they read in the book, in the Torah of God, distinctly; and they gave the sense, and caused them to understand the reading.
>
> Nehemiah 8:2, 7–8

The Book of Nehemiah tells us that the Torah was also read on the second day of Rosh HaShanah and on each day of Sukkot.

Torah and Shabbat

It is likely that from the time of Ezra to the development of the synagogue, the Torah was read on Festivals and celebrations. It was, however, with the birth of the synagogue, sometime after 300 B.C.E., that the reading of the Torah became a regular practice within Jewish life.

The Rabbis and the people of the synagogue made קְרִיאַת הַתּוֹרָה part of their prayer experience on Shabbat and other holidays. They believed that the study of Torah within the synagogue was so important that they even introduced the reading of Torah at their services on Mondays and Thursdays as well.

Rabbi Meir, who lived in the second century C.E., told his students: "Take time off from your business and engage in Torah" (*Pirkei Avot* 6:1). Moses Maimonides wrote that "every Jew, rich or poor, or even a beggar, healthy or not, young or old is obliged to study Torah" (*Yad HaChazakah*). A Sage, who may have lived during the period in which the synagogue was developing and the Torah reading was being accepted as a regular part of its worship, once put forth the question: "Why is Israel called God's people?" He answered his own question by saying: "Because of the Torah" (*Tanchuma, Va-eira* 9a).

In light of these statements, why do you think the Rabbis and those who developed the synagogue were anxious to make the reading of Torah a regular part of their worship services?

We know that after Alexander the Great conquered the Middle East (in about 333 B.C.E.), he introduced the culture and way of life of Hellenism, which included athletic games, study, debates, musical and dramatic festivals, and worship of many gods. Many Jews began to forsake their Judaism for the attractive Greek lifestyle. The Rabbis and Jewish leaders of that period worried about the growing assimilation in their midst. Do you think that might explain why they introduced the tradition of reading and studying the Torah in the synagogue? How might such a custom have helped prevented assimilation? Look at the quotation in "Different Because of Torah." Would you agree with the statement? How does the Torah still play a part in making us different "from the nations of the world"?

The Weekly Torah Portion

Where did the custom of reading a פָּרָשָׁה, or weekly Torah portion, originate? We don't know!

We do know that by the time of Rabban Gamliel (80–120 C.E.), under whose leadership many of the prayers of the synagogue were arranged, the custom of reading the Torah was accepted practice. Rabban Gamliel lived in the first century C.E. Rabbi Meir, who lived in the century just after Gamliel, ruled that the Torah should be read consecutively so that those studying it would ultimately cover the entire text (BT *M'gillah* 31b). Sometime during the latter part of the second century C.E., assigned פָּרָשִׁיּוֹת (*parashiyot*), weekly Torah portions, were drawn up by the Rabbis.

Those who were responsible for developing the Torah portions and the order of readings in the Land of Israel divided the Torah into 154 sections. This meant that the Torah was read from the first chapter in Genesis to the last chapter in Deuteronomy once every three years. This triennial cycle became the accepted custom in the Land of Israel.

The Jews of Babylonia, however, developed another division of the Torah. They chose to divide it into 54 sections and to complete its reading and study once each year. On each Simchat Torah they would finish reading Deuteronomy and immediately begin reading Genesis. In this way the cycle of Torah readings and study never ended. As the Babylonian Jewish community grew in size and importance, and as the Jewish community of Israel dwindled in size, the Babylonian custom of reading the entire Torah in one year became the dominant practice of Jews throughout the world. If you look in your Bible at the Torah (also called the Five Books of Moses, or the *Chumash*), you will notice that it is divided into the 54 weekly sections suggested by the Sages of Babylonian Jewry.

Why do you think that in the Land of Israel the Rabbis thought it sufficient to read the entire Torah over a period of three years but in Babylonia they chose a yearly cycle? What might have been some of the factors that influenced their decision? Rabbi Israel Goldman, commenting in 1938 on Jewish survival, told an audience: "The learned Jew is the complete Jew.... The Jew who knows Jewish culture is the Jew who knows himself. To know oneself is to have integrity." What does Rabbi Goldman's observation have to do with a regular reading of the Torah? How does a knowledge of Torah strengthen Jewish survival?

Talmud Torah

The Torah has been called "the map of the world" by devoted Jews. The talmudic Rabbis taught that the study of Torah "promotes peace in heaven and on earth" (BT *Sanhedrin* 99b). In another place they suggest that "the existence of the world depends upon three things: upon Torah, upon worship, and upon deeds of loving-kindness" (*Pirkei Avot* 1:2). The great sage Hillel taught: "The more Torah, the more life" (*Pirkei Avot* 2:8).

Why?

Why did Jewish tradition consider the study of Torah so important?

One answer may be found in the Mishnah of Rabbi Y'hudah HaNasi, which is also included in many prayer books. He taught: "These are things for which a person enjoys the fruits in this world and the principal in the world to come: the honoring of parents, the practice of charity, and making peace between neighbors. But the study of Torah is more important than them all" (*Mishnah Pei-ah* 1:1). What do you think Rabbi Y'hudah meant by the statement "the study of Torah is more important than them all"? How could he consider the study of Torah more important than doing charity or making peace? The Reform prayer book, *Gates of Prayer,* adds that the study of Torah is the most important mitzvah because it leads to all the other mitzvot. Do you agree?

Another well-known teacher, Isaac ben Samuel, who lived in Babylonia during the fourth century C.E., taught that the "study of Torah is superior to honoring parents" (BT *M'gillah* 16b). How could he teach such a lesson when one of the Ten Commandments is "Honor your father and mother"? How might we apply the statement in *Gates of Prayer* to Isaac ben Samuel's teaching?

There are no simple answers to these questions. Perhaps, however, if we try to understand what the Torah has meant to the Jewish people throughout the ages, we will begin to comprehend its importance, not only to the past, but to our lives as well.

A Tree of Life!

The Chasidic leader known as the Gerer Rebbe once related the following parable: A man fell from a boat into the sea. The captain of the boat threw him a rope and shouted: "Take hold of this rope, and do not let go. If you do, you will lose your life."

"What is the meaning of the parable?" his students asked. The Gerer replied: "When we return the Torah to the ark, we say: 'It is a tree of life to those who hold fast to it.' If you let the Torah go, you will lose your life."

Speaking as the Torah, Dr. Ellen Frankel comments: "My words provided the blueprint for creation, and they contain the script for redemption [for making the world a just and caring place for all human beings].... The tradition teaches: '[Torah] is a tree of life to all that hold fast to [it].' And I am."

What do you think the Gerer Rebbe and Dr. Frankel meant by their teachings? Why is Torah described as a "tree of life"? Does it have roots, a trunk, and leaves? How does holding onto the Torah help us to stay alive? How does living by the Torah help us to find redemption?

175

The Rabbis of the Talmud comment: "If it were not for the Torah, Israel would not be different from the nations of the world" (*Sifra* 112c). What does this comment have to do with the Gerer Rebbe's parable and Dr. Frankel's comment? How is the Torah a "tree of life" for the Jewish people? Would you agree that without the Torah "Israel would not be different from the nations of the world"?

A Torah-Person!

The Baal Shem Tov once said to his followers: "The object of the whole Torah is that a person should become a Torah!" How is that possible? What is a "Torah-person"?

In the Talmud, we find a fascinating definition of a Torah-person. We are told that he or she possesses forty-eight qualities. They are as follows:

1 a listening ear, **2** studying aloud, **3** developing an ability to grasp ideas, **4** developing an ability to understand issues, **5** respect for one's teachers, **6** reverence for God, **7** humility, **8** cheerfulness, **9** helping one's teachers, **10** associating with one's fellow students, **11** a disciplined approach to one's studies, **12** knowledge in Bible and Talmud, **13** fairness in business practices, **14** courteous manners, **15** avoiding of extremes in pleasures, **16** avoiding of extremes in sleep, **17** avoiding of extremes in conversation, **18** avoiding of extremes in laughter, **19** patience, **20** sensitivity, **21** trusting in teachers, **22** knowing how to accept troubles and suffering, **23** knowing when to keep silent and when to speak, **24** appreciating one's self, **25** taking care with words, **26** not needing to claim credit for good deeds, **27** being beloved, **28** loving God, **29** loving one's fellow human beings, **30** loving justice, **31** loving righteousness, **32** appreciating criticism, **33** shunning honors, **34** not being boastful, **35** not delighting in giving decisions, **36** sharing burdens with other human beings, **37** judging others fairly, **38** leading others to truth, **39** leading others to peace, **40** being calm in the midst of learning, **41** knowing how to ask questions, **42** knowing how to answer questions, **43** knowing how to add to what he or she hears, **44** learning in order to teach, **45** learning in order to practice, **46** adding to his or her teachers' knowledge, **47** knowing how to listen to the lessons of a teacher, **48** always repeating a matter honestly in the name of whoever said it (*Pirkei Avot* 6:6).

If you were to list all of the characteristics of a "good person," which of the forty-eight qualities listed above would you select? Which of them do you feel are the most important, and why?

Divide your study group into three groups. Have two groups draw up what they feel are the characteristics of a modern Torah-person. Each list ought to be rated with the more important qualities on the top and the less important toward the bottom. Have the third group arrange the above forty-eight qualities in the order of most important to least important. Then compare and contrast the lists. Each group should be ready to defend its presentation.

Two Torahs?

In Jewish tradition, Torah is more than just the Five Books of Moses (Genesis, Exodus, Leviticus, Numbers, and Deuteronomy). "Torah" means all of Jewish teaching throughout the ages. The Rabbis taught that two Torahs had been given to Moses at Mount Sinai. One was the תּוֹרָה שֶׁבִּכְתָב (*Torah Shebichtav*), the "Written Torah," and the other they called the תּוֹרָה שֶׁבְּעַל פֶּה (*Torah Sheb'al Peh*), the "Oral Torah." According to the Sages, the Oral Torah contains all of the interpretations of the Written Torah that would be discovered and taught throughout the ages.

The teachers of Judaism have always realized that changes in society require changes and adjustments in the application of Torah. One example will help us understand. The Torah tells us: "You may not make a fire on Shabbat" (Exodus 35:3). That law seems clear enough. But, what about our modern times and the use of electric lights? Is the use of an electric light the same as making a "fire"? In other words, with the invention of electricity, the Torah must be applied to a new situation. The Baal Shem Tov taught: "The Torah is eternal, but its explanation and interpretation are to be made by the leaders of Judaism in accordance with the age in which they are living."

It has often been observed that ideas that are written down or printed seem more permanent and more difficult to change than ideas or suggestions that are shared by word of mouth. Why do you think this is so? What might have been the reason the Rabbis taught that an Oral Torah was given on Mount Sinai? In the United States, we have a Constitution. It might be considered as our "Written Torah." Do we have an "Oral Torah"?

Actually, in the course of history, the Oral Torah also became a written document. After about 200 years of teaching the interpretations by word of mouth from one generation to the next, it was decided to organize the laws. This was done first by Rabbi Akiva and then, finally, by Rabbi Y'hudah HaNasi in about 200 C.E. Rabbi Y'hudah's collection became known as the Mishnah. There was a 300-year period in which the interpretations of the Mishnah were passed on orally. Finally, in about the sixth century C.E., that

TORAH

With the Torah freedom came into the world.
B'reishit Rabbah

Why is Israel God's people? Because of the Torah!
Tanchuma Va-eira 9a

Do not make the Torah a crown to magnify yourself, nor a spade with which to dig.
Pirkei Avot 4:5

Approach the Torah with joy and also with trembling.
BT Yoma 4b

What might these quotes have to do with becoming a Torah-person?

177

oral tradition, known as Gemara, was also put down in writing. Together the Mishnah and Gemara form what is known as the Talmud.

The vast books of the Talmud, however, were not considered to contain the whole Oral Torah. Rabbis and students of Jewish tradition have continued the process of interpretation to this very day. Why? How does the process of continued interpretation help to keep Judaism alive and vital? What would happen if Jews stopped interpreting our tradition?

Rabbi Levi Yitzchak was once asked by his students: "Why does each book of the Talmud begin with page two and not with page one?" He replied: "To remind us that no matter how much we study and learn, we have not yet come to the first page." What do you think Levi Yitzchak meant? How might his statement relate to the interpretation of Torah within Judaism?

A Life-Giving Medicine!

Rabbi Y'hudah bar Chiya, who lived in the Land of Israel during the third century C.E., once observed: "A drug may be beneficial to one and not to another. The Torah, however, is a life-giving medicine for all Israel" (BT *Eiruvin* 54a).

The Sages of Jewish tradition believed that the Torah contained the knowledge and directions for a good life. For them, the Torah was a "map" or a "prescription" of the ethical ways in which a human being ought to live. Yosef Albo, a medieval Jewish philosopher, commented: "The purpose of the Torah is to guide human beings to obtain spiritual happiness." And other rabbis taught: "Each מִצְוָה is a branch of the Torah, and the person who honors the Torah by performing מִצְוֹת will receive honor." In another place we are taught: "Through Torah, humanity becomes God's partner in creation" (*Maalot HaTorah*).

Can the modern Jew still consider the Torah a "life-giving medicine"? In what ways? How can the Torah, written and oral, help us obtain "spiritual happiness"?

Look at Exodus 21:33–37; 22:24–26; 23:1–9; and Leviticus 19:9–18. Ask: How can these passages be applied to modern society? How can they help us achieve spiritual happiness? How in the doing of these מִצְוֹת are we partners with God? You may wish to divide into groups for this project and then report your findings. You may also wish to develop your own talmudic commentary on the meaning of these Torah quotations. If you do, remember that the Talmud records both majority and minority opinions.

AT THE ARK

At the Ark

אֵין כָּמְוֹךָ בָאֱלֹהִים, אֲדֹנָי, וְאֵין כְּמַעֲשֶׂיךָ.

There are no gods that can compare to You, Eternal God, and there are no works like Yours.

יְיָ עֹז לְעַמּוֹ יִתֵּן, יְיָ יְבָרֵךְ אֶת עַמּוֹ בַשָּׁלוֹם.

Eternal God, give strength to Your people; Eternal God, bless Your people with peace.

וַיְהִי בִּנְסֹעַ הָאָרֹן וַיֹּאמֶר מֹשֶׁה: קוּמָה יְיָ.

And when the Ark was about to be moved, Moses would say: Rise up, Eternal our God.

כִּי מִצִּיּוֹן תֵּצֵא תוֹרָה, וּדְבַר יְיָ מִירוּשָׁלָיִם.

For out of Zion will go forth the Torah and the word of the Eternal from Jerusalem.

בָּרוּךְ שֶׁנָּתַן תּוֹרָה לְעַמּוֹ יִשְׂרָאֵל בִּקְדֻשָּׁתוֹ.

Praised be the One who in holiness gives Torah to our people Israel.

COMMENTARY

The Torah service is the dramatic center of the Shabbat worship service. In taking the Torah from the ark and reading it, Jews relive the giving of the Torah on Mount Sinai, the carrying of it across the wilderness, and the study of it in synagogues for over 2,000 years. In order to help celebrate such a special moment, those who composed the prayer book selected special sentences from the Bible and from Jewish tradition. They then wove these passages together as poetry expressing the special significance of Torah to the Jewish people and the joy of taking it from the ark and studying it.

There Are No Gods

The אֵין כָּמֽוֹךָ (Ein Kamocha) is taken from Psalm 86:8. In that psalm the poet proclaims: "All nations that You have created, O God, will come and bow themselves before You.... For You are great and do wonderful things—You are God alone!" (Psalm 86:9–10).

Why would the authors of the Torah service begin it with the words of Psalm 86? What is so special about the declaration of the אֵין כָּמֽוֹךָ? Why did the poet's declaration "There are no gods that can compare to You, Eternal God" seem so appropriate?

Perhaps the authors of the Torah service wanted to remind those who were about to take the Torah from the ark of the time when the Torah was first given to the people of Israel. According to tradition, that moment took place on Mount Sinai with the giving of the Ten Commandments. The first two commandments read as follows:

> I am *Adonai*, your God, who brought you out of the land of Egypt, out of the house of bondage.
> You shall have no other gods before Me.
>
> Exodus 20:2–3

Do you see a connection between the אֵין כָּמֽוֹךָ prayer and the first two commandments? Jews believe that God's power can be seen not only in the wonderful works of nature but in human history as well. How do both the אֵין כָּמֽוֹךָ prayer and the first two commandments express the Jewish idea that God is to be found in human history and in nature?

No Gods That Can Compare to You

The second commandment forbids idolatry. After the words: "You shall have no other gods before Me" is the following:

> You shall not make for yourself a graven image, nor any likeness of any thing that is in the heavens above, or that it is on the earth beneath, or that is in the water under the earth; you shall not bow down to them nor serve them.
>
> Exodus 20:4–5

The אֵין כָּמוֹךְ reminds us of the commandment that forbids idolatry. It declares: "There are no gods that can compare to You." Why did ancient Jews deplore idolatry? Why did some Jews, even though their laws forbade it, build and worship idols? What is so attractive and dangerous about idol worship?

The prophet Isaiah tells about a carpenter who cuts down a tree. He chops it in two. With one half he "makes the figure of a man," and with the other he builds a fire to warm himself and cook his food. Then he sets up the image he has made, bows down to it, and prays: "Save me, for you are my god." Having given us this description of idolatry, Isaiah comments about those who worship idols:

> They do not know, neither do they understand;
> For their eyes are blinded so they cannot see,
> And their hearts, that they cannot understand.
> They are incapable of saying to themselves:
> "I have burned the one half of it for fire,
> And have baked bread on the coals....
> How, then, can I make an idol with the other half
> And bow down to the stock of a tree?"
> Such a man strives after ashes,
> He has been turned aside by a deceived heart.
>
> Isaiah 44:18–20

According to Isaiah, why do people worship idols? What does he find foolish and wrong about idol worship? What does idol worship do to the worshiper?

Does idol worship still exist in modern times? Psychiatrist Dr. Erich Fromm has written: "Words can become idols, and machines.... Science and the opinion of one's neighbors can become idols, and God has become an idol for many" (*Psychoanalysis and Religion*). The medieval Jewish philosopher Bachya observed in his times: "People make their bellies, their fine clothes, and their homes their gods" (*Chovot HaL'vavot*). What do you think Fromm and Bachya meant by their statements? How do people make the things they mention idols? What is the danger when "science" or "religion" becomes an idol? The well-known Zionist leader Shemarya Levin once remarked: "Every idol demands sacrifices." What do you suppose he meant? How do the modern idols, described by Fromm, demand "sacrifices" from human beings?

181

The Chasidic leader Rabbi Menachem Mendel of Kotzk once warned his followers: "The Torah prohibits us from making idols out of the מִצְווֹת." Perhaps Rabbi Menachem Mendel was referring to the times that fulfilling a מִצְוָה might require us to hurt another person or otherwise cause harm. Judaism instructs us to transgress almost any מִצְוָה in order to save a life. How does this teaching keep us from making "idols" of the מִצְווֹת? What if by fulfilling a מִצְוָה, you would discriminate against women or show dishonor to non-Jews? Might there be another way of making "idols" of the מִצְווֹת?

> *Divide your study group into small research groups. The task is to find objects of which modern people have made idols. Take your evidence from newspapers, magazines (watch for the ads!), radio and television (watch for the commercials!), the Internet, and any other areas where you can find good examples. Don't overlook your school classroom, the sports field, and your house. After you have compiled your evidence, make a list indicating the idol, the evidence, why you think people today worship the idol, and whether you feel it is dangerous for people to have such an idol. Then, share the results with the members of your study group.*

Eternal God, Give Strength to Your People
Eternal God, Bless Your People with Peace

These words, taken from Psalm 29:11, are used not only in the Torah service but in many other places in Jewish worship as well. In the Torah service, however, they have a special meaning, for they apply to the Torah and to its role in the life of the Jew.

The teachers of Jewish tradition believed that the Torah was a source of strength for the Jewish people and that its purpose was to help people to achieve peace. "Without the Torah," the Rabbis teach, "a person stumbles and does not know which path to take; with the Torah, however, a person walks like one who has a lantern in the dark. The person can find the way" (*Sh'mot Rabbah* 36:3). What do you suppose the Rabbis meant by this analogy?

Can you think of examples where the Torah helps us decide between right and wrong or between justice and injustice? (Some good examples may be found in Deuteronomy 16:18–20; 19:15–19; 20:19–20; 22:1–3.) How do these examples fulfill Rabbi Yosef's observation that "the whole Torah exists only for the sake of peace" (BT *Gittin* 59b)?

Moses Would Say

Just as the ark is opened, the congregation says: "And when the Ark was about to be moved, Moses would say: 'Rise up, Eternal our God.'"

While the Jewish people were in the desert, their מִשְׁכָּן (*Mishkan*), "Sanctuary," and its Ark were portable. Each time the camp moved, the Sanctuary was taken down and the Ark was carried by the people. The Ark was given the honor of being placed ahead of the people so that they could follow it.

The words "And when the Ark was about to be moved..." remind us of the honor given by our ancestors to the Ark and to the Torah. Together with the words taken from Isaiah 2:3—"For out of Zion will go forth the Torah..."—they help us celebrate the importance of Torah to our people in the past and to our hopes for the future.

What are these hopes? Look at Isaiah 2:1–4. There the prophet expresses the hope for a messianic time. What does he envision, and how will the Torah help us achieve his hopes? In what ways might the State of Israel help the Torah "go forth...from Jerusalem"?

Who in Holiness Gives Torah to Our People Israel

The בָּרוּךְ שֶׁנָּתַן (*Baruch Shenatan*) thanks God for giving the Torah to the people of Israel.

In some congregations this praise is followed by a prayer found in the *Zohar*, a book containing all mystical interpretations of the Torah. Some believe the *Zohar* was written by Rabbi Shimon bar Yochai, who lived in the second century C.E. Most likely, however, it was written in Spain during the thirteenth century and attributed to Rabbi Shimon.

In one place, the *Zohar* teaches: "The Torah is a garment for God's presence." In another it says: "If one is far from Torah, one is far from God." How can the Torah be a "garment for God"? If we are known by what we say and what we do, how is the Torah also known by what it "says" and "does" in the lives of those who cherish it?

Just after the בָּרוּךְ שֶׁנָּתַן, we have a place for private devotion. In it a person can use the words of the *Zohar*, found on page 184, or compose some expression of his or her own. The theme of this special prayer from the *Zohar* is the meaning of the Torah to the people of Israel and to us as individuals.

Prayer from the *Zohar*

יְהֵא רַעֲוָא קֳדָמָךְ, דְּתִפְתַּח לִבִּי בְּאוֹרַיְתָא. וְתַשְׁלִים מִשְׁאֵלִין דְּלִבִּי, וְלִבָּא דְכָל עַמָּךְ יִשְׂרָאֵל, לְטָב וּלְחַיִּין וְלִשְׁלָם. אָמֵן.

May it be Your will, O *Adonai*, to open my heart to Your Torah and to fulfill the wishes of my heart and the hearts of all Your people Israel for good, for life, and for peace.

TAKING THE TORAH FROM THE ARK

Taking the Torah from the Ark

שְׁמַע יִשְׂרָאֵל: יהוה אֱלֹהֵינוּ, יהוה אֶחָד!

Hear, O Israel: the Eternal One is our God, the Eternal God alone!

אֶחָד אֱלֹהֵינוּ, גָּדוֹל אֲדוֹנֵינוּ, קָדוֹשׁ שְׁמוֹ.

Our God is One; great and holy is the Eternal One.

גַּדְּלוּ לַיהוה אִתִּי, וּנְרוֹמְמָה שְׁמוֹ יַחְדָּו.

Magnify the Eternal One with me, and together let us exalt God's name.

לְךָ, יְיָ, הַגְּדֻלָּה וְהַגְּבוּרָה וְהַתִּפְאֶרֶת וְהַנֵּצַח וְהַהוֹד כִּי כֹל בַּשָּׁמַיִם וּבָאָרֶץ. לְךָ, יְיָ, הַמַּמְלָכָה וְהַמִּתְנַשֵּׂא לְכֹל לְרֹאשׁ. רוֹמְמוּ יְיָ אֱלֹהֵינוּ, וְהִשְׁתַּחֲווּ לַהֲדֹם רַגְלָיו, קָדוֹשׁ הוּא. רוֹמְמוּ יְיָ אֱלֹהֵינוּ וְהִשְׁתַּחֲווּ לְהַר קָדְשׁוֹ, כִּי קָדוֹשׁ יְיָ אֱלֹהֵינוּ.

Yours, God, is the greatness, the power, the glory, the victory, and the majesty; for all that is in heaven and earth is Yours. You, God, are sovereign; You are supreme over all. Praised be the Eternal. Worship at God's Temple. Holy is the Eternal. Praised be the Eternal. Worship at God's holy mountain, for the Eternal is holy.

184

COMMENTARY

The drama of the Torah service now turns to taking the Torah from the ark. Notice, however, that nothing is said here about the importance or significance of Torah. Indeed, the word "Torah" is not even mentioned. Why not? Wouldn't it be logical for us to say something about how much the Torah means to us as we take it out of the ark?

Notice, also, that the words spoken here are very few. The שְׁמַע and the אֶחָד אֱלֹהֵינוּ (Echad Eloheinu) both say the same thing. The גַּדְּלוּ (Gad'lu) is taken from Psalm 34:4. It is simply a call to the congregation to magnify and praise God. But how is that to be done? We are not told; we are just challenged.

Is "Doing" the Essential Thing?

The fact that there is no mention of Torah or its importance when we take it from the ark may provide a significant lesson. Let's see if we can understand why the authors of the Torah service omitted the mention of Torah or its meaning at this point.

Rabbi Elazar ben Azaryah served as the vice president and president of the Sanhedrin at Yavneh during the Roman persecutions from the 80 to 135 C.E. He was a man of wisdom, political insight, and action. Together with Rabbi Akiva, he represented the Jewish people in Rome before the leaders of the Roman empire.

One of Rabbi Elazar's best-known teachings is the following:

> To what shall one be compared whose wisdom exceeds one's deeds? To a tree whose branches are many, but whose roots are few. What happens to such a tree when a strong wind comes along? It is plucked up and over-turned on its face!
>
> To what shall one be compared whose deeds exceed one's wisdom? To a tree whose branches are few, but whose roots are many. What happens to such a tree when a strong wind comes along? Even if all the winds in the world blow upon it, it cannot be uprooted from its place!
>
> *Pirkei Avot* 3:22

Practice makes the artist.
Rabbi Hanau

It is in the deed that God is revealed in life.
Rabbi Leo Baeck

True wisdom can be obtained only through practice.
Moses Maimonides

My deeds are both my witnesses and my judges.
Moses ibn Ezra

We can judge people faithful or unfaithful only by their deeds.
Baruch Spinoza

STUDY

Do not neglect the knowledge of the wise.
Ben Sira

Study from love, and honor will follow.
Bachya

Study strengthens our good powers for victory over our evil ones.
Bratzlaver Rebbe

The ignorant person cannot be religious.
Hillel

Learning! Learning! Learning! That is the secret of Jewish survival.
Achad Ha-Am

What is the meaning of Rabbi Elazar's observation? What is the difference between the two people he describes? Rabbi Elazar's traveling companion, Rabbi Akiva, taught: "Everything depends upon deeds" (*Pirkei Avot* 3:15). What do you think he meant? What is the relationship of his statement to Rabbi Elazar's?

A Debate

The issue of what is more important, knowledge or deeds, is a very old one. We have already seen that Judaism emphasizes the study of Torah. The Rabbis taught that תַּלְמוּד תּוֹרָה כְּנֶגֶד כֻּלָם (*talmud Torah k'neged kulam*), "the study of Torah comes before everything else." On the other hand, they also taught that "the pursuit of knowledge is not essential, but rather the doing of it" (*Pirkei Avot* 1:17). In one place Shammai teaches his pupils: "Say little and do much" (*Pirkei Avot* 1:15), and in another Abahu tells his students: "Study must precede practice" (BT *Kiddushin* 40b).

Whom are we to follow here? Who is right? Which is more important—study or practice?

About 120 C.E., the leaders of the Jewish people in the Land of Israel met in the town of Lod. At their meeting, they debated several issues. One of them was the question: "Which is more important—study or practice?" Rabbi Tarfon said, "Practice." Rabbi Akiva said, "Study." Have two groups prepare and reenact each side of the debate, and then vote on which your study group believes to be more important. Your reasons for favoring one over the other ought to be based on examples taken from the past and from the present. Note the quotes in the box dealing with both sides of the issue.

Why We Say Nothing

We still have not answered the question asked earlier in this section: "Why is nothing said about the Torah when we take it from the ark"?

Perhaps the authors of this part of our service wanted to teach us that the very act of taking the Torah from the ark speaks for itself. It is the tradition to lift the Torah from the ark and hold it high above the head when the congregation recites the שְׁמַע and the אֶחָד אֱלֹהֵינוּ. Then the leader challenges the congregation with the words of Psalm 34: "Magnify the Eternal One with me, and together let us exalt God's name." That challenge is to "live the Torah"—to incorporate its teachings into one's practice and deeds.

How Do We "Magnify the Eternal One"?

Look at Psalm 34. Notice that it is written in the form of an acrostic. It begins with א *(alef)*, the first letter of the Hebrew alphabet, and ends with ת *(tav)*, the last letter. The first words of the psalm are:

I will bless *Adonai* at all times;
God's praise shall continually be in my mouth.

Those first lines provide us with a clue as to why the author may have used the acrostic form and the twenty-two letters of the Hebrew alphabet. Perhaps he wished to suggest that just as one can praise God using every letter of the alphabet, so one can also serve God with every human ability and deed.

The poet who wrote Psalm 34 not only voiced the challenge "Magnify the Eternal One with me..." but he tried to describe how human beings should "magnify the Eternal One." Notice especially verses 12–16. How, according to the Psalmist, does a person express "fear of *Adonai*"?

Yours, God, Is the Greatness

Just before his death, King David called his people together and announced that his son Solomon would become king of Israel. At the same time, he told the people that during his reign, Solomon would build a Temple in Jerusalem. David's announcement was made in the form of a prayer found in I Chronicles 29:10–19. That prayer includes the words: "Yours, God, is the greatness...." These words are usually sung while the Torah is being taken to the reading desk. Look at the whole prayer in Chronicles. Why do you think a part of it was chosen for this particular place in the Torah service? Could it be that those who placed the words "Yours, God, is the greatness..." wished to teach that just as David handed tradition to his son Solomon, each generation of parents has the task of handing that tradition to its children? How is a bar or bat mitzvah ceremony the fulfillment of such a task?

THE *ALIYAH* AND THE TORAH SERVICE

The *Aliyah*

Before the Reading

בָּרְכוּ אֶת־יְיָ הַמְבֹרָךְ!

בָּרוּךְ יְיָ הַמְבֹרָךְ לְעוֹלָם וָעֶד!

בָּרוּךְ אַתָּה יְיָ, אֱלֹהֵינוּ מֶלֶךְ הָעוֹלָם, אֲשֶׁר בָּחַר־בָּנוּ מִכָּל־
הָעַמִּים, וְנָתַן־לָנוּ אֶת־תּוֹרָתוֹ. בָּרוּךְ אַתָּה יְיָ, נוֹתֵן הַתּוֹרָה.

Praise the One to whom our praise is due!
Praised be the One to whom our praise is due, now and for ever!
We praise You, Eternal God, Sovereign of the universe: You have called us to Your service by giving us the Torah. We praise You, O God, Giver of the Torah.

After the Reading

בָּרוּךְ אַתָּה יְיָ, אֱלֹהֵינוּ מֶלֶךְ הָעוֹלָם, אֲשֶׁר נָתַן־לָנוּ תּוֹרַת
אֱמֶת, וְחַיֵּי עוֹלָם נָטַע בְּתוֹכֵנוּ. בָּרוּךְ אַתָּה יְיָ, נוֹתֵן הַתּוֹרָה.

We praise You, Eternal God, Sovereign of the universe: You have given us a Torah of truth, implanting within us eternal life. We praise You, O God, Giver of the Torah.

COMMENTARY

Among many ancient peoples, the priests were the privileged, educated class. They were charged with the responsibility of knowing and preserving the tribal traditions. Often, their knowledge was kept a secret from others and passed on only to members of their families.

Among Jews, however, even though there were priests, the Torah was considered the possession of all the people. When Ezra read and taught the Torah, he did so "before the congregation, both men and women, all that could hear...." Jewish tradition revolutionized and democratized religion. In Judaism the Torah was open to everyone, and each Jew became responsible for both knowing Torah and living according to its מִצְווֹת.

The reading of the Torah in the ancient synagogue demonstrated the democratic spirit of Jewish tradition. From biblical times the Jewish people had been divided among כֹּהֲנִים (kohanim), "priests," לְוִיִּם (L'viyim), "Levites," and יִשְׂרְאֵלִים (Yisr'eilim), "Israelites." The synagogue gave ceremonial honor to these divisions during the Torah service. When it came time to read from the Torah, first the כֹּהֵן (kohein) was called, then a לֵוִי (Leivi), and then a יִשְׂרָאֵל (Yisrael). Once called to the Torah, however, each person did the same thing. Each would read a designated portion.

In Orthodox and many Conservative synagogues today, you will find that these ceremonial honors are still given. During the Torah service, the first person called to the Torah is a *kohein* (someone thought to be descended from the ancient priests, often with a last name like Cohen, Kahn, or Kagan). Next to be called is a Levite (a person thought to be a descendant of the tribe of Levi, often with the last name Levy, Levine, or Levitt). The third person called to the Torah is a *Yisrael* (a person not descended from the ancient priests or Levites). In maintaining this tradition, Orthodox and Conservative Jews link their Torah service to the Torah service of the ancient synagogue and show honor to the descendants of the earliest priests and Levites. In preserving this ancient ritual, they feel that they are reliving the experience of our historic people.

Among most Reform Jews, however, you will find that these ceremonial honors are not given. Because thousands of years have passed since the Jewish people lived as separate tribes, it is impossible to know for certain who the true descendants of the ancient priests and Levites are. Also, Reform Jews see all Jews as equal and do not distinguish among *kohanim, L'viyim,* or *Yisr'eilim.* Therefore, during the Torah service in a Reform synagogue, there are no designated portions for the descendants of priests, Levites, and Israelites. People are called to the Torah not to represent their ancestors' tribes, but on their own individual merit. Each Jew is considered equal to another.

If you were leading a Torah service, would you follow the traditional or the Reform practice of calling people to the Torah? Why did you choose the way you did?

What Is an *Aliyah*?

The privilege of being "called up" to read from the Torah is known as עֲלִיָּה
(aliyah). Why?

Do you remember the passage sung while the Torah is being placed on
the reading desk? Its words are "Praise be the Eternal. Worship at God's holy
mountain...." In Psalm 24:3 the poet asks:

> Who shall ascend to the mountain of *Adonai*?
> And who shall stand in God's holy place?

For the Jew in biblical times, the "mountain of *Adonai*" was Mount Zion in
Jerusalem, where the Temple stood. From there was the Torah to go forth to
all nations. In order to visit Jerusalem, one must "go up," or "ascend," for it
is located on one of the highest places in the Land of Israel. In biblical times,
"going up" to Jerusalem for a Festival was called עֲלִיָּה לְרֶגֶל *(aliyah l'regel)*. In
our own times, the word used for immigration to Israel is עֲלִיָּה.

Now, how did the word עֲלִיָּה come to be associated with being called up
to read from the Torah? Perhaps because the Torah was associated with
Jerusalem, the reading of it became a substitute for "going up" to the holy
city. It follows that the reader became known as an עוֹלֶה *(oleh)* because the
reader "goes up" to the pulpit to read the Torah. Whatever the explanation,
over the course of years the word עֲלִיָּה came to designate the privilege of
reading from the Torah.

The בַּעַל קוֹרֵא—*Baal Korei*

From about 300 B.C.E., the language of Aramaic began to replace Hebrew as
the spoken language of the Jewish people. Gradually, over the years, many
Jews lost the art of reading from the Torah or even being able to understand
all of the Hebrew of the Torah. As one might imagine, this posed a serious
problem for the future of Judaism.

In order to solve the problem, the Rabbis created the position of בַּעַל
קוֹרֵא, the trained reader of the Torah. In this way they could be sure that the
text would be read correctly. Their solution, however, brought with it another
problem. It removed the privilege of reading the Torah from most Jews. In
order to solve that problem, the Rabbis assigned the blessings before and after
the reading of Torah to the עוֹלֶה. This meant that all Jews, whether they could
read from the Torah or not, could be called upon for an עֲלִיָּה. In this way, the
Rabbis preserved the democracy of the synagogue.

190

Translating the Torah

As we have already discovered, the introduction of Aramaic as the spoken language of the people meant that many were unable to understand the Hebrew of the Torah. Again, in order to preserve the democratic nature of Jewish knowledge, the Rabbis introduced the position of מְתוּרְגְּמָן (m'turg'man), "translator," into the synagogue. They also developed and accepted an Aramaic translation of the Torah, which was read by the translator. That translation is known as *Targum Onkelos*. It is interesting to note that the Jews of Egypt, who spoke Greek, developed a translation of the Torah in Greek.

And Caused Them to Understand the Reading

When Ezra and his fellow priests read the Torah to the people of Israel, we are told that "they gave the sense and caused them to understand the reading." What, exactly, does it mean to "give the sense" or "cause" someone to understand the Torah?

The Sages of Jewish tradition believed that Ezra sought to "interpret" the Torah and provide the people with its application in their lives. The task of "interpreting Torah" required knowledge and skill. In the ancient synagogue, the interpretation of Torah was called a דְּרָשָׁה (d'rashah). The word דְּרָשָׁה is derived from the root דרש, which means to search, to investigate, or to explain. Today, we call the דְּרָשָׁה a sermon.

Creating the Sermon

In the ancient synagogue, as in most modern ones, the דְּרָשָׁה was delivered just after the reading of the haftarah. (For a discussion of the haftarah, see pp. 193–201.)

The Rabbis developed the sermon in order to explain the Torah and inspire Jews toward its fulfillment. To make their points clear, the Sages used stories, analogies, legends, and incidents from their own experiences. Most of their sermons were organized in the following way:

a. The first section called attention to the story, theme, or subject of the Torah or haftarah they wished to interpret.

b. The Rabbis then asked questions about the most challenging parts of the section.

c. Having asked the questions, they tried to answer them and apply their answers to the lives of their listeners.

d. The conclusion of the sermon included a summary as well as a statement meant to inspire the listeners to "take to heart" the message of the Torah or haftarah interpretation.

This outline of the דְּרָשָׁה ought to be helpful to you when you are called upon to write a sermon for your congregation. Remember that your task is to help others appreciate and understand the Torah or haftarah text.

Contributions

The practice of reading from Torah and haftarah, as well as delivering the sermon, were borrowed by Christianity and Islam. In both the church and the mosque, Scripture is read and interpreted. In the church, Scripture includes the Hebrew Bible and the New Testament. In the mosque, Scripture is the Koran, which Moslems believe was dictated to Muhammad by the angel Gabriel. The Hebrew word for biblical verse, קְרָא *(k'ra)*, and the Arabic word "Koran" both come from the same root that means "to read aloud."

The Blessings before and after the Reading of Torah

Who wrote the blessings that come before and after the reading of Torah? We do not know! We really do not even know when they were composed. In the Book of Nehemiah, we are told that when Ezra read from the Torah he "blessed *Adonai*, the great God. And all the people answered, 'Amen, Amen,' with the lifting up of their hands..." (Nehemiah 8:6).

It seems that by the end of the first century C.E., the custom of saying blessings before and after the reading of Torah was accepted. The blessings we recite today are those most likely used by Jews since that time.

You Have Given Us the Torah
Giver of the Torah

Notice that in both the blessings before and after the reading of Torah, the author used the words נָתַן (natan), "gave," and נוֹתֵן (notein), "gives." Why do you supposed Jews utilize both past and present tenses when thanking God for the Torah?

A Sage known by the strange name of Ben Bag Bag once taught: "Turn the Torah, and turn it over again, for everything is in it!" (*Pirkei Avot* 5:25). What might Ben Bag Bag's statement have to do with the use of past (נָתַן) and present (נוֹתֵן) in the blessings for the reading of Torah?

Is Torah still in the process of being given today? In what ways? Look again at the quote from the Baal Shem Tov. He said: "The Torah is eternal, but its explanation is to be made by the spiritual leaders of Judaism...in accordance with the age." How are new "explanations" a modern giving of the Torah?

SINAI IS EVER PRESENT

Sinai is ever present—not
  only a past event.
Wherever people gather
  to seek God's presence,
To renew the covenant,
  to discover God's will;
Whenever they listen and
  hear, receive and
  transmit—
They stand at Sinai.
                Rabbi Eugene Mihaly

Remember that the Jewish people received the Torah at Mount Sinai. Rabbi Mihaly says that we stand at Sinai whenever we search for God, study Torah, and try to understand what God requires of us. What do you think it means to "stand at Sinai"? How does Rabbi Mihaly's teaching relate to the idea that Torah is still being given to us today?

THE HAFTARAH BLESSINGS

Blessings before Haftarah Reading

בָּרוּךְ אַתָּה יי, אֱלֹהֵינוּ מֶלֶךְ הָעוֹלָם, אֲשֶׁר בָּחַר בִּנְבִיאִים טוֹבִים, וְרָצָה בְדִבְרֵיהֶם הַנֶּאֱמָרִים בֶּאֱמֶת. בָּרוּךְ אַתָּה יי, הַבּוֹחֵר בַּתּוֹרָה, וּבְמֹשֶׁה עַבְדּוֹ, וּבְיִשְׂרָאֵל עַמּוֹ וּבִנְבִיאֵי הָאֱמֶת וָצֶדֶק.

We praise You, Eternal God, Sovereign of the universe: You have called faithful prophets to speak words of truth. We praise You, O God, for the revelation of Torah, for Moses Your servant and Israel Your people, and for the prophets of truth and righteousness.

Among Moslems, Jews have historically been known as "the people of the Book." We were given that name because of our devotion to our Bible. While the Torah occupies a special place not only in the ark but in the history of the Jewish people, the rest of the Hebrew Bible is also considered holy. The "Prophets" of Israel were believed to have spoken "in the name of God," and the "Writings" (such as Psalms, Proverbs, and the Book of Job) were all considered sacred.

When Jews refer to the Hebrew Bible, we call it תַּנַ״ךְ *(Tanach)*. That name is made up of the three first letters taken from the titles of the three sections of the Hebrew Bible:

Torah	תּוֹרָה	ת =	*tav*
Prophets *(N'vi-im)*	נְבִיאִים	נ =	*nun*
Writings *(K'tuvim)*	כְּתוּבִים	ך =	*chaf* (the final *chaf*)

The תּוֹרָה section, as we have indicated, includes the Five Books of Moses. נְבִיאִים begins with the Book of Joshua and concludes with the Book of Malachi. כְּתוּבִים begins with Psalms and ends with the final book of the Hebrew Bible, Second Chronicles.

What Is the הַפְטָרָה—Haftarah?

The word הַפְטָרָה means "conclusion" or "dismissal." Why would a reading from the Bible be given such a name? We are not sure.

It could be that it was the custom in the ancient synagogue to follow the reading of the Torah with a reading from the Prophets and then dismiss or conclude the worship services. We do know that such a custom did exist in some synagogues, and this may explain how the reading selected from the Prophets came to be known as הַפְטָרָה.

Selecting the Haftarah

By the second century C.E., the practice of reading a selection from the Prophets was well established. The blessings before and after the reading had been written and were used throughout the Jewish world. The selection of the specific הַפְטָרָה reading, however, was left to those in charge of each local synagogue.

How did they make their selection of an appropriate הַפְטָרָה for each Shabbat? Interestingly enough, the New Testament gives us a good description:

> [Jesus] came to Nazareth, where he had been brought up, and as was his custom, he went to the synagogue on the Shabbat day. While there, he was called upon to read, and the Book of Isaiah was given to him....
>
> Luke 4:16–17

It seems clear from this description of Jesus at the synagogue in Nazareth that it was the custom to call upon a member of the congregation to come forward to read from the הַפְטָרָה. We are not sure whether the selection of a passage from Isaiah was made by the leaders of the synagogue or by Jesus. The description in Luke, however, does indicate that after he had completed the reading, Jesus went on to deliver a sermon based upon it.

There are those who believe that by the time of Jesus it had become the custom to select a הַפְטָרָה reading that would have some connection with the Torah portion. This, too, is entirely possible. By the seventh century C.E., a full cycle of הַפְטָרָה readings had been developed. All of these were selected by the Rabbis because they complemented or developed the subject found in the Torah portion. For example, when the first chapters of Genesis are read, the הַפְטָרָה is taken from Isaiah, chapter 42. The theme of the first chapters of Genesis is the creation of the world by God. The chapter of Isaiah that is read as the הַפְטָרָה includes the following words:

> Thus says *Adonai*,
> Who created the heavens and stretched them forth,
> Who spread forth the earth and that which comes out of it,
> Who gives breath to the people upon it,
> And spirit to them that walk therein.
>
> Isaiah 42:5

THE HEBREW BIBLE

Torah תּוֹרָה
  Genesis
  Exodus
  Leviticus
  Numbers
  Deuteronomy

Prophets נְבִיאִים
  Joshua
  Judges
  First Samuel
  Second Samuel
  First Kings
  Second Kings
  Isaiah
  Jeremiah
  Ezekiel
  Hosea
  Joel
  Amos
  Obadiah
  Jonah
  Micah
  Nahum
  Habakkuk
  Zephaniah
  Haggai
  Zechariah
  Malachi

Writings כְּתוּבִים
  Psalms
  Proverbs
  Job
  Song of Songs
  Ruth
  Lamentations
  Ecclesiastes
  Esther
  Daniel
  Ezra
  Nehemiah
  First Chronicles
  Second Chronicles

You may wish to compare the order of the Hebrew Bible with the order of the Christian Bible. What is the difference, and why do you think Christians have arranged the books of the Hebrew Bible in a different order?

As indicated on page 195, the הַפְטָרָה was selected on the basis of its having something in common with the Torah portion. Below are some Torah portions and their הַפְטָרָה selections. Divide them up, and have two or three groups examine them. Try to figure out the relationship of the הַפְטָרָה to the Torah selection. Then share your results.

1. *Genesis 6:9–11:22 and Isaiah 54.*
2. *Exodus 6:2–9:35 and Ezekiel 28.*
3. *Exodus 13:17–17:16 and Judges 5.*
4. *Exodus 21:1–24:18 and Jeremiah 34.*
5. *Numbers 22:1–25:9 and Micah 6.*
6. *Deuteronomy 3:23–7:11 and Isaiah 40.*
7. *Deuteronomy 33:1–34:12 and Joshua 1.*

The Maccabees and the הַפְטָרָה

Some Jewish scholars trace the beginning of the custom of reading a הַפְטָרָה to the time of the Maccabees. Just before the revolt led by Mattathias and his sons, Antiochus Epiphanes decreed that there should be no public reading of the Torah. Some Jews responded to this form of persecution by substituting a reading from the Prophets for the Torah portion. After the Jewish uprising and the defeat of the Greek-Syrians, the custom of the הַפְטָרָה reading was continued.

Do you think that substituting the הַפְטָרָה reading for the Torah portion was a good way to handle Antiochus Epiphanes' decree? What would be your reaction if a modern government prohibited the reading of Torah in the synagogue? What might you do if your government began to force Jews to close their synagogues? What do you believe would be the most effective response to such anti-Semitism? How have Jews in the past reacted to such persecution? How should Jews today react to attacks on synagogues or Jewish centers, or to anti-Semitic websites?

What do you think of the following four statements and responses to anti-Semitism? How do they differ? With which, if any, would you agree?

Anti-Semitism is a mad passion, akin to the lowest perversities of diseased human nature. It is the will to hate.

Leo Tolstoy

Anti-Semitism is not to be overcome by getting people to forget us but to know us.

Meyer Levin

A Jewish group with firmly established rights can—when the fine balance of the people amid whom it lives is disturbed—suddenly find itself faced with hostility. The system has not yet been found which will insure the Jew living in the Diaspora the complete normalization of [life] as a part of society and as an individual.

Leni Yahil

For the Jews, the moral is to answer anti-Semitism with more Semitism . . . greater devotion to the great ideals which Judaism proclaimed to the world.

Israel Abrahams

Blessings before Haftarah Reading

The blessings before the reading of the הַפְטָרָה praise God for "the prophets of truth and righteousness." They also thank God for the Torah and for those who have passed the Torah from generation to generation. We are not sure when the blessings before the reading of the הַפְטָרָה were written. It is likely that they were composed sometime during the second to the seventh century C.E.

> *Study the blessings before the reading of the הַפְטָרָה. Notice that their themes are God's choosing "good prophets," the "truthfulness" of their messages, and the faithful passing on of the tradition from generation to generation.*
>
> *On the basis of these themes, what would you include today if you were challenged to write a new a הַפְטָרָה prayer? Take up the challenge and write one!*

Blessings after Haftarah Reading

The blessings after the reading of the הַפְטָרָה are divided into four sections. We might expect that their theme would have to do with the importance of the prophets or their message. However, that is not what we find. Rather, the first section praises the truthfulness and fulfillment of God's words. The second section asks for mercy upon Zion and the people of Israel. The third section voices the hope for the coming of Elijah and the messianic era. And the fourth thanks God for the Torah, the prophets, worship, and the Shabbat day.

Blessings after Haftarah Reading

I

בָּרוּךְ אַתָּה יְיָ אֱלֹהֵינוּ מֶלֶךְ הָעוֹלָם, צוּר כָּל־הָעוֹלָמִים, צַדִּיק בְּכָל־הַדּוֹרוֹת, הָאֵל הַנֶּאֱמָן, הָאוֹמֵר וְעוֹשֶׂה, הַמְדַבֵּר וּמְקַיֵּם שֶׁכָּל־דְּבָרָיו אֱמֶת וָצֶדֶק.

We praise You, Eternal God, Sovereign of the universe, the Rock of all creation, the Righteous One of all generations, the faithful God whose word is deed, whose every command is just and true.

נֶאֱמָן אַתָּה הוּא, יְיָ אֱלֹהֵינוּ, וְנֶאֱמָנִים דְּבָרֶיךָ, וְדָבָר אֶחָד מִדְּבָרֶיךָ, אָחוֹר לֹא יָשׁוּב רֵיקָם, כִּי אֵל מֶלֶךְ נֶאֱמָן וְרַחֲמָן אָתָּה. בָּרוּךְ אַתָּה יְיָ, הָאֵל הַנֶּאֱמָן בְּכָל־דְּבָרָיו.

You are faithful, Eternal our God, and all of Your words are to be trusted. Not one of Your words is empty, for You are a faithful and merciful God. We praise You, Eternal God, whose words can be trusted.

II

רַחֵם עַל צִיּוֹן, כִּי הִיא בֵּית חַיֵּינוּ, וְלַעֲלוּבַת נֶפֶשׁ תּוֹשִׁיעַ בִּמְהֵרָה בְיָמֵינוּ. בָּרוּךְ אַתָּה יְיָ, מְשַׂמֵּחַ צִיּוֹן בְּבָנֶיהָ.

Have mercy upon Zion, for it is the source of our life. Save the oppressed of soul speedily in our days. We praise You, Eternal God, who makes Zion rejoice in her children.

III

שַׂמְּחֵנוּ, יְיָ אֱלֹהֵינוּ, בְּאֵלִיָּהוּ הַנָּבִיא עַבְדֶּךָ, וּבְמַלְכוּת בֵּית דָּוִד מְשִׁיחֶךָ. בִּמְהֵרָה יָבֹא, וְיָגֵל לִבֵּנוּ. עַל כִּסְאוֹ לֹא יֵשֶׁב זָר, וְלֹא יִנְחֲלוּ עוֹד אֲחֵרִים אֶת כְּבוֹדוֹ, כִּי בְשֵׁם קָדְשְׁךָ נִשְׁבַּעְתָּ לוֹ, שֶׁלֹּא יִכְבֶּה נֵרוֹ לְעוֹלָם וָעֶד. בָּרוּךְ אַתָּה יְיָ, מָגֵן דָּוִד.

Make us happy, Eternal God, with the coming of Your servant, Elijah the prophet, and with the establishment of the house of David, Your messiah. May Elijah soon come and bring joy to our hearts. May no stranger sit on his throne, nor others take for themselves his glory. For You have promised by Your holy name that his light would never go out. We praise You, Eternal God, Shield of David.

IV

עַל־הַתּוֹרָה, וְעַל־הָעֲבוֹדָה, וְעַל־הַנְּבִיאִים, וְעַל־יוֹם הַשַּׁבָּת
הַזֶּה, שֶׁנָּתַתָּ־לָּנוּ, יְיָ אֱלֹהֵינוּ, לִקְדֻשָּׁה וְלִמְנוּחָה, לְכָבוֹד
וּלְתִפְאָרֶת. עַל־הַכֹּל, יְיָ אֱלֹהֵינוּ, אֲנַחְנוּ מוֹדִים לָךְ, וּמְבָרְכִים
אוֹתָךְ. יִתְבָּרַךְ שִׁמְךָ בְּפִי כָל־חַי תָּמִיד לְעוֹלָם וָעֶד. בָּרוּךְ
אַתָּה יְיָ, מְקַדֵּשׁ הַשַּׁבָּת.

For the Torah, for the privilege of worship, for the prophets, and
for this Sabbath day that You, our Eternal God, have given us
for holiness and rest, for honor and glory, we thank and praise
You. May Your name be praised for ever by every living being.
We praise You, O God, for the Sabbath and its holiness.

COMMENTARY

Why is it that these four sections, which comprise the blessings after the
reading of the הַפְטָרָה, barely mention the prophets or the meaning of their
message? Are they really appropriate as blessings after the reading of the
הַפְטָרָה? How were they chosen? By whom? And when?

Origins of the Final הַפְטָרָה Blessings

If you reread the הַפְטָרָה blessings, you will note that we have studied their
themes before. Look back at the *Amidah* sections on בּוֹנֵה יְרוּשָׁלַיִם, "Rebuilding
Jerusalem"; קֶרֶן יְשׁוּעָה, "the Messianic Hope"; and קְדוּשַׁת הַיּוֹם, "the
Sanctification of the Day."

What we seem to have here in the final blessings of the הַפְטָרָה is an
abbreviated עֲמִידָה! How is this possible? Why would the Rabbis have
concluded the הַפְטָרָה with such a group of prayers?

Some scholars believe that the four sections that make up the final הַפְטָרָה
blessings were written sometime before the first century C.E. Like the rest of
the prayers of the עֲמִידָה, they were in existence when the Rabbis, under the
leadership of Rabban Gamliel II, head of the Academy at Yavneh, chose those
prayers that would be included in the עֲמִידָה. We know that several prayers
were not chosen. These, however, remained in the possession of Jewish
scholars, and some of them were later included in different sections of the
prayer book. A good example of this is the שָׁלוֹם רָב prayer. The Rabbis chose
the שִׂים שָׁלוֹם for the concluding prayer of the עֲמִידָה rather than the שָׁלוֹם רָב.

Later, as we have already seen (see page 157), the שָׁלוֹם רָב was added to the prayer book.

Jewish scholars believe that the four sections of the final הַפְטָרָה blessings were once a version of an עֲמִידָה. After the עֲמִידָה was formulated at Yavneh, the blessings were preserved. When the tradition of concluding the worship service with the הַפְּטָרָה developed, it is likely that the abbreviated version of the עֲמִידָה was reintroduced as a final set of prayers for the worship service. In other words, the four sections were not thought of as a blessing for the reading of the הַפְּטָרָה but rather as concluding prayers for the whole worship service. This would explain why there is practically no mention of the prophets or of the הַפְטָרָה in the four sections.

What do you think would be an appropriate prayer after the reading of the הַפְטָרָה? What themes would you include in such a prayer? Would you retain any of the older sections?

Here you will find an abbreviated version of the blessings after the reading of the הַפְּטָרָה from the Reform prayer book, *Gates of Prayer.* How does this version differ from the traditional one? The version of *Gates of Prayer* published in 1975 includes both the traditional version and this abbreviated one.

Abbreviated Final Haftarah Blessings

בָּרוּךְ אַתָּה יי אֱלֹהֵינוּ מֶלֶךְ הָעוֹלָם, צוּר כָּל־הָעוֹלָמִים, צַדִּיק
בְּכָל־הַדּוֹרוֹת, הָאֵל הַנֶּאֱמָן, הָאוֹמֵר וְעוֹשֶׂה, הַמְדַבֵּר וּמְקַיֵּם,
שֶׁכָּל־דְּבָרָיו אֱמֶת וָצֶדֶק.
עַל־הַתּוֹרָה וְעַל־הָעֲבוֹדָה וְעַל־הַנְּבִיאִים וְעַל־יוֹם הַשַּׁבָּת
הַזֶּה, שֶׁנָּתַתָּ־לָּנוּ, יי אֱלֹהֵינוּ, לִקְדֻשָּׁה וְלִמְנוּחָה, לְכָבוֹד
וּלְתִפְאָרֶת, עַל־הַכֹּל, יי אֱלֹהֵינוּ, אֲנַחְנוּ מוֹדִים לָךְ, וּמְבָרְכִים
אוֹתָךְ. יִתְבָּרַךְ שִׁמְךָ בְּפִי כָּל־חַי תָּמִיד לְעוֹלָם וָעֶד. בָּרוּךְ
אַתָּה יי, מְקַדֵּשׁ הַשַּׁבָּת.

We praise You, Eternal God, Sovereign of the universe, the Rock of all creation, the Righteous One of all generations, the faithful God whose word is deed, whose every command is just and true.

For the Torah, for the privilege of worship, for the prophets, and for this Sabbath day that You, our Eternal God, have given us for holiness and rest, for honor and glory, we thank and praise You. May Your name be praised for ever by every living being. We praise You, O God, for the Sabbath and its holiness.

THE NEW MONTH

The New Month (Traditional Version)

יְהִי רָצוֹן מִלְּפָנֶיךָ יְיָ, אֱלֹהֵינוּ וֵאלֹהֵי אֲבוֹתֵינוּ, שֶׁתְּחַדֵּשׁ עָלֵינוּ אֶת־הַחֹדֶשׁ הַזֶּה, לְטוֹבָה וְלִבְרָכָה. וְתִתֶּן־לָנוּ חַיִּים אֲרֻכִּים, חַיִּים שֶׁל־שָׁלוֹם, חַיִּים שֶׁל־טוֹבָה, חַיִּים שֶׁל־בְּרָכָה, חַיִּים שֶׁל־פַּרְנָסָה, חַיִּים שֶׁל־חִלּוּץ עֲצָמוֹת, חַיִּים שֶׁיֵּשׁ בָּהֶם יִרְאַת שָׁמַיִם וְיִרְאַת חֵטְא, חַיִּים שֶׁאֵין בָּהֶם בּוּשָׁה וּכְלִמָּה, חַיִּים שֶׁל עֹשֶׁר וְכָבוֹד, חַיִּים שֶׁתְּהִי בָנוּ אַהֲבַת תּוֹרָה וְיִרְאַת שָׁמַיִם, חַיִּים שֶׁיִּמָּלְאוּ מִשְׁאֲלוֹת לִבֵּנוּ לְטוֹבָה, אָמֵן סֶלָה.

May it be Your will, Eternal, our God and God of our ancestors, to renew us with goodness and blessing in the new month ahead. Grant us life—a life of length of days, a life of peace, a life of goodness, a life of blessings, a life of sustenance, a life of strength, a life of reverence for God, fear of sin, without shame or disgrace, a life of riches and honor, a life marked by our love of Torah, a life in which the wishes of our hearts may be fulfilled for good. Amen. Selah.

מִי שֶׁעָשָׂה נִסִּים לַאֲבוֹתֵינוּ וְגָאַל אוֹתָם מֵעַבְדוּת לְחֵרוּת, הוּא יִגְאַל אוֹתָנוּ בְּקָרוֹב, וִיקַבֵּץ נִדָּחֵינוּ מֵאַרְבַּע כַּנְפוֹת הָאָרֶץ, חֲבֵרִים כָּל־יִשְׂרָאֵל, וְנֹאמַר: אָמֵן.

May the Eternal, who has done wonderful things for our ancestors, who redeemed them from slavery to freedom, soon redeem us and gather our scattered people from the four corners of the earth. Israel is one united people! And let us say: Amen.

רֹאשׁ חֹדֶשׁ . . . יִהְיֶה בַּיּוֹם . . . הַבָּא עָלֵינוּ וְעַל־כָּל־יִשְׂרָאֵל לְטוֹבָה.

The new month of _____ will begin on _____ . May it bring goodness to us and to all of Israel.

יְחַדְּשֵׁהוּ, הַקָּדוֹשׁ בָּרוּךְ הוּא, עָלֵינוּ וְעַל־כָּל־עַמּוֹ, בֵּית יִשְׂרָאֵל, לְחַיִּים וּלְשָׁלוֹם, לְשָׂשׂוֹן וּלְשִׂמְחָה, לִישׁוּעָה וּלְנֶחָמָה, וְנֹאמַר: אָמֵן.

May the Holy One renew in the new month, life and peace, rejoicing and happiness, salvation and consolation for us, and for all of the people of the house of Israel. And let us say: Amen.

The New Month (Reform Version)

יְהִי רָצוֹן מִלְּפָנֶיךָ, יי אֱלֹהֵינוּ וֵאלֹהֵי אֲבוֹתֵינוּ וְאִמּוֹתֵינוּ, שֶׁתְּחַדֵּשׁ עָלֵינוּ אֶת־הַחֹדֶשׁ הַזֶּה, (הַבָּא,) לְטוֹבָה וְלִבְרָכָה. וְתִתֶּן־לָנוּ חַיִּים אֲרֻכִּים, חַיִּים שֶׁל־שָׁלוֹם, חַיִּים שֶׁל־טוֹבָה, חַיִּים שֶׁל־בְּרָכָה, חַיִּים שֶׁל־פַּרְנָסָה, חַיִּים שֶׁל־חִלּוּץ עֲצָמוֹת, חַיִּים שֶׁיֵּשׁ בָּהֶם יִרְאַת חֵטְא, חַיִּים שֶׁתְּהֵא בָנוּ אַהֲבַת תּוֹרָה וְיִרְאַת שָׁמַיִם, חַיִּים שֶׁיִּמָּלְאוּ מִשְׁאֲלוֹת לִבֵּנוּ לְטוֹבָה. אָמֵן.

Our God and God of our ancestors, may the new month bring us renewed good and blessing. May we have long life, peace, prosperity and health, a life full of blessing, a life exalted by love of Torah and reverence for the Divine; a life in which the longings of our hearts are fulfilled for good.

מִי שֶׁעָשָׂה נִסִּים לַאֲבוֹתֵינוּ וּלְאִמּוֹתֵינוּ וְגָאַל אוֹתָם מֵעַבְדוּת לְחֵרוּת, הוּא יִגְאַל אוֹתָנוּ בְּקָרוֹב, חֲבֵרִים כָּל־יִשְׂרָאֵל, וְנֹאמַר: אָמֵן.

Wondrous God, in ancient days You led our people from bondage to freedom; redeem us now out of our exile from one another, making all Israel one united people.

202

רֹאשׁ חֹדֶשׁ . . . יִהְיֶה בְּיוֹם . . .

The new month of _____ will begin on _____ .

or

רֹאשׁ חֹדֶשׁ . . . הוּא הַיּוֹם.

The new month of _____ begins today.

יְחַדְּשֵׁהוּ הַקָּדוֹשׁ בָּרוּךְ הוּא עָלֵינוּ וְעַל־כָּל־עַמּוֹ בֵּית יִשְׂרָאֵל: לְחַיִּים וּלְשָׁלוֹם, לְשָׂשׂוֹן וּלְשִׂמְחָה, לִישׁוּעָה וּלְנֶחָמָה, וְנֹאמַר: אָמֵן.

God of holiness, let the new month bring for us, and for the whole House of Israel, life and peace, happiness and joy, deliverance and comfort; and let us say: Amen.

COMMENTARY

One of the most ancient celebrations among Jews is the observance of רֹאשׁ חֹדֶשׁ (Rosh Chodesh), "the New Month." It was celebrated even before the Temple came into existence. During Temple times, special sacrifices were brought to the sanctuary and offered by the priests (Numbers 28:11 ff.). It was the task of the High Court, or Sanhedrin, which sat in the Hall of Hewn Stone in the Temple, to determine the time of the New Month and then to announce it to the Jewish community.

Determining the New Month

The Jewish calendar consists of twelve months with a little more than 29½ days in each. Each month begins at the time of a new moon, and an entire year contains about 354⅓ days. That is 11 less than the solar calendar year of 365¼ days. As a result, every few years, an extra month is added to the Jewish calendar in the form of a leap year in order to keep the adjustment of months to the seasons accurate. The extra month is known as אֲדָר שֵׁנִי *(Adar Sheini),* Adar II.

What are the origins of the Jewish calendar?

In the Torah, the names of only four months are mentioned. They are Aviv, Ziv, Etanim, and Bul. The rest of the months are designated by numbers. For example, when the Torah calls upon Israelites to observe Passover, it says: "In the first month, on the fourteenth day of the month at dusk, is God's Passover" (Leviticus 23:5).

The names of the months of the Jewish calendar were taken from the Babylonian calendar by Jews during the Babylonian exile. When Jews returned to the Land of Israel, they continued to use the Babylonian names. The months and their lengths are as follows:

Nisan	30 days	נִיסָן
Iyar	29 days	אִיָּיר
Sivan	30 days	סִיוָן
Tammuz	29 days	תַּמּוּז
Av	30 days	אָב
Elul	29 days	אֱלוּל
Tishrei	30 days	תִּשְׁרֵי
Cheshvan	29 or 30 days	חֶשְׁוָן
Kislev	29 or 30 days	כִּסְלֵו
Tevet	29 days	טֵבֵת
Sh'vat	30 days	שְׁבָט
Adar	29 days	אֲדָר

(In a leap year, Adar I has 30 days and Adar II has 29 days.)

The Talmud gives us a good description of how רֹאשׁ חֹדֶשׁ, the New Month, was determined and announced during the time of the Temple. Witnesses would watch for the new moon and its appearance to report to the Sanhedrin. The Sanhedrin would examine the testimony of the witnesses and then announce רֹאשׁ חֹדֶשׁ. A fire signal would then be lit on a special mountain top; from there to Babylonia, signal fires would be kindled to carry the announcement of רֹאשׁ חֹדֶשׁ to all Jewish communities. When enemies of the Jews ruined this method by lighting fires early, the Jewish community developed a system of messengers whose task it was to carry the news of רֹאשׁ חֹדֶשׁ.

Why Two Days for Some Holidays?

You may have wondered why Orthodox and Conservative Jews celebrate an extra day of Rosh HaShanah and add one extra day to the celebration of

204

Sukkot, Pesach, and Shavuot. In the biblical tradition, Rosh HaShanah is celebrated for one day, and Sukkot and Pesach are celebrated for seven days. Why did Jews living outside the Land of Israel add an extra day to their observance of these holidays?

Problems with the calendar explain the addition of the extra days. Since there were often problems with both the accuracy of lighting fires and the arrival of messengers, those who lived outside the Land of Israel decided to celebrate their holidays for two days so that if they happened to be a day late, they would still be observing at the proper time.

When, in the middle of the fourth century C.E., Hillel II, the head of Jewry living in Israel, developed and published scientific rules for determining the calendar, the use of signals and messengers was stopped. By then, however, the celebration of extra days had become a tradition for Jews living outside of the Land of Israel. To this day, Jews in Israel celebrate according to the biblical tradition. Orthodox and Conservative Jews living outside of Israel still continue the practice of observing the extra days. Reform Judaism did away with the extra days in the middle of the nineteenth century, and most Reform Jews continue to observe only one day of the Festivals. In recent years, however, a number of Reform synagogues have returned to the practice of observing a second day of the holidays, especially on Rosh HaShanah.

Do you think it is still valid for Jews living outside of the Land of Israel to observe extra days of the Festivals and Rosh HaShanah? Should there be a difference between Jews who live in Israel and Jews who live outside the Land? Why?

Find a chart of the Zodiac. Compare the symbols of the months with those of the Jewish months. What are the similarities and differences?

Notice which Jewish holidays fall into which months. Do you notice any relationship between the meaning of the holiday or holidays and the symbol of the month?

Prayers for Announcing the New Month

As we have already indicated, the practice of announcing רֹאשׁ חֹדֶשׁ was an ancient one. Even with the development of Hillel II's rules of calculation, it was still necessary to inform the people of the beginning of רֹאשׁ חֹדֶשׁ. This was done in the synagogue on the Shabbat preceding the first day of the month. The announcement was made in the form of a simple statement: "The new month of _____ will begin on _____ . May it bring goodness to us and to all of Israel."

About two hundred years ago, the other prayers that we have included in *B'chol L'vavcha* were added to the announcement. The first paragraph, "May it be Your will...," is based upon an ancient prayer written by the sage Rav, the founder of Sura, the most important academy of Jewish learning in Babylonia. Rav wrote his prayer in the third century C.E. as a personal expression to be recited after the עֲמִידָה. His original prayer did not include the words "...to renew us with goodness and blessing in the new month ahead."

Read Rav's prayer without the addition above. What is the theme? What are the things that Rav considered important for a "fulfilled life"? Would you agree with him? If you could ask for twelve things meant to give you a happy, fulfilled life, what would they be?

Have each person in your study group make up a list of the twelve things he or she believes would bring joy and happiness for a lifetime. Each list should go from the most important to the least important, and each person should develop some reasons why one thing is more important than another. Then discuss the three most important items on everyone's list. Put each list on the board. Don't forget the last three on your lists. What makes them the least important for achieving happiness in life? Compare your lists with that of Rav. Also ask yourselves why the author of our רֹאשׁ חֹדֶשׁ ceremony thought that Rav's prayer was appropriate.

Israel Is One United People

What does the second prayer, "May the Eternal, who has done wonderful things...," mean to express? Does it remind you of a prayer in the עֲמִידָה? Which one and why?

The prayer contains the phrase חֲבֵרִים כָּל־יִשְׂרָאֵל (*chaveirim kol Yisrael*), "Israel is one united people." What does that statement have to do with the theme of the prayer? Of what does it remind us? During the bitter persecution of Jews in Russia from 1870 through the 1880s, Rabbi Israel Kagan wrote: "All Jews constitute one soul and one body." What do you think he meant? What does Rabbi Kagan's statement mean when read together with the prayer that says "Israel is one united people"? In what ways are Jews still "one soul and one body"? What about the Jews of Israel and the Jews of the United States? What about our relationship to Jews who suffer persecution and oppression?

The modern philosopher Martin Buber once wrote: "We have been held together and upheld by common remembering." Would you agree? Is there more that holds us together as Jews? What are the elements that "unite" us as a people?

As the Moon Goes...So Israel

The modern scholar Abraham Millgram has written the following about the "May the Eternal, who has done wonderful things..." prayer:

> The monthly reappearance of the moon became the symbol of Israel's restoration. As the moon emerges from its total eclipse into brightness, so will Israel be redeemed from its exile and brought back to the land of its ancestors.
>
> *Jewish Worship*

What does Rabbi Millgram mean? What is Israel's eclipse? What is meant by "Israel's restoration"? The Second Book of Maccabees (1:27) contains a prayer that defines redemption or restoration. It reads:

> Gather our dispersion, free those in bondage,
> Look upon them that are despised, and let the
> Nations know that You are God!

Does this description seem to say what our prayer says? How does it compare with Rabbi Millgram's idea?

A Holiday for Women

While all Jewish Festivals should be observed by men and women alike, Jewish tradition teaches that רֹאשׁ חֹדֶשׁ is a holiday especially for women! Why are women singled out in the celebration of רֹאשׁ חֹדֶשׁ?

Remember that when the Israelites were in the wilderness waiting for Moses to come down from Mount Sinai, they grew fearful at his long absence. They lost faith in God and decided to construct an idol that they could worship instead. The Israelite men went through the camp ordering the women to give up their necklaces, bracelets, and earrings so that there would be more gold to build the Golden Calf. According to Jewish legend, the women remained loyal to God and refused to surrender their jewelry. In honor of the Israelite women's righteousness and loyalty to God, God proclaimed רֹאשׁ חֹדֶשׁ a holiday especially for women (*Pirkei D'Rabbi Eliezer* 45).

In recent years, a number of Jewish women have begun to observe רֹאשׁ חֹדֶשׁ in special ways. More and more synagogues are sponsoring רֹאשׁ חֹדֶשׁ groups, where women—or men and women together—gather to pray, study, and share their thoughts and feelings. Modern prayers and services have been composed for these new רֹאשׁ חֹדֶשׁ celebrations.

If you were invited to create your own רֹאשׁ חֹדֶשׁ group, what would you do? What kinds of activities would you plan? Would your group be for women only, or would you include men as well? Why? Look again at the traditional and the Reform prayers for the New Month. Which version do you prefer, and why? What other prayers might you choose for your רֹאשׁ חֹדֶשׁ group?

HONORING THE TORAH

Hagbahah

וְזֹאת הַתּוֹרָה אֲשֶׁר שָׂם מֹשֶׁה לִפְנֵי בְּנֵי יִשְׂרָאֵל, עַל פִּי יְיָ בְּיַד מֹשֶׁה.

This is the Torah that Moses placed before the children of Israel, in accordance with God's command through Moses.

Returning the Torah to the Ark

יְהַלְלוּ אֶת־שֵׁם יהוה, כִּי־נִשְׂגָּב שְׁמוֹ לְבַדּוֹ.

Let us praise the Eternal God, whose name alone is exalted.

הוֹדוֹ עַל־אֶרֶץ וְשָׁמָיִם, וַיָּרֶם קֶרֶן לְעַמּוֹ, תְּהִלָּה לְכָל־חֲסִידָיו, לִבְנֵי יִשְׂרָאֵל, עַם־קְרֹבוֹ, הַלְלוּיָהּ!

Your splendor covers heaven and earth; You are the strength of Your people, making glorious Your faithful ones, Israel, a people close to You. Hallelujah!

תּוֹרַת יהוה תְּמִימָה, מְשִׁיבַת נָפֶשׁ;
עֵדוּת יהוה נֶאֱמָנָה, מַחְכִּימַת פֶּתִי.

God's Teaching is perfect, reviving the soul;
God's word is unfailing, making wise the simple.

פִּקוּדֵי יהוה יְשָׁרִים, מְשַׂמְּחֵי־לֵב;
מִצְוַת יהוה בָּרָה, מְאִירַת עֵינָיִם.

God's precepts are right, delighting the mind;
God's mitzvah is clear, giving light to the eyes.

יִרְאַת יהוה טְהוֹרָה, עוֹמֶדֶת לָעַד;
מִשְׁפְּטֵי־יהוה אֱמֶת, צָדְקוּ יַחְדָּו.

God's doctrine is pure, enduring for ever;
God's guidance is true, and altogether just.

כִּי לֶקַח טוֹב נָתַתִּי לָכֶם, תּוֹרָתִי אַל־תַּעֲזֹבוּ.
עֵץ־חַיִּים הִיא לַמַּחֲזִיקִים בָּהּ, וְתֹמְכֶיהָ מְאֻשָּׁר.
דְּרָכֶיהָ דַרְכֵי־נֹעַם, וְכָל־נְתִיבוֹתֶיהָ שָׁלוֹם.

Behold, a good doctrine has been given you—My Torah; do not forsake it.

It is a tree of life to those who hold it fast, and all who cling to it find happiness.

Its ways are ways of pleasantness, and all its paths are peace.

הֲשִׁיבֵנוּ יהוה אֵלֶיךָ, וְנָשׁוּבָה. חַדֵּשׁ יָמֵינוּ כְּקֶדֶם.

Help us to return to You, O God; then truly shall we return. Renew our days as in the past.

COMMENTARY

We are told that when Ezra first read the Torah to the people of Israel, he "opened the book in the sight of all..., and when he opened it, all the people stood up" (Nehemiah 8:5). For centuries now, it has been the custom, after the Torah is read, to lift it up so that the entire congregation can see it. The honor of "lifting the Torah" is called הַגְבָּהָה (hagbahah), "lifting." The person given the honor of הַגְבָּהָה holds the Torah so that the members of the congregation can see at least three columns of the Torah text. As the Torah is lifted, the congregation stands, and everyone says: "This is the Torah that Moses placed before the children of Israel, in accordance with God's command through Moses."

This Is the Torah

The words for the statement "This is the Torah..." are taken from Deuteronomy 4:44. The whole statement reads:

This is the Torah that Moses placed before the children of Israel; these are the testimonies, and the statutes, and the ordinances that Moses spoke unto the children of Israel when they came forth out of Egypt....

Deuteronomy 4:44–45

The words "...in accordance with God's command through Moses" are taken from Numbers 9:23.

210

Why do you think the Sages who composed the Torah service combined both statements? Why are they said by the entire congregation, rather than just by the one who holds up the Torah? What do they have to do with the "action" of holding up the Torah? Look at the statements about the relationship of the Jewish people to Torah. What do these statements have to do with the declaration from Numbers 9:23?

Honor for the Torah

Some of the decorations for the Torah once had a practical purpose. For instance, the breastplate was first used in order to mark which Torah should be read at which time. On some holidays, more than one Torah section is read. Rather than having to roll the Torah from one place to the next, two Torahs would be used. The first breastplates were markers indicating when each Torah should be read. Later, artists were invited to create the beautiful ornamental breastplates now used. Some of them still have a place where the Torah reader can mark the holiday for which the Torah is ready to be read.

The יָד (yad), "hand" or "Torah pointer," also has a very practical use. It was developed in about the sixteenth century in Germany as an aid to the person reading from the Torah.

The רִמּוֹנִים (rimonim), "Torah crowns," are purely decorative and symbolic. They are meant to serve the same purpose as the crown worn by a king or queen. The Torah crowns (or crown) symbolize the devotion, commitment, and love the Jew has for Torah.

Usually, while the congregation is singing the עֵץ־חַיִּים הִיא (Eitz Chayim Hi), "It is a Tree of Life," the Torah is rolled, tied, and covered; then the breastplate and crowns are placed upon it.

The rolling of the Torah is called גְּלִילָה (g'lilah).

The acts of הַגְבָּהָה and גְּלִילָה, the congregation rising as the Torah is lifted, the use of beautiful ornaments for the Torah—all confirm the Jew's appreciation of Torah. That appreciation is also spoken or sung in the words "It is a tree of life..." (Proverbs 3:18, 17). How do these words about Torah relate to what we have already learned about the Jew's relationship to it?

The famous Rabbi Akiva, who was arrested and put to death by the Romans for teaching Judaism, was once approached by a fellow teacher, Pappos ben Judah. The Talmud records their conversation:

Rabbi Pappos ben Judah said to Akiva: "Are you not afraid of what the Romans will do if they catch you teaching and studying Torah?" Akiva replied: "I will tell you a parable. The matter may be compared to a fox who was walking along the bank of a stream. He saw some fish gathering together to move from one place to another. He said to them: 'What are you fleeing from?' They answered: 'From the nets of fishermen.' So the fox said: 'Why don't you come up here on dry land, and we will dwell together?' 'O fox,' they replied, 'you are the cleverest of animals, but you are a fool! If we are afraid to be in a place vital for our survival, how much more dangerous would it be for us to go to a place that is certain death for us?'

"So it is with us," Rabbi Akiva said to Rabbi Pappos ben Judah. "It is better for the Jew to stay in an atmosphere vital for our survival, and face Roman threats, than to abandon our Torah, for it is our 'tree of life' and the 'length of our days.'"

BT B'rachot 61b

Would you agree with Rabbi Akiva's argument? How does his view of Torah as "vital for our survival" compare with the Gerer Rebbe's point of view and Ellen Frankel's teaching (see page 175)? Is Akiva's position realistic or unrealistic?

Rabbi Julie Greenberg's earlier statement takes another view of what it means to live by the Torah. She teaches: "We are teaching Torah daily by the way we solve problems, stand up for justice, take care of one another, protect the earth, put out love and kindness, persistence and forgiveness.... That is how we make a holy Torah for today." For example, Torah teaches us to stand up for justice when it says "Justice, justice shall you pursue" (Deuteronomy 16:20). Torah teaches us to love and take care of one another as it says "Love your neighbor as yourself" (Leviticus 19:18). How does Rabbi Greenberg's teaching relate to the other ways of honoring the Torah we have just studied? What are some other ways a Jew can show honor to the Torah?

212

סִיּוּם הָעֲבוֹדָה

The Conclusion of the Service

Siyum HaAvodah

THE ALEINU

Aleinu   עָלֵינוּ

עָלֵינוּ לְשַׁבֵּחַ לַאֲדוֹן הַכֹּל, לָתֵת גְּדֻלָּה לְיוֹצֵר בְּרֵאשִׁית, שֶׁלֹּא
עָשָׂנוּ כְּגוֹיֵי הָאֲרָצוֹת, וְלֹא שָׂמָנוּ כְּמִשְׁפְּחוֹת הָאֲדָמָה. שֶׁלֹּא
שָׂם חֶלְקֵנוּ כָּהֶם וְגֹרָלֵנוּ כְּכָל־הֲמוֹנָם.
וַאֲנַחְנוּ כּוֹרְעִים וּמִשְׁתַּחֲוִים וּמוֹדִים לִפְנֵי מֶלֶךְ מַלְכֵי
הַמְּלָכִים, הַקָּדוֹשׁ בָּרוּךְ הוּא.

It is our duty to praise the God of all, to praise the Creator of
the universe, for God has not made us like the nations of other
lands, nor like other families of the earth. The Eternal One has
not made our portion like theirs, nor our lot like all others.
Therefore we bend the knee, bow, and give thanks before God,
the Holy and Blessed One.

שֶׁהוּא נוֹטֶה שָׁמַיִם וְיוֹסֵד אָרֶץ, וּמוֹשַׁב יְקָרוֹ בַּשָּׁמַיִם מִמַּעַל,
וּשְׁכִינַת עֻזּוֹ בְּגָבְהֵי מְרוֹמִים. הוּא אֱלֹהֵינוּ, אֵין עוֹד. אֱמֶת
מַלְכֵּנוּ, אֶפֶס זוּלָתוֹ, כַּכָּתוּב בְּתוֹרָתוֹ: וְיָדַעְתָּ הַיּוֹם וַהֲשֵׁבֹתָ
אֶל לְבָבֶךָ, כִּי יְיָ הוּא הָאֱלֹהִים בַּשָּׁמַיִם מִמַּעַל וְעַל הָאָרֶץ
מִתָּחַת. אֵין עוֹד.

For God stretched out the heavens and laid the foundations of
earth. God's glory is in the heavens above, and God's mighty
power is in the height of heights. We worship the Eternal alone,
there is none else. Truly God is supreme, there is none other. As
it is written in the Torah: And you shall know this day, and
reflect upon it, that the Eternal One is God in the heavens
above and upon the earth beneath. There is none else.

עַל כֵּן נְקַוֶּה לְּךָ, יְיָ אֱלֹהֵינוּ, לִרְאוֹת מְהֵרָה בְּתִפְאֶרֶת עֻזֶּךָ,
לְהַעֲבִיר גִּלּוּלִים מִן הָאָרֶץ, וְהָאֱלִילִים כָּרוֹת יִכָּרֵתוּן. לְתַקֵּן
עוֹלָם בְּמַלְכוּת שַׁדַּי, וְכָל־בְּנֵי בָשָׂר יִקְרְאוּ בִשְׁמֶךָ, לְהַפְנוֹת
אֵלֶיךָ כָּל־רִשְׁעֵי אָרֶץ.

Therefore, we put our hope in You, Eternal our God, that we may soon see the glory of Your power—when all evil will be removed from the earth—when false gods will be completely destroyed—when the world will be perfected under Your rule and all human beings will call upon Your name—and when the wicked of the earth will turn and worship you.

יַכִּירוּ וְיֵדְעוּ כָּל־יוֹשְׁבֵי תֵבֵל, כִּי לְךָ תִּכְרַע כָּל־בֶּרֶךְ תִּשָּׁבַע כָּל־לָשׁוֹן. לְפָנֶיךָ, יְיָ אֱלֹהֵינוּ, יִכְרְעוּ וְיִפֹּלוּ, וְלִכְבוֹד שִׁמְךָ יְקָר יִתֵּנוּ, וִיקַבְּלוּ כֻלָּם אֶת־עוֹל מַלְכוּתֶךָ, וְתִמְלוֹךְ עֲלֵיהֶם מְהֵרָה לְעוֹלָם וָעֶד, כִּי הַמַּלְכוּת שֶׁלְּךָ הִיא, וּלְעוֹלְמֵי עַד תִּמְלוֹךְ בְּכָבוֹד, כַּכָּתוּב בְּתוֹרָתֶךָ: יְיָ יִמְלֹךְ לְעוֹלָם וָעֶד. וְנֶאֱמַר: וְהָיָה יְיָ לְמֶלֶךְ עַל־כָּל־הָאָרֶץ, בַּיּוֹם הַהוּא יִהְיֶה יְיָ אֶחָד וּשְׁמוֹ אֶחָד.

May all the inhabitants of earth know that to You every knee must bend and every tongue swear allegiance. Before You, Eternal our God, let all bow, worship, and give honor. And let all of them accept the yoke of Your kingdom, and rule over them for ever. For Yours is the Power, and You will rule for ever and ever. As it is written in Your Torah: The Eternal will rule over all the earth. On that day the Eternal will be one and God's name will be one.

COMMENTARY

The עָלֵינוּ (Aleinu) marks the actual conclusion of the worship service. However, it was not always considered the final prayer. As we have already seen, the Shabbat service, at one time, may have concluded with the final blessings after the הַפְטָרָה reading.

What, then, are the origins of the עָלֵינוּ prayer? How and when did it become the final prayer of the Shabbat service?

A Fascinating History

Seldom do we come across a poem or prayer that is ancient, has brought persecution and death upon those who used it, and has become a symbol of a people's courage and bravery. The עָלֵינוּ is one of those rare pieces of literature.

We are not sure when the עָלֵינוּ was first written, and we are not sure who its author was. However, most Jewish scholars agree that it was composed around the time of the Maccabees. It is likely that whoever wrote "...when all evil will be removed from the earth—when false gods will be completely destroyed..." had in mind the idol worship of the Greek-Syrians and their attempt to force Jews into abandoning their worship of one God.

The author of the עָלֵינוּ also sought to express the uniqueness of the Jewish people. The prayer declares: "For God has not made us like the nations of other lands, nor like other families of the earth. The Eternal One has not made our portion like theirs, nor our lot like all others." In other words, the prayer expresses the thought that Jews are different from all other peoples of the earth!

When the sage Rav, who headed the Academy of Sura in Babylonia during the third century C.E., composed the Rosh HaShanah prayers, he included the עָלֵינוּ in the Shofar Service. This was most likely done because it voiced hope for the day when "all the inhabitants of earth" would worship God and be united in justice and peace.

About the thirteenth century, the עָלֵינוּ was introduced into the Shabbat and daily services as a final prayer. Apparently, there were many Jews who thought that it was an appropriate and beautiful conclusion to their worship. For them it was a hope that soon the "messianic days" would come and God would rule over the whole earth.

Persecution and Death

What was meant to be a prayer of hope, however, became a prayer of controversy. If we look at the original prayer carefully, we can see why it might have been misunderstood. The first paragraph of the עָלֵינוּ prayer originally read as follows:

It is our duty to praise the God of all, to praise the Creator of the universe, for God has not made us like the nations of other lands, nor like other families of the earth. The Eternal One has not made our portion like theirs, nor our lot like all others. <u>For they bow down to vanity and emptiness, and pray to a god that cannot save.</u>

Therefore we bend the knee, bow, and give thanks before God, the Holy and Blessed One.

The words underlined were part of the original prayer. They were based upon two sentences found in the Book of Isaiah (30:7 and 45:20). Look at those sentences in the Book of Isaiah and see if you can figure out what the prophet meant by them and why the author of the עָלֵינוּ used them for this prayer.

Not long after the עָלֵינוּ had been introduced into the daily and Shabbat worship, Christians and Jewish converts to Christianity accused Jews of slandering the beliefs of Christianity in their worship. Those who made the accusation claimed that the words "For they bow down to vanity and emptiness, and pray to a god that cannot save" were meant as a deliberate slur against Christianity.

During the Crusades and most of the Middle Ages, the words of the עָלֵינוּ were held up as evidence of Jewish prejudice and slander against Christians. When Jews tried to explain that the words being used against them had been written by the prophet Isaiah over seven hundred years before the birth of Jesus, their arguments were dismissed as untruth and trickery. During the Spanish Inquisition, Jews suffered death and torture at the hands of church leaders who accused them of reciting the עָלֵינוּ prayer and thereby slandering the beliefs of Christians. In many cases, it is reported that Jews went to their deaths with the עָלֵינוּ on their lips.

What is your opinion of the accusations by church leaders? Why would a convert to Christianity from Judaism accuse his abandoned faith and people of such slander? What do you think about the older (full) version of the עָלֵינוּ prayer?

In about the year 1400, a convert to Christianity from Judaism sought to prove that the עָלֵינוּ prayer was a deliberate slander and attack upon Christianity. What was his proof? He pointed to the word וָרִיק (varik), "emptiness," in the sentence "For they bow down to vanity and emptiness." He claimed that the word וָרִיק had a numerical value of 316 (ו = 6, ר = 200, י = 10, ק = 100) and that Jesus' name in Hebrew, יֵשׁוּ (Yeishu), also had the numerical value of 316 (י = 10, שׁ = 300, ו = 6). In this way he claimed that Jews were really saying: "For they [Christians] bow down to vanity and emptiness (וָרִיק) [which is Jesus]." What do you think about such an argument? How would you attempt to answer it? The words "vanity and emptiness" are found in Isaiah 30:7. That verse reads: "Egypt's help will be vanity and emptiness." What do you suppose Isaiah meant by his statement?

Changing the עָלֵינוּ Prayer

At the beginning of the eighteenth century, the Prussian government censored the Jewish prayer book and issued a decree forbidding Jews to include the words "For they bow down to vanity and emptiness and pray to a god that cannot save" in the עָלֵינוּ prayer or anywhere within their worship. From that time on, the עָלֵינוּ prayer has not included those words.

Should Jews have given in to the Prussian authorities and government and changed their prayer book? If you were printing a new prayer book today, would you include the controversial words? Why? One of the freedoms guaranteed by the U.S. Constitution is "free exercise of religion." What is this? Did the Jews of Prussia have this freedom? How might their situation have influenced their decision to obey the Prussian authorities?

We Put Our Hope in You

The second section of the עָלֵינוּ prayer declares that God is the power responsible for the heavens and the earth and that there is none else. This Jewish idea of God is found throughout the Torah and the rest of תַּנַ״ךְ. The words of עָלֵינוּ, however, are very close to those expressed by the prophet Isaiah. Look, for instance, at Isaiah 40:12–20; 42:5–8; 43:10–11; 44:6–8; 45:4–8; and 45:18–46:13.

Compare the quotes from the prophet Isaiah with the second section of the עָלֵינוּ prayer. What do they teach us about the Jewish idea of God? Why was Isaiah so opposed to idol worship? If you were to write a prayer about the "greatness of God" or the "power of God," what passages or thoughts from Isaiah would you include?

The third section of the עָלֵינוּ prayer expresses the hope for the dominion of God, or the messianic days. What is mentioned in this section of the prayer that could lead to the coming of an age of justice and peace? How does this section compare with the hope for the "messianic days" voiced by Isaiah (2:1–21)?

On That Day

Judaism was the first religion to teach the idea that there is one God over all nations and human beings. And it was the first faith to put forward the hope that all human beings would, one day, be united. The prophet Malachi put this teaching of Judaism into the form of a question. He asked: "Have we not all one Source? Has not one God created all of us? Why, then, do we deal treacherously every person against one's neighbor?" (Malachi 2:10).

The hope that someday all human beings would live together in peace was also expressed by the prophet Zechariah. He said:

> And it shall come to pass in that day
> That living waters shall go out from Jerusalem:
> Half of them toward the eastern sea,
> And half of them toward the western sea;
> In summer and in winter shall it be.
> And the Eternal will rule over all the earth;
> On that day the Eternal will be one and God's name will be One.
>
> Zechariah 14:8–9

The authors of the עָלֵינוּ prayer chose these last words of Zechariah as the conclusion of the עָלֵינוּ prayer. For them, Zechariah's words represented the highest hope for humanity. Would you agree with them? Were both Malachi and Zechariah saying the same thing?

Would human beings need to share the same religion in order to fulfill Zechariah's or Malachi's hope? Does the עָלֵינוּ prayer say that all people must have the same religion in order for God's name to be One?

Moses Maimonides describes the "messianic days" as follows: "In the Messiah's days there will be no hunger, nor war, nor jealousy, nor strife; there will be plenty for all, and the world's chief occupation will be to know the Eternal One" *(Mishneh Torah)*. How does Maimonides' statement compare to the עָלֵינוּ prayer? Does he seem to believe that all human beings will have to share the same religion in the days of the Messiah?

Prayers on the עָלֵינוּ Theme

And I Tell You

And I tell you the good in man will win
Over all his wickedness, over all the wrongs he has done.

219

He will look at the pages of written history and be amazed,
And then he will laugh and sing.

And the good that is in man, children in their cradles, will have won.

Here I stand, the Jew marked by history, for who can count how long?

Wrapped in compassion as in a *Tallit,* staring every storm in the face.

Write songs of pain, sing prayers of torment, refresh yourself with suffering.

Too much for one people, small and weak—it is enough to share out among
the whole human race.

But God has planted in me goodness, compassion, as a father loves
his children,

So I writhe with pain, weep and sing, sing and weep,
For the blood knows the heart of the world is not made of stone;

The wonderful light of God's face is for all eternity stamped on it firm
and deep;

And the heart feels that there is a day and an hour, and a mountain
called Zion;

And then all the sufferings will gather there and will all become song,

Ringing out into every corner of the earth, from end to end,

And the nations will hear it, and like caravans in the desert will all to that
mountain throng.

Hugh A. Nisenson, translated by Joseph Leftwich

It is up to us to sing the praises of the Source of all,
to recognize the greatness of the Author of Creation,
Who has made the world a web of languages and peoples,
endowing all of them with the ability to know God's ways.
And when they act in kindness, and turn away from cruelty,
and call to God in their own tongues,
God listens to their prayer.

Arthur Green

Eternal God, we face the morrow with hope made stronger by the vision of Your kingdom, a world where poverty and war are banished, where injustice and hate are gone.

Teach us more and more to share the pain of others, to heed Your call for justice, to pursue the blessing of peace. Help us, O God, to gain victory over evil, to bring nearer the day when all the world shall be one.

Gates of Prayer (1975)

And then all that has divided us will merge
And then compassion will be wedded to power
And then softness will come to a world that is harsh and unkind
And then both men and women will be gentle
And then both women and men will be strong
And then no person will be subject to another's will
And then all will be rich and free and varied
And then the greed of some will give way to the needs of many
And then all will share equally in the Earth's abundance
And then all will care for the sick and the weak and the old
And then all will nourish the young
And then all will cherish life's creatures
And then all will live in harmony with each other and the Earth
And then everywhere will be called Eden once again.

Judy Chicago, "Merger"

May the time not be distant, O God,
When Your enduring rule shall be established in the midst of the earth;
When justice shall prevail in the land,
Evil destroyed,
And the strong shall no more oppress the weak;
May sin be taken away from every person,
And, heir to a royal covenant,
May we each exercise the just power that is our birthright
As human beings.
In youth may we gain wisdom,
Overflowing like a river with understanding;
Our soul profound enough to cover the earth,

Loved, each of us,
For the peace we bring to others.
May our deeds exceed our speech,
And may we never lift up our hand
But to conquer fear and doubt and grave despair.
Rise up like the sun, O God, over all humanity,
Cause light to go forth over all the lands between the seas,
And light up the universe with the joy of wholeness, of freedom and of peace.

On Wings of Awe

It is up to us
to hallow Creation,
to respond to Life
with the fullness of our lives.
It is up to us
to meet the World,
to embrace the Whole
even as we wrestle
with its parts.
It is up to us
to repair the World
and to bind our lives to Truth.

Therefore we bend the knee
and shake off the stiffness that keeps us
from the subtle
graces of Life
and the supple
gestures of Love.
With reverence
and thanksgiving
we accept our destiny
and set for ourselves
the task of redemption.

Rami M. Shapiro

It really is a wonder that I haven't dropped all my ideals, because they seem so absurd and impossible to carry out. Yet I keep them, because in spite of everything, I still believe that people are really good at heart.

I simply can't build up my hopes on a foundation consisting of confusion, misery, and death. I see the world gradually being turned into a wilderness. I hear the ever-approaching thunder, which will destroy us, too.

I can feel the suffering of millions, and yet, if I look up into the heavens, I think that it will all come out right, that this cruelty too will end, and that peace and tranquillity will return again.

In the meantime, I must uphold my ideals, for perhaps the time will come when I shall be able to carry them out.

Anne Frank, July 15, 1944

THE KADDISH

Kaddish   קַדִּישׁ

יִתְגַּדַּל וְיִתְקַדַּשׁ שְׁמֵהּ רַבָּא בְּעָלְמָא דִּי־בְרָא כִרְעוּתֵהּ,
וְיַמְלִיךְ מַלְכוּתֵהּ בְּחַיֵּיכוֹן וּבְיוֹמֵיכוֹן וּבְחַיֵּי דְכָל־בֵּית יִשְׂרָאֵל,
בַּעֲגָלָא וּבִזְמַן קָרִיב, וְאִמְרוּ: אָמֵן.

יְהֵא שְׁמֵהּ רַבָּא מְבָרַךְ לְעָלַם וּלְעָלְמֵי עָלְמַיָּא.

יִתְבָּרַךְ וְיִשְׁתַּבַּח, וְיִתְפָּאַר וְיִתְרוֹמַם וְיִתְנַשֵּׂא, וְיִתְהַדָּר
וְיִתְעַלֶּה וְיִתְהַלָּל שְׁמֵהּ דְּקוּדְשָׁא, בְּרִיךְ הוּא, לְעֵלָּא מִן־כָּל־
בִּרְכָתָא וְשִׁירָתָא, תֻּשְׁבְּחָתָא וְנֶחֱמָתָא דַּאֲמִירָן בְּעָלְמָא,
וְאִמְרוּ: אָמֵן.

יְהֵא שְׁלָמָא רַבָּא מִן־שְׁמַיָּא וְחַיִּים עָלֵינוּ וְעַל־כָּל־יִשְׂרָאֵל,
וְאִמְרוּ: אָמֵן.

עֹשֶׂה שָׁלוֹם בִּמְרוֹמָיו, הוּא יַעֲשֶׂה שָׁלוֹם עָלֵינוּ וְעַל־
כָּל־יִשְׂרָאֵל, וְאִמְרוּ: אָמֵן.

> Let the glory of God be extolled, and God's great name be hallowed in the world whose creation God willed. May God rule in our own day, in our own lives, and in the life of all Israel, and let us say: Amen.
>
> Let God's great name be blessed for ever and ever.
>
> Beyond all the praises, songs, and adorations that we can utter is the Holy One, the Blessed One, whom yet we glorify, honor, and exalt. And let us say: Amen.
>
> For us and for all Israel, may the blessing of peace and the promise of life come true, and let us say: Amen.
>
> May the One who causes peace to reign in the high heavens, cause peace to reign among us and all Israel, and let us say: Amen.

COMMENTARY

The קַדִּישׁ (Kaddish) may be the best known and most often recited prayer in all of Jewish tradition. Why? What are its origins? What is its meaning? Why has it become so important a prayer within Judaism?

Origins of the קַדִּישׁ

As with many prayers within Judaism, we are not sure who wrote the קַדִּישׁ or when it was written. It may be that it began as a brief, one-sentence prayer and, over the ages, gathered additions and increased in size.

Some scholars believe that the original קַדִּישׁ prayer is found in either the Book of Daniel (2:20) or Psalms (113:2). Those sentences read as follows:

לֶהֱוֵא שְׁמֵהּ דִּי אֱלָהָא מְבָרַךְ מִן עָלְמָא וְעַד עָלְמָא.

Blessed be the name of God for ever and ever.

Daniel 2:20

יְהִי שֵׁם יְהֹוָה מְבֹרָךְ מֵעַתָּה וְעַד עוֹלָם.

May the name of the Eternal One be blessed now and for ever.

Psalm 113:2

Compare the two quotes above with the second paragraph of the קַדִּישׁ prayer. What are the similarities and differences?

One of the differences is that of language. The sentence from the Book of Daniel and the קַדִּישׁ prayer are both written in Aramaic, not Hebrew. The sentence from Psalm 113 is in Hebrew. Aramaic was spoken by Jews from the time of the Babylonian exile (586 B.C.E.) until about the fifth century C.E. According to the Talmud, when teachers finished a lesson or when Rabbis finished their sermon in the synagogue, they would dismiss their listeners with the words: "May God's great name be blessed now and forever" (BT *B'rachot* 3a, 21b).

That sentence of dismissal formed the kernel of what became the קַדִּישׁ prayer. Gradually, over the course of centuries, five different versions of the קַדִּישׁ developed.

The Half *Kaddish*

The Half *Kaddish*, חֲצִי קַדִּישׁ (*Chatzi Kaddish*), is the most frequently recited version of the קַדִּישׁ prayer. It consists of the first three paragraphs found on page 223. It is traditionally recited by the reader and congregation at the end of each section of the prayer service, at the end of the פְּסוּקֵי דְזִמְרָה, and at the end of the Torah service.

The Full *Kaddish*

The Full *Kaddish*, קַדִּישׁ שָׁלֵם (*Kaddish Shaleim*), is traditionally recited after the עֲמִידָה by the reader and congregation. It is also known as קַדִּישׁ תִּתְקַבֵּל (*Kaddish Titkabeil*) because of its petition for acceptance of the prayer. Just after the third paragraph, it contains this sentence:

תִּתְקַבֵּל צְלוֹתְהוֹן וּבָעוּתְהוֹן דְּכָל־יִשְׂרָאֵל קֳדָם אֲבוּהוֹן דִּי בִשְׁמַיָּא, וְאִמְרוּ אָמֵן.

May the prayers and supplications of all Israel be acceptable to their God, who is in heaven. And let us say, Amen.

The Mourner's *Kaddish*

The Mourner's *Kaddish*, קַדִּישׁ יָתוֹם (*Kaddish Yatom*), is traditionally recited at the conclusion of every service for eleven months by those who have lost a parent. In many Reform congregations, it is customary for the entire community to rise and recite the קַדִּישׁ together in order to express solidarity with those who mourn as well as to honor those Jews who have no descendants to say קַדִּישׁ for them. The version of the קַדִּישׁ found on page 223 is the קַדִּישׁ יָתוֹם.

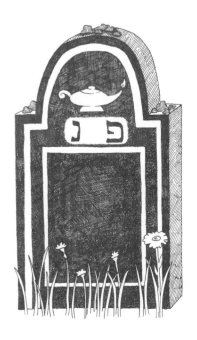

225

Why did the קַדִּישׁ become a prayer for mourners? There are several possible answers to our question. We know that it was the custom during talmudic times to devote time to the study of Torah during days of mourning. At the conclusion of each study session, the קַדִּישׁ was recited. This may have been the beginning of the custom.

Another explanation is found in a legend about Rabbi Akiva. It is said that he once came upon a man who was wandering in a cemetery and carrying a heavy load of wood. Rabbi Akiva asked the man: "What are you doing here? Are you a man or a demon?" The man replied: "I am dead, but I have been condemned to carry wood in the cemetery." "What did you do?" asked Akiva. "Why have you been condemned to such a fate?" The man answered: "I was a tax collector who favored the rich and oppressed the poor." Akiva then inquired: "Is there no way that you can be saved from such a terrible fate?" The man replied: "If my son will recite the קַדִּישׁ, I will be saved from this punishment and will rest in heaven." It is said that Akiva went to find the son and taught him the קַדִּישׁ prayer, so that the man might finally come to rest in heaven.

What is the point or lesson of this legend? How might it have inspired Jews to recite the קַדִּישׁ for their parents? It is reported that there were many Jews who strongly disagreed with the idea that the קַדִּישׁ prayer would enable a parent to reach heaven. Rabbi Avraham bar Chiya, one of the great leaders of Spanish Jewry during the twelfth century, declared: "Those who hope that the קַדִּישׁ of their children will benefit them after death are hoping in vain." What did Rabbi Avraham bar Chiya mean by his statement? To whom was his criticism directed? Why? How might the saying of the קַדִּישׁ prayer help us honor the memory of our parents?

The English version of the קַדִּישׁ יָתוֹם in the *Union Prayer Book* included the following paragraph:

The departed, whom we now remember, have entered into the peace of life eternal. They still live on earth in the acts of goodness they performed and in the hearts of those who cherish their memory. May the beauty of their life abide among us as a loving benediction.

What do you think is meant by the sentence "They still live on earth in the acts of goodness they performed and in the hearts of those who cherish their memory"? How might the saying of קַדִּישׁ help us "cherish their memory"?

It is interesting to note that the קַדִּישׁ יָתוֹם contains no mention of death, immortality, or the afterlife. Look at it carefully. What is its theme? Why did it become a mourners' prayer? How is a prayer of praise for God—one that voices the hope for the "establishment of God's dominion"—appropriate for the mourners' prayer?

In the sixteenth century, Abraham Hurwitz wrote the following about the קַדִּישׁ:

> ...The קַדִּישׁ is not a prayer of the son that the father may be brought up [into heaven] but a recognition of the parent's merit, since through its recital the child best vindicates [claims honor for] the memory of his parent by causing the congregation to respond to him with the praise "Amen. May His great name be blessed now and forever."

Would you agree with Abraham Hurwitz? How does a praise of God, said in the memory of a parent, honor him or her?

The Rabbis' *Kaddish*

The fourth version of the קַדִּישׁ is known as the קַדִּישׁ דְּרַבָּנָן (*Kaddish D'Rabanan*), the Rabbis' *Kaddish*. It is recited after the study of Torah or Talmud. The following paragraph is added after the third paragraph of our version:

עַל יִשְׂרָאֵל וְעַל רַבָּנָן, וְעַל תַּלְמִידֵיהוֹן, וְעַל כָּל תַּלְמִידֵי תַלְמִידֵיהוֹן, וְעַל כָּל מָאן דְּעָסְקִין בְּאוֹרַיְתָא, דִּי בְּאַתְרָא הָדֵין, וְדִי בְכָל אֲתַר וַאֲתַר. יְהֵא לְהוֹן וּלְכוֹן שְׁלָמָא רַבָּא, חִנָּא וְחִסְדָּא וְרַחֲמִין, וְחַיִּין אֲרִיכִין, וּמְזוֹנָא רְוִיחָא, וּפוּרְקָנָא מִן קֳדָם אֲבוּהוֹן דִּי בִשְׁמַיָּא וְאַרְעָא, וְאִמְרוּ: אָמֵן.

Unto Israel and unto the rabbis and their students, and to all the students of their students, and to all who study the Torah in this or in any other place, to you and to them may there be abundant peace, grace, loving-kindness, mercy, long life, plenty to eat, and salvation from God, who is in heaven. And let us say, Amen.

The Funeral *Kaddish*

The fifth version of the קַדִּישׁ is the only one that mentions death or eternal life. It is called קַדִּישׁ לְאִתְחַדְתָּא (*Kaddish L'itchad'ta*), the *Kaddish* of Renewal. It is traditionally said by the mourner at the grave just after the burial, and it includes the words: "May God's great name be magnified and sanctified in the world that is to be created anew, where God will make the dead live again and raise them up unto life eternal—where God will rebuild the city of Jerusalem and establish the Temple in its midst, and destroy false worship from the earth, and restore the worship of the true God. O may the Holy One, blessed be God, rule in power and glory...."

The קַדִּישׁ לְאִתְחַדְתָּא may be one of the last versions of the קַדִּישׁ prayer written. It is the only one to make mention of the rebuilding of Jerusalem and the Temple. Its authors believed that the coming of the messianic days would also bring with them a new world with the possibility of all the dead being brought back to life.

Do Jews Believe in Life after Death?

As we have noticed, the mention of life after death is found only in the fifth version of the קַדִּישׁ prayer called קַדִּישׁ לְאִתְחַדְתָּא. We have already discussed some aspects of the Jewish belief in life after death (see the *G'vurot*, starting on page 111).

There has always been a variety of views within Jewish life about immortality or עוֹלָם הַבָּא (*olam haba*), the world-to-come. The closest that Jews have come to a binding statement on the subject is found in the Thirteen Principles of Faith drawn up by Moses Maimonides. He wrote:

> I believe with perfect faith that there will be a revival of the dead at the time when it shall please the Creator, blessed be God's name and exalted be God's name for ever and ever.

Maimonides' Thirteen Principles of Faith have been printed in most prayer books for the past eight hundred years, and many Jews have accepted them as the most important beliefs of Judaism.

Disagreement and Controversy

There are, however, many Jews who do not believe in the עוֹלָם הַבָּא, the world-to-come, and who reject the idea that there is a life after death. They argue that the Hebrew Bible makes no mention of it and that it is a foreign idea to Judaism. In the Book of Job, we are told: "One who goes down to the grave will not come up again" (Job 7:9), and the author of Ecclesiastes writes: "The dust returns to the earth from where it came, and the spirit returns to God, who gave it" (Ecclesiastes 12:7). In another place the same author tells us: "There is no work, no advice, no knowledge, no wisdom in the grave" (Ecclesiastes 9:10).

What do the statements of Job and Ecclesiastes say about death and immortality? Is there a life after death for them? Do you think they would agree with the observation made by Moses Montefiore in 1903: "As to what happens to us after death, we have no conception and we form no theory." Would you agree with Montefiore's statement?

Reform Judaism eliminated mention of the "resurrection of the dead" from the prayer book. It does, however, say the following about life after death: "Death is not the end; the earthly body vanishes, the immortal spirit lives on with God." How does that view compare with those of Job and Ecclesiastes?

You may wish to look at the views on immortality found in *Gates of Prayer* (1994), pages 151–153, and also in *B'chol L'vavcha*, pages 230–233. Which of those prayers do you find more in harmony with your own view of immortality, and why?

Heaven and Hell

We have already mentioned heaven. What is it? Do Jews believe in heaven and hell?

While modern Jews do not often speak of such beliefs, our ancient Rabbis believed very strongly in what we might call heaven and hell. The Hebrew phrase for heaven is *Gan Eden*, the Garden of Eden. Our Sages imagined that the Garden of Eden was the most beautiful and peaceful place ever created and that the righteous would be able to spend eternity in its wonderful surroundings. The midrash contains many vivid descriptions of the Garden of Eden, or heaven. Here is one example:

> Rabbi Y'hoshua ben Levi taught: When righteous people come to *Gan Eden*, they are clothed in clouds of glory. Crowns of precious stones, pearls, and gold are places on their heads. Then they are brought to a riverbank surrounded by 800 kinds of roses and myrtle plants. Four rivers flow forth: one of wine, one of balsam, one of milk, one of honey. Sixty groups of angels sing in the Garden of Eden. The Tree of Life is in the center, and it bears 500,000 kinds of fruit. Under the tree sit students studying Torah.
>
> *Otzar Hamidrashim* 84:1

What do you think of this description? Is it how you would imagine heaven? If you believe in heaven, what do you think it might be like?

The Sages whose observations make up the midrash also speak of a terrible place called *Geihinom*, which might be considered hell. The name גֵּיא בֶּן־הִנֹּם (*Gei ben Hinom*) means "the valley of the son of Hinom." It was a place near Jerusalem where idolators sacrificed human beings. For this reason, the valley was known as a place of torture, suffering, and bloodshed. We are not sure when, but gradually it became associated with punishment after a wicked life. It apparently became common to say that a wicked person would suffer like those who had suffered in גֵּיהִנּוֹם (Geihinom).

Another name for hell in the Bible is שְׁאוֹל (Sheol). We are not sure what שְׁאוֹל originally meant. It is likely that it referred to the grave or to the realm of death.

The existence of a גֵּיהִנּוֹם was debated by the talmudic Rabbis. Here is a part of their argument:

> Yannai and Shimon ben Lakish say: "There is no גֵּיהִנּוֹם, but the sun will burn up the wicked." The rest of the Rabbis say: "There will be a גֵּיהִנּוֹם." Y'hudah bar Ilai said: "There will be neither a consuming sun nor a גֵּיהִנּוֹם but, rather, a fire issuing from the wicked will burn them up."
>
> BT *N'darim* 8b

Why did ancient people make a connection between destruction by fire (sun) and wickedness? Do you think it is possible to speak in terms of a hell for those who are unethical in their lives?

Usually, just before the Mourner's Kaddish is recited, a brief prayer about life or immortality is read. Following you will find some examples. Compare and contrast them. Discuss them, asking the question: "Does this prayer say what I believe and feel?" When you are called upon to do the Kaddish section of your service, you may wish to use one of the following or you may want to write your own introduction to the Kaddish.

In death, only the body dies. The spirit lives through God's love and mercy. Our loved ones continue to be with us when we remember their deeds and the precious times we shared with them. Now, their kindness, the beautiful words they spoke, and their inspiration give us courage and direction along life's path.

Do not stand at my grave and weep;
I am not there, I do not sleep.
I am a thousand winds that blow;
I am the diamond glints on the snow;
I am the sunlight on ripened grain;
I am the gentle autumn's rain.

When you awaken in the morning's hush
I am the swift uplifting rush of quiet birds
    in circled flights.
I am the soft star that shines at night.
Do not stand at my grave and cry.
I am not there.
I am the glance of two people
Who just fell in love.

Anonymous

The Life of Eternity

The light of life is a finite flame. Like the Sabbath candles, life is kindled, it burns, it glows, it is radiant with warmth and beauty. But soon it fades; its substance is consumed, and it is no more.

In light we see; in light we are seen. The flames dance and our lives are full. But as night follows day, the candle of our life burns down and gutters. There is an end to the flames. We see no more and are no more seen. Yet we do not despair, for we are more than a memory slowly fading into the darkness. With our lives we give life. Something of us can never die: we move in the eternal cycle of darkness and death, of light and life.

Gates of Prayer (1975)

Each Man Has a Name

Each man has a name,
given him by God,
and given him by his father and mother.
Each man has a name
given him by his stature and
his way of smiling,
and given him by his clothes.
Each man has a name
given him by the mountains
and given him by his walls.
Each man has a name
given him by the planets
and given him by his neighbours.

Each man has a name
given him by his sins
and given him by his longing.
Each man has a name
given him by his enemies
and given him by his love.
Each man has a name
given him by his feast days
and given him by his craft.
Each man has a name
given him by the seasons of the year
and given him by his blindness.
Each man has a name
given him by the sea
and given him by his death.

Zelda, translated by T. Carmi

The first time that Adam saw the sun go down and an ever-deepening gloom enfold creation, his mind was filled with terror. Then God took pity on him, and endowed him with the divine intuition to take two stones—the name of one was Darkness and the name of the other Shadow of Death—and rub them against each other, and to discover fire. Thereupon Adam exclaimed with grateful joy: "Blessed be the Creator of Light!"

Based on BT Avodah Zarah 8b, adapted in Likrat Shabbat

Stars

There are stars up above
So far away we only see their light
Long long after the star itself is gone
And so it is with people that we loved
Their memories keep shining ever brightly
Though their time was with us is done
But the stars that light up the darkest night
These are the lights that guide us
As we live our days
These are the ways we remember.

Hannah Senesh

In Praise of Lives Now Gone

יִתְגַּדַּל וְיִתְקַדַּשׁ שְׁמֵהּ רַבָּא

This the profound praise of the living,
Praise for the generous gift of life.
Praise for the presence of loved ones,
    the bonds of friendship,
    the link of memory.
Praise for the toil and searching,
    the dedication and vision,
    the ennobling aspirations.
Praise for the precious moorings of faith,
    for courageous souls,
    for prophets, psalmists, and sages.
Praise for those who walked before us,
    the sufferers in the valley of shadows,
    the steadfast in the furnace of hate.

יִתְגַּדַּל וְיִתְקַדַּשׁ שְׁמֵהּ רַבָּא

Praise for the God of our people,
    the Source of all growth and goodness.
    the Promise on which we build tomorrow.

HJF

ADON OLAM

Adon Olam   אֲדוֹן עוֹלָם

אֲדוֹן עוֹלָם אֲשֶׁר מָלַךְ, בְּטֶרֶם כָּל־יְצִיר נִבְרָא;

לְעֵת נַעֲשָׂה בְחֶפְצוֹ כֹּל, אֲזַי מֶלֶךְ שְׁמוֹ נִקְרָא.

וְאַחֲרֵי כִּכְלוֹת הַכֹּל, לְבַדּוֹ יִמְלֹךְ נוֹרָא;

וְהוּא הָיָה וְהוּא הֹוֶה, וְהוּא יִהְיֶה בְּתִפְאָרָה.

וְהוּא אֶחָד, וְאֵין שֵׁנִי, לְהַמְשִׁיל לוֹ, לְהַחְבִּירָה;

בְּלִי רֵאשִׁית, בְּלִי תַכְלִית, וְלוֹ הָעֹז וְהַמִּשְׂרָה.

וְהוּא אֵלִי, וְחַי גֹּאֲלִי, וְצוּר חֶבְלִי בְּעֵת צָרָה;

וְהוּא נִסִּי וּמָנוֹס לִי, מְנָת כּוֹסִי בְּיוֹם אֶקְרָא.

בְּיָדוֹ אַפְקִיד רוּחִי, בְּעֵת אִישָׁן וְאָעִירָה;

וְעִם רוּחִי גְּוִיָּתִי, יְיָ לִי, וְלֹא אִירָא.

You are the Eternal God, who reigned before any before any being had been created; when all was done according to Your will, already then You were Sovereign. And after all has ceased to be, still will You reign in solitary majesty; You were, You are, You will be in glory. And You are One; none other can compare to You, or consort with You; You are without beginning, without end; Yours alone are power and dominion. And You are my God, my living Redeemer, my Rock in time of trouble and distress; You are my banner and my refuge, my benefactor when I call on You. Into Your hands I entrust my spirit, when I sleep and when I wake; and with my spirit, my body also: You are with me, I shall not fear.

COMMENTARY

The אֲדוֹן עוֹלָם (Adon Olam) is one of the best loved and best known of all Jewish songs. We are not sure when it was written. Some say it was composed by the great Spanish Jewish poet Solomon ibn Gabirol during the eleventh century C.E. Others say that the אֲדוֹן עוֹלָם was written much earlier, perhaps at the time Jews lived under Moslem rule in Babylonia. For the past

234

six centuries, it has been included in the prayer book, and it has become one of the most popular of all Jewish songs.

The theme of אֲדוֹן עוֹלָם is the greatness and eternity of God. Actually, its verses contain a definition of God. Look at them carefully. What do they tell us about the Jewish understanding of God? How would you compare the definition of God in the song with the Christian understanding of God?

There are many different musical settings of אֲדוֹן עוֹלָם. Since it was sung on Shabbat, at *Kol Nidrei* on Yom Kippur, at the daily service by those gathered about the bed of a dying person, and by Moroccan Jews at weddings, its music reflects a variety of moods and meanings.

Make a collection of as many different musical versions of אֲדוֹן עוֹלָם as you can find. Compare and contrast them, and try to relate them to the times and cultures in which they were created.

EIN KEILOHEINU

Ein Keiloheinu

אֵין כֵּאלֹהֵינוּ

אֵין כֵּאלֹהֵינוּ, אֵין כַּאדוֹנֵינוּ,
אֵין כְּמַלְכֵּנוּ, אֵין כְּמוֹשִׁיעֵנוּ.
מִי כֵאלֹהֵינוּ? מִי כַאדוֹנֵינוּ?
מִי כְמַלְכֵּנוּ? מִי כְמוֹשִׁיעֵנוּ?
נוֹדֶה לֵאלֹהֵינוּ, נוֹדֶה לַאדוֹנֵינוּ,
נוֹדֶה לְמַלְכֵּנוּ, נוֹדֶה לְמוֹשִׁיעֵנוּ.
בָּרוּךְ אֱלֹהֵינוּ, בָּרוּךְ אֲדוֹנֵינוּ,
בָּרוּךְ מַלְכֵּנוּ, בָּרוּךְ מוֹשִׁיעֵנוּ.
אַתָּה הוּא אֱלֹהֵינוּ, אַתָּה הוּא אֲדוֹנֵינוּ,
אַתָּה הוּא מַלְכֵּנוּ, אַתָּה הוּא מוֹשִׁיעֵנוּ.

There is none like our God, our Sovereign, our Redeemer.
Who is like our God, our Sovereign, our Redeemer?
We give thanks to our God, our Sovereign, our Redeemer.
Praised be our God, our Sovereign, our Redeemer.
You are our God, our Sovereign, our Redeemer.

Like the אֲדוֹן עוֹלָם, the אֵין כֵּאלֹהֵינוּ (Ein Keiloheinu) is one of the most popular songs at worship services. It was composed about the eighth century C.E., and it has been included in Jewish prayer ever since. Originally, it began with the second stanza, which was followed by אֵין כֵּאלֹהֵינוּ. Later someone reversed the stanzas. Some say this was done so that when the first letters of the first three stanzas were combined they would spell אָמֵן (amen).

YIGDAL

Yigdal　　　　　　　　　　　　　　　　　　　　יִגְדַּל

יִגְדַּל אֱלֹהִים חַי וְיִשְׁתַּבַּח, נִמְצָא וְאֵין עֵת אֶל־מְצִיאוּתוֹ.

אֶחָד וְאֵין יָחִיד כְּיִחוּדוֹ, נֶעְלָם וְגַם אֵין סוֹף לְאַחְדוּתוֹ.

אֵין לוֹ דְמוּת הַגּוּף וְאֵינוֹ גוּף, לֹא נַעֲרוֹךְ אֵלָיו קְדֻשָּׁתוֹ.

קַדְמוֹן לְכָל־דָּבָר אֲשֶׁר נִבְרָא, רִאשׁוֹן וְאֵין רֵאשִׁית לְרֵאשִׁיתוֹ.

הִנּוֹ אֲדוֹן עוֹלָם. לְכָל־נוֹצָר יוֹרֶה גְּדֻלָּתוֹ וּמַלְכוּתוֹ.

שֶׁפַע נְבוּאָתוֹ נְתָנוֹ, אֶל־אַנְשֵׁי סְגֻלָּתוֹ וְתִפְאַרְתּוֹ.

לֹא קָם בְּיִשְׂרָאֵל כְּמֹשֶׁה עוֹד, נָבִיא וּמַבִּיט אֶת־תְּמוּנָתוֹ.

תּוֹרַת אֱמֶת נָתַן לְעַמּוֹ אֵל, עַל יַד נְבִיאוֹ נֶאֱמַן בֵּיתוֹ.

לֹא יַחֲלִיף הָאֵל, וְלֹא יָמִיר דָּתוֹ, לְעוֹלָמִים לְזוּלָתוֹ.

צוֹפֶה וְיוֹדֵעַ סְתָרֵינוּ, מַבִּיט לְסוֹף דָּבָר בְּקַדְמָתוֹ.

גּוֹמֵל לְאִישׁ חֶסֶד כְּמִפְעָלוֹ, נוֹתֵן לְרָשָׁע רַע כְּרִשְׁעָתוֹ.

יִשְׁלַח לְקֵץ יָמִין פְּדוּת עוֹלָם, כָּל־חַי וְיֵשׁ יַכִּיר יְשׁוּעָתוֹ.

חַיֵּי עוֹלָם נָטַע בְּתוֹכֵנוּ, בָּרוּךְ עֲדֵי עַד שֵׁם תְּהִלָּתוֹ.

Magnified be the living God, praised, whose existence is eternal, One and Unique in that unity, the unfathomable One whose Oneness is infinite.

A God with no bodily form, incorporeal, whose holiness is beyond compare, who preceded all creation, the Beginning who has no beginning.

Your are Eternal Might, who teach every creature Your greatness and sovereignty, with the gift of prophecy inspiring those whom You chose to make Your glory known.

Never has there been a prophet like Moses, whose closeness to You is unmatched. A Torah of truth You gave Your people through Your prophet, Your faithful servant.

A changeless God, ever the same, whose teaching will stand, who watches us and knows our inmost thoughts, who knows all outcomes before events begin.

You give us each what we deserve, the good and bad alike. In the end of days You will send an everlasting redemption; all that lives and has being shall witness Your deliverance.

You have implanted eternal life within us; praised be Your glory to all eternity!

COMMENTARY

It is said that יִגְדַּל (Yigdal), written sometime in the fourteenth century, was based on the Thirteen Principles of Moses Maimonides. The Thirteen Principles were considered so important that they were included in most prayer books. Look them up (*Daily Prayer Book,* Joseph H. Hertz, Bloch Publishing Co., 1955, pages 248–255 or in the *Encyclopaedia Judaica*, Vol. 3, col. 655), and compare them to the יִגְדַּל. The יִגְדַּל was more than a song for the Jewish people. It was recited at the beginning of each daily service as a statement of belief.

Some people have asked why Maimonides included thirteen principles and not more or less. What is the significance of thirteen? There are several interesting answers. Among them are the following: the numerical value of the word אֶחָד (echad), referring to the *one* God, (א = 1, ח = 8, and ד = 4) is thirteen; the bar and bat mitzvah age of thirteen; and the Torah's mention of thirteen powers of God (Exodus 34:6–7). What relationship might these explanations have to the Thirteen Principles?

KIDDUSH FOR SHABBAT DAY

Kiddush for Shabbat Day קִדּוּשׁ לְיוֹם שַׁבָּת

וְשָׁמְרוּ בְנֵי־יִשְׂרָאֵל אֶת־הַשַּׁבָּת, לַעֲשׂוֹת אֶת־הַשַּׁבָּת לְדֹרֹתָם
בְּרִית עוֹלָם. בֵּינִי וּבֵין בְּנֵי יִשְׂרָאֵל אוֹת הִיא לְעֹלָם. כִּי־שֵׁשֶׁת
יָמִים עָשָׂה יהוה אֶת־הַשָּׁמַיִם וְאֶת־הָאָרֶץ, וּבַיּוֹם הַשְּׁבִיעִי
שָׁבַת וַיִּנָּפַשׁ.

The people of Israel shall keep the Sabbath, observing the Sabbath in every generation as a covenant for all time. It is a sign for ever between Me and the people of Israel. For in six days the Eternal One made heaven and earth, but on the seventh day God rested and was refreshed.

זָכוֹר אֶת־יוֹם הַשַּׁבָּת לְקַדְּשׁוֹ. שֵׁשֶׁת יָמִים תַּעֲבֹד וְעָשִׂיתָ כָּל־
מְלַאכְתֶּךָ. וְיוֹם הַשְּׁבִיעִי שַׁבָּת לַיָי אֱלֹהֶיךָ. לֹא־תַעֲשֶׂה כָל־
מְלָאכָה—אַתָּה וּבִנְךָ־וּבִתֶּךָ, עַבְדְּךָ וַאֲמָתְךָ וּבְהֶמְתֶּךָ, וְגֵרְךָ
אֲשֶׁר בִּשְׁעָרֶיךָ. כִּי שֵׁשֶׁת־יָמִים עָשָׂה יְיָ אֶת־הַשָּׁמַיִם וְאֶת־
הָאָרֶץ, אֶת־הַיָּם, וְאֶת־כָּל־אֲשֶׁר־בָּם, וַיָּנַח בַּיּוֹם הַשְּׁבִיעִי.
עַל־כֵּן בֵּרַךְ יְיָ אֶת־יוֹם הַשַּׁבָּת וַיְקַדְּשֵׁהוּ.

Remember the Sabbath day and keep it holy. Six days you shall labor and do all your work, but the seventh day is a Sabbath of the Eternal your God: you shall not do any work—you, your son or daughter, your male or female slave, or your cattle, or the stranger who is within your settlements. For in six days the Eternal One made heaven and earth and sea, and all that is in them, and God rested on the seventh day. Therefore the Eternal One blessed the seventh day and called it holy.

בָּרוּךְ אַתָּה יְיָ, אֱלֹהֵינוּ מֶלֶךְ הָעוֹלָם, בּוֹרֵא פְּרִי הַגָּפֶן.

We praise You, Eternal God, Sovereign of the universe, Creator of the fruit of the vine.

HaMotzi / הַמוֹצִיא

בָּרוּךְ אַתָּה יי, אֱלֹהֵינוּ מֶלֶךְ הָעוֹלָם, הַמּוֹצִיא לֶחֶם מִן הָאָרֶץ.

We praise You, Eternal God, Sovereign of the universe, for You cause bread to come forth from the earth.

COMMENTARY

Wine is a symbol of the joy of the Shabbat celebration. It is shared three times on Shabbat: first when Shabbat is welcomed with the קִדּוּשׁ (Kiddush) on Friday evening; at the conclusion of Shabbat morning worship; and, finally, at הַבְדָּלָה (Havdalah), the ceremony that concludes Shabbat.

The קִדּוּשׁ לְיוֹם שַׁבָּת (Kiddush L'Yom Shabbat), Kiddush for Shabbat Day, is also known as קְדֻשָׁה רַבָּה (K'dushah Rabbah), the Great Kiddush. We are not sure how it came to be known by that name, but we do know that the first two paragraphs were added to the blessing over the wine in order to give the Kiddush importance. For an explanation of the first paragraph of the קִדּוּשׁ, known as V'shamru, see page 135. The first paragraph is taken from Exodus 31:16–17, and the second is from Exodus 20:8–11.

In the third paragraph, we have the בְּרָכָה for wine, קִדּוּשׁ, and in the fourth, the בְּרָכָה for bread, הַמּוֹצִיא (HaMotzi). According to tradition, the blessings for bread and wine are derived from the following words found in Psalm 104:14:

מַצְמִיחַ חָצִיר לַבְּהֵמָה וְעֵשֶׂב לַעֲבֹדַת הָאָדָם; לְהוֹצִיא לֶחֶם מִן הָאָרֶץ וְיַיִן יְשַׂמַּח לְבַב אֱנוֹשׁ.

Who causes the grass to spring up for the cattle,
And herb for the service of humanity;
To bring forth bread out of the earth,
And wine that makes glad the hearts of all.

239

Praising God

The קָדוֹשׁ and הַמּוֹצִיא are praises of God.

Y'hudah HaLevi, the great Jewish philosopher who lived in Spain between 1085 and 1140, once commented on the meaning of "praising God" before eating and drinking. He wrote: "Preparing for a pleasure doubles the enjoyment" *(Kuzari)*. How is a בְּרָכָה before drinking wine or eating bread a form of "preparation"? In what ways can a בְּרָכָה help us to "double the enjoyment" of the wine, or bread, or anything else we may eat?

Dr. Ernst Simon, who once taught education at Hebrew University in Jerusalem, told the following story about his son:

Once, when my son was four years old, he happened to see some beautiful flowers and said to me: "Abba, I am happy with these flowers. What is the proper benediction (בְּרָכָה) for them?" Though a small child,

240

he expressed a universal human sentiment. Children can love and enjoy flowers just as deeply as adults can, perhaps even more so. But this child was a little Jew who had already learned in his parents' home that nothing is eaten or experienced without a בְּרָכָה, a benediction. Hence it was natural for him to seek a specific Jewish religious formulation to express a general human emotion.

Ernst Simon, *On the Meaning of Prayer*

Other Reasons

Prayer is one of the things that distinguishes human beings from animals. This is especially true of the הַמּוֹצִיא, the prayer before eating bread. Animals simply eat when food is placed before them. Human beings can pause, give thought to the incredible process through which food reaches them, and give thanks to God.

There are those who believe that, in saying the בְּרָכָה for wine and bread, we remind ourselves of how dependent we are upon nature, upon other human beings, and upon God. Others say that when we say a בְּרָכָה, we reaffirm our identity with the Jewish people and its faith.

Which of these views appeals to you? Why do you think it is important to say a בְּרָכָה?

FINALLY, WHAT IS PRAYER?

Asking difficult religious questions can sometimes lead to loud arguments and even angry attacks. Why we pray and what we believe about God are very personal matters and very touchy subjects! That, however, should not drive us to keep silent or avoid such issues. Through a sensitive and open discussion, we can learn from one another and increase our understanding of God and prayer.

Each of us is a highly unique individual. We are different from one another in our talents, interests, and abilities. Some of us are satisfied with what we believe; others are struggling with doubts and difficult questions. As individuals, we see the world, its wonder, and human history from a variety of perspectives. It should not surprise us, then, to discover that Jews today, and throughout the ages, have developed a number of very different definitions of prayer. This chapter includes some of the most important of these various approaches to the meaning of prayer.

Prayer Is Natural

Some people believe that prayer is as natural a response to the universe as the growth of a flower toward the sun. Just as a flower, even on a cloudy day, will turn toward the light as a source of its growth, so too will the human spirit reach out to a sustaining Spirit in the universe. Prayer, in this sense, is something that all human beings do whether they recognize it or not. When a person pauses to observe beauty, or feels hope in a moment of sadness, or reaches out for strength in a time of trouble—that may be called prayer.

Some scientists believe that the evolution and development of all life are responses to a creative spirit at work in the universe. Dr. Edmond Sinnot, former director of the Sheffield Scientific School at Yale University, has written:

> If there were not something in the universe that draws us, as the moon draws the sea, man's high aspirations would have no meaning. Tides prove the moon is *there,* even though clouds may cover it.... Aspiration is an expression of something deeper than intellect; a profound certainty that beyond man's body and beyond his mind there is a spiritual content

in the universe with which his own spirit can from time to time communicate and from which he can draw strength and comfort... this sense of Presence, this central, orienting core of things, is what we mean by God.

The Bridge of Life

The belief that prayer is a natural aspiration or response to the universe is expressed throughout Jewish literature. The author of Psalm 19 went so far as to exclaim that the heavens, and day and night, declare the glory of God. Other similar expressions may be found throughout the Book of Psalms (see especially Psalms 36:6–10, 84:2–13, 96, 98, 104, and 148). Your discussion group may wish to compare and contrast the following statements about prayer. What do they have in common with Dr. Sinnot's understanding of prayer as "aspiration"? Do you find these statements and the argument that prayer is a "natural response to the universe" satisfying or convincing?

We are formed by the same forces—chemical, physical, and spiritual—which hold the stars in their orbit, thrust up the mountains, scoop out the seas, bring the rose to bloom, teach the hawk to fly, the horse to neigh. "If I climb up unto the heavens, behold Thou art there, and, if I go to the ends of the earth, behold Thou art there" (Psalm 139:8).

Prayer is not the lonely cry of a "tailless monkey playing ape to his dreams," nor a shout into an empty void answered only by its own echo. Prayer is the spirit within us reaching out to the Spirit of the universe, and prayer is that Spirit responding to us.

Rabbi Robert I. Kahn, *Prayer and Its Expression*

It is not you alone who pray, or we, or those others; all things pray and all things pour forth their souls. The heavens pray, the earth prays, every creature and every living thing. In all life, there is longing. Creation is itself but a longing, a kind of prayer to the Almighty. What are the clouds, the rising and the setting of the sun, the soft radiance of the moon, and the gentleness of the night? What are the flashes of the human mind and the storms of the human heart? They are all prayers—the outpouring of boundless longing for God.

Micah Joseph Ben Gurion Berdichevski [1865–1921], translated by Rabbi Aharon Opher

Every plant and bush, every grain of sand and clod of earth, everything in which life is revealed or hidden, the smallest and the biggest in creation—longs and yearns and reaches out toward its celestial Source. And, at every moment, all these cravings are gathered up and absorbed by man who is himself lifted up by the longing for holiness within him. It is during prayer that all these pent-up desires and yearnings are released. Through his prayer, man unites in himself all being and lifts all creation up to the Fountainhead of blessing and life.

Abraham Isaac Kook, *Jewish Thought*

Praise Me, says God, and I will know that you love Me.
Curse Me, I will know that you love Me.
    Praise Me or curse Me, I will know that you love Me.
Sing out My graces, says God.
Raise your fist against Me and revile, says God.
    Sing My graces or revile, reviling is also praise, says God.
But if you sit fenced off in your apathy,
    Entrenched in "I couldn't care less," says God,
If you look at the stars and yawn, says God,
    If you see suffering and don't cry out,
If you don't praise and don't revile,
    Then I created you in vain, says God.

Aaron Zeitlin, "Praise Me, Says God," translated by Emanuel Goldsmith

We Need Help

Human beings often feel fear and loneliness. We encounter times of sickness, hunger, oppression, failure, and death. In such moments of trial and pain, prayer can be an expression of our need for help. Rabbi Sheila Peltz Weinberg teaches: "God is sought as the source of spiritual healing—soul healing. In union with the divine we find release from the pain of our futile cycle of searching and disappointment." Such expressions are found throughout the Book of Psalms and the traditional prayer book. Here are a few examples, including one sung in many synagogues today.

Heal us, Eternal God, and we shall be cured. Save us and we shall be saved.

Amidah

O, Sovereign of the universe! Redeem, help, save, and assist Your people from disease, the sword, famine, want, and all evils that trouble the world.

BT *K'tubot* 8a

Give ear, O God, to my prayer;

And hide not Yourself from my supplication.

Attend to me, and answer me;

I am filled with sorrow and will cry out;

Because of the voice of the enemy,

Because of the oppression of the wicked;

For they cast mischief upon me,

And in anger they persecute me.

Psalm 55:2–4

O, my God, rescue me out of the hand of the wicked,

Out of the grasp of the unrighteous and ruthless man.

For You are my hope;

O Eternal God, my trust from my youth.

Psalm 71:4–5

מִי שֶׁבֵּרַךְ אֲבוֹתֵינוּ

מְקוֹר הַבְּרָכָה לְאִמּוֹתֵינוּ

Mi shebeirach avoteinu

M'kor hab'rachah l'imoteinu

May the Source of strength

Who blessed the ones before us

Help us find the courage

To make our lives a blessing

And let us say: *A-mein.*

מִי שֶׁבֵּרַךְ אִמּוֹתֵינוּ

מְקוֹר הַבְּרָכָה לְאֲבוֹתֵינוּ

Mi shebeirach i-moteinu

M'kor hab'rachah la-a-voteinu

Bless those in need of healing

With *r'fuah sh'lei-mah*

The renewal of body

The renewal of spirit

And let us say: *A-mein.*

Debbie Friedman and Drorah Setel

Does God Hear Prayer?

Each of the above prayers is based upon a trust, hope, and faith that God can and will help those who call out in prayer. Those who voice such prayers believe that God is a שׁוֹמֵעַ תְּפִלָּה (Shomei-a T'filah), a Power who hears our prayers and may answer them. The immediate and difficult question to be faced by one who believes in God as a שׁוֹמֵעַ תְּפִלָּה is: "Does God really hear and answer prayer?" Those who have faith in God as a שׁוֹמֵעַ תְּפִלָּה have developed a variety of answers to that question. Your discussion group may wish to explore the following ones. How do they differ? Which comes closest to your own belief?

Is it superstition to believe that God hears prayer and answers us? Yes, if we believe that whenever we say something or do something magical then God must jump to our command. But, it is not superstitious to hope that, if we call, He will hear. What would stop Him from hearing us? Why should He not hear? Magic tries to accomplish something against God. Prayer tries to tell Him something, leaving it to Him to do what He wishes. Magic accomplishes something or tries to. Prayer is itself accomplishment.

To be heard by God is to be forgiven of our errors and changed into better people. Prayer does not insure that we get what we want, but only what God wants. It cannot cure cancer or win races, but it can change lives. It has.

Rabbi Arnold Wolf, *Challenge to Confirmands*

Perhaps an analogy will help. Like all analogies, it is not perfect and therefore should not be pressed too far. It tends to make God seem too mechanical and distant, yet it may clarify what we mean in asserting that the proper kind of prayer is answered. Each of us has a series of faucets in his home. These faucets are the terminal points of water pipes which are connected to mains, going back ultimately to a pumping station. When we feel thirsty and want a drink of water, what happens? We proceed to a faucet, turn it on, and help ourselves. Has the engineer at the pumping station met our needs? Obviously so, but not in the sense that he is aware of our thirst whenever we feel it. He has constructed and maintained an ingenious system of pipes and valves which makes it possible for us to have water—provided we understand the system and our relationship to it, provided we fulfill our responsibility of operating the system correctly. If we merely stand before the faucet, piteously begging for a drink but doing nothing to activate the system, our thirst will never be slaked.

Similarly, God has initiated and maintains an incredibly complicated system through which most of our physical and spiritual needs may be satisfied. Here again, however, we must become knowledgeable as to how the system operates and must meet our responsibilities in activating it. In a sense, God has answered our prayers even before we utter them, even before we are aware of them. He sustains the system, keeping it in good working order, whether we pray or not. Our prayers affect, not His support of the system, but whether or not we shall reap full benefit from it. Prayer is the experience through which we remind ourselves of how our most urgent needs can be met and activate ourselves to "turn the faucet." In this sense, mature prayer is always answered.

Rabbi Roland B. Gittelsohn, *Wings of the Morning*

Thus, at the core of prayer is its richest content—the awareness that there is a God to whom man responds. But out of this comes the frightening question—does God respond to man? "Praised be Thou, O God, who hearest prayer." What sense does this statement make? If by response we mean a reply, a "Yes, I will" or "No, I won't," then there is no response. God does not answer our requests.

I stood in a hospital room where a young woman was feeding her mother, a victim of a heart attack. Suddenly the mother began to gasp for breath. Nurses were summoned. Within seconds, doctors rushed into the room to attempt to save the patient. The daughter was taken to an adjoining room where she pleaded with me, "Rabbi, how do I pray?" Then she moaned again and again, "God, help my mother to live." But the mother died. Did God deny the prayer? It would be cruel to say this. Yet, even if we know in advance that such a prayer cannot help the patient, it must nevertheless be spoken because the grief-stricken person must express his desperate need for help. Sometimes, as in this instance, prayers are altogether nonrational. The one who prays does not ask in his anguish, "Is this reasonable?" He only knows his grief and he must release it. How wisely the rabbis said, "The heart knows its own bitterness." Anguish demands expression, and, however unreasonable it may be, it must not be denied.

But, if God does not reply, what kind of response can we expect?—the response which God gave to the suffering and questing Job, "I am God." . . . God responds to man. How? By disclosing Himself to us. God hears prayer, not by fulfilling our requirements, not by satisfying our needs, but by making Himself known to us as a living reality in our lives. When we pray we become aware, like Moses who sought to know who God was, that God "is what He is."

Rabbi David Polish, "The Need to Pray," in *The Theological Foundations of Prayer*

I do not waste time pleading with God to make me well. I believe that prayer is not to be invoked to ask God for things for oneself or even for others. Rather, prayer is a medium through which I ask God to show me God's will, and to give me the strength to carry out that will.

Arthur Ashe, *Days of Grace*

[Arthur Ashe was a tennis champion who died of AIDS]

Do not think that the words of prayer
    as you say them
    go up to God.
It is not the words themselves that ascend;
    it is rather the burning desire of your heart
    that rises like smoke toward heaven.
If your prayer consists only of words and letters,
    and does not contain your heart's desire—
    how can it rise up to God?

Or Ha-Me'ir 3:16c, as translated in *Your Word Is Fire*

A Soldier Fulfilling Orders

Professor Yeshayahu Leibowitz was a scientist, philosopher, and traditional Jew who lived in Jerusalem. He taught organic chemistry and neurophysiology at Hebrew University and was one of Israel's best-known and most controversial figures. Professor Leibowitz was a practicing, praying, and observant Jew who argued that prayer is not reasonable and that human beings cannot praise or influence God. Nevertheless, Professor Leibowitz prayed three times a day with devotion.

In an interview with Paula Hirth, which appeared in *Israel Magazine,* Professor Leibowitz was asked to explain why he prayed:

Q: Can you honestly, every day, say something you do not believe?

LEIBOWITZ: Why not? The prayer is not my prayer—it is prescribed. Our prayer is not meant to be an expression of my feelings; it has nothing to do with my feelings. I have no need to inform God about my needs—I am simply fulfilling the obligation of prayer, just as a soldier has to obey orders. It is impossible for man to praise God, and you can't influence God—if you believe in God and not in an idol. Therefore, the prayer, in Judaism, does not express human needs; it is a prescribed form of worship of God.

By "the prayer," Professor Leibowitz means the עֲמִידָה. For him, prayer is an obligation and responsibility. It is a מִצְוָה. The idea that prayer is an obligation that each Jew must fulfill is expressed many times in Jewish literature. In the *Zohar,* a book that first appeared in thirteenth-century Spain but that Jewish mystics claim was revealed by God to Rabbi Shimon bar Yochai (100–160 C.E.), we are told: "We should be like a servant before our master when we stand up to recite the *Amidah.*" The great Jewish philosopher Moses Maimonides also stressed that prayer was a מִצְוָה, an obligation. In his *Sefer HaMitzvot,* he wrote: "To pray to God daily is a positive מִצְוָה, as it is said: 'And you shall serve the Eternal One your God' (Exodus 23:25). The oral tradition teaches that this *service* is prayer.... The obligation in this מִצְוָה is for each of us to pray every day according to our ability."

What do Professor Leibowitz, the *Zohar,* and Maimonides all have in common? What does it mean to pray as if you are a "servant"? Does that make sense to you? What are the positive aspects of their arguments? What can be gained by viewing prayer as an obligation, a מִצְוָה, or something that we must do? What are some of the dangers in such an approach? How does this definition of prayer compare with the others in this chapter?

THE CHALLENGES WE FACE

Prayer is a perspective from which to behold, from which to respond to, the challenges we face. Man in prayer does not seek to impose his will upon God; he seeks to impose God's will and mercy upon himself. Prayer is necessary to make us aware of our failures, backsliding, transgressions, sins.
Rabbi Abraham Joshua Heschel, *On Prayer*

To Change Ourselves

Quite opposite from Professor Leibowitz's argument that prayer "has nothing to do with my feelings" is the belief, held by many, that the purpose of prayer is to change ourselves.

Dr. Emil L. Fackenheim, in his book *Paths to Jewish Belief*, writes: "We pray not to change God's purposes but our own—so as to make them conform to God's. Having thus changed them, we become willing to act as God's co-workers. And this too is part of God's will. But it is not done for us. We can only do it ourselves—through prayer."

The Hebrew verb לְהִתְפַּלֵל (l'hitpaleil), "to pray," may be translated as to judge or examine oneself. Prayer is meant to be a time of honest self-searching where we struggle with the gap between what we say and what we do—between our ideals and our actions. This kind of prayer is meant to bother and trouble a person. It should make us ashamed of our selfishness, aware of our apathy, embarrassed by our callous indifference. And it should force us to see the opportunities we may have wasted or the rich potentials we may have squandered.

The following meditation by the Chasidic teacher Rabbi Nachman of Breslov (1772–1810) is a good example of prayer that is meant to help us judge ourselves:

> O God,
> Help me perfect
> every element
> of my humanness.
> Help me overcome
> all my negative traits,
> all my evil motivations.
> Teach me to turn bad
> into good.
>
> Rebbe Nachman of Breslov

Many prayers contain phrases and sections that invite us to reflect on our relationships with others, even on how we treat ourselves. When, for instance, we read, "In loving-kindness You sustain the living," we may be moved to ask ourselves, "What have I done as a partner of God in helping to feed the hungry and care for the sick or the aged?" When we pray, "Grant peace...to all who worship You," we ought to be asking, "What have I done to make

peace possible within my family, among friends, and in my community?" In other words, by using the prayers of Jewish tradition, we may challenge ourselves with questions that can change our behavior.

Your discussion group may wish to take a prayer from *B'chol L'vavcha* and make a list of the questions we might ask ourselves if we wanted to use the prayer as a means for judging our ethical behavior and challenging ourselves to be better, more sensitive human beings.

Try an experiment! Have each member of your discussion group prepare a series of questions and/or comments alongside a prayer. Then use the prayers and comments in a service. Afterward, discuss how our prayer experience might help us to change our attitudes and relationships with others and the world. An example using the last section of the הוֹדָאָה follows:

O God our Redeemer and Helper, let all who live affirm You and praise Your name in truth.
How aware have I been of the beauty of earth? Have I given thanks for what I have eaten and enjoyed?
Have I praised God by helping others in need or saving them from pain? What have I done to make the world a happier and better place in which to live?

Eternal God, whose nature is Goodness, we give You thanks and praise.
We are faithful to God when we are sensitive and loving with God's creatures and creation. How good and pleasant have I been with friends and family? Can I really give thanks to God without being more grateful to others?

251

A Means of Jewish Identity

When we recite the words אֱלֹהֵינוּ וֵאלֹהֵי אֲבוֹתֵינוּ וְאִמּוֹתֵינוּ, "our God, the God of our fathers and our mothers," we identify ourselves with Jews of all ages and throughout the world.

Speaking personally, when I enter a synagogue or join with other Jews in prayer, a special dimension is added to my life. In those moments, I renew my connection with centuries of Jewish experience and tradition. Since the prayer book is filled with the words of the prophets and the writings of rabbis and poets, I become a part of my people's engagement with God. For me, Jewish worship is the bridge that links me to the past, the present, and the future of the Jewish people. It is a reaffirmation of my identity as a Jew.

Jewish tradition has always emphasized the importance of community prayer. While it does not forbid private prayer, it teaches that a human being is not only an individual, but also a participant in a community. Rabbi Milton Steinberg, in his book *Basic Judaism*, captures this emphasis of Jewish tradition when he writes: "But a Jew is also an Israelite, a fellow in the Jewish people. Wherefore Judaism has established a schedule of times and seasons at which he shall come to God in this capacity."

Your discussion group ought to discuss the variety of ways in which Jewish prayer helps us to express our Jewish identity and feelings as Jews. For instance, you may wish to examine the use of Hebrew, the participation in a מִנְיָן (minyan), the use of a common prayer book, the reading of Torah, the recitation of prayers composed thousands of years ago, and the wearing of a כִּפָּה (kippah) and טַלִית (tallit). How might these aid us in expressing our Jewishness and our devotion to the Jewish tradition and people?

To Enlarge Sensitivity

There is a story told about a Chasidic rebbe who was always late to his synagogue for the daily שַׁחֲרִית (Shacharit), morning prayers. One morning, a few of his students asked him: "Rebbe, why do you come so late each morning?" He was quiet for a moment as if afraid to answer. Then he explained: "I cannot help myself! When I awaken each morning, I immediately recite the morning prayer. I say מוֹדֶה אֲנִי לְפָנֶיךָ [Modeh ani l'fanecha], 'I give thanks to You.' Having said those words, I cannot go on. I tremble, and I ask myself: 'Who is the I, and who is the You?' The I is a tiny and passing creature of clay; the You is the eternal Creator of the universe. The contrast amazes me, and soon I am lost in wonder and silence before the vast beauty and order of the world. That is why I am late, each morning, in arriving at the synagogue."

Like that Chasidic rebbe, prayer for many people is a powerful and poetic way through which human beings enlarge their vision and deepen their sensitivities to the wonder, awe, and beauty of the universe. We cannot always stand in the midst of a beautiful forest or at the top of a mountain. Yet prayer allows us the opportunity to attune ourselves to the feelings we might have had at such special moments. It also provides us with insights through which to open our hearts to new sacred experiences and recognitions. We may, in the midst of our prayer, realize more deeply the meaning and mystery of the love we share with others, or the health of our body, or the wondrous capacities of our mind. Prayer is meant to enlarge and open our sensitivities to the world and to ourselves. The poet and liturgist Marcia Falk explains that when she prays, she seeks "to acknowledge the uniqueness of each day and, by extension, the individuality and preciousness of each moment. . . . I try to allow myself not to focus on my desires but to let go of them; not to wish but simply to accept what is." The author of Psalm 8 echoes this idea:

> How glorious is Your name in all the earth! . . .
> When I behold Your heavens, the work of Your fingers,
> The moon and the stars, which You have established;
> What is humanity, that You are mindful of us,
> that You consider us?
>
> Psalm 8:2, 4–5

Many psalms (see especially Psalms 19, 24, 93, 95–98, and 104) are filled with poetic expressions of reverence for God and the wonder of life. Our prayer book, as we have discovered, contains countless meditations that seek to capture our relationship with the Life-Power pervading all nature. Prayer, in this sense, is meant to enlarge our awareness and enrich our perception. It should open us to the divine margin that energizes all existence.

Your discussion group may wish to compare and contrast the statements about prayer found in the marginal notes on pages 253–254. Select a prayer from B'chol L'vavcha, or one of the suggested psalms, and read it after you have studied the quotations from Rabbi Heschel, Rabbis Green and Prager, Rabbi Kaplan, Rabbi Greenberg, and Rabbi Weinberg. How did the prayer-writer or the Psalmist express wonder and mystery? How do their words help us to new insights and awareness—to a deeper appreciation of ourselves?

TO PRAY IS . . .

To pray is to take notice of the wonder, to regain a sense of the mystery that animates all beings, the divine margin in all attainments. Prayer is our humble answer to the inconceivable surprise of living. . . . It is so embarrassing to live! How strange we are in the world, and how presumptuous our doings! Only one response can maintain us: gratefulness for witnessing the wonder, for the gift of our unearned right to serve, to adore, and to fulfill. It is gratefulness which makes the soul great.
> Abraham Joshua Heschel,
> *Man's Quest for God*

The external mouthing of words alone cannot move us. It is the inward flame of devotion that brings our prayer close to God. The phrase *lahav tefilatam*, "the flame of Israel's prayer," recalls that feeling of *hitlahavut*: the "in-burning" flame of passionate devotion. To attain *hitlahavut* in prayer is to soar with the rapturous ecstasy of divine communion, to access the infinite and be aflame with the nearness of God.
> Rabbi Arthur Green and
> Rabbi Marcia Prager

Public worship aids us by liberating personality from the confining walls of the individual ego. Imprisoned in self, we easily fall prey to morbid brooding. . . . With a whole wide world of boundless opportunities about us, we permit our minds, as it were, to pace

(continued on the next page)

To pray is to feel and to give expression to a deep sense of gratitude. No intelligent, healthy, normal human being should take for granted, or accept without conscious, grateful acknowledgment, the innumerable blessings which God in His infinite love bestows upon him daily—the blessings of parents and loved ones, of friends and country, of health and understanding.

Simon Greenberg, *Sabbath and Festival Prayer Book*

Prayer is awareness not only of God but of oneself as well. God is what He is and we are what we are whether we recognize and welcome it or not. Prayer is joyous recognition and deliberate thankful accept-ance of what we are.

Dudley Weinberg, *The Efficacy of Prayer*

In Conclusion—A Story

Far away from the highways of civilization there was a small village. In it were all the trades and crafts essential to the community except one. There was no watchmaker. As a result, over the years, all the clocks in the village became inaccurate. Many of their owners, therefore, stopped using them.

One day a watchmaker came to the village. He was greeted with much excitement. Everyone rushed to him with a clock. He carefully examined all the clocks before him and then told their owners: "I am sorry, I can fix only those that have been kept running. The others are too corroded by rust. They are ruined beyond repair."

Our ability to pray and derive meaning out of prayer demands effort and skill. *Prayer is an art,* and its success, as in all art, depends upon the artist. The cultivation of prayer requires the constant exercise of our spiritual powers and capacities.

The age in which we live challenges us with many difficult questions about ourselves and the world in which we live. Should we conform to the crowd? What is our connection with the cosmos into which we were born? How can we achieve self-fulfillment? How can we face the fears we have and express the joys we feel? What is our responsibility to our people and to all human beings? Living with such questions, we require prayer. We need sacred moments set aside for struggling toward renewed perspective and faith.

We cannot afford to let our capacities for prayer become corroded by neglect. Our lives are too precious, and our tasks as partners with God in creation are too important. The Torah teaches: "Choose life!" Yet, life is constantly evolving and confronting us with novel choices. It is not enough just to exist. The vital question before us is how to exist. For us, prayer can be the indispensable art through which we probe our place in the universe, purify our souls in the white-heat of self-scrutiny, and link our lives to the goals, values, and visions of our people.

A Selected Bibliography

Books on Prayer

Bradshaw, Paul F., and Lawrence A. Hoffman (eds.). *The Making of Jewish and Christian Worship*. Notre Dame, Ind.: University of Notre Dame Press, 1991.

Donin, Hayim Halevy. *To Pray as a Jew: A Guide to the Prayer Book and the Synagogue Service*. New York: Perseus Books Group, 1980.

Efron, Benjamin. *Pathways through the Prayerbook*. New York: Ktav Publishing House, 1962.

Elbogen, Ismar. *Jewish Liturgy: A Comprehensive History*. Philadelphia: Jewish Publication Society, 1993.

Falk, Marcia. *The Book of Blessings*. Boston: Beacon Press, 1996.

Garfiel, Evelyn. *Service of the Heart*. Hollywood: Wilshire Book Company, 1978.

Green, Arthur. *These Are the Words: A Vocabulary of Jewish Spiritual Life*. Woodstock, Vt.: Jewish Lights Publishing, 1999.

Hammer, Reuven. *Entering Jewish Prayer*. New York: Schocken Books, 1994.

Hoffman, Lawrence A. *The Art of Public Prayer: Not for Clergy Only*. Woodstock, Vt.: SkyLight Paths Publishing, 1999.

_____, ed. *My People's Prayer Book: Traditional Prayers, Modern Commentaries*. Vol. 1, *The Sh'ma and Its Blessings*. Woodstock, Vt.: Jewish Lights Publishing, 1997.

_____. *My People's Prayer Book: Traditional Prayers, Modern Commentaries*. Vol. 2, *The Amidah*. Woodstock, Vt.: Jewish Lights Publishing, 1998.

_____. *My People's Prayer Book: Traditional Prayers, Modern Commentaries*. Vol. 3, *P'sukei D'zimrah*. Woodstock, Vt.: Jewish Lights Publishing, 1999.

_____. *My People's Prayer Book: Traditional Prayers, Modern Commentaries*. Vol. 4, *Seder K'riat Hatorah*. Woodstock, Vt.: Jewish Lights Publishing, 2000.

Isaacs, Ronald H. *Every Person's Guide to Jewish Prayer*. London: Jason Aronson Inc., 1997.

Kirzner, Yitzchok, and Lisa Aiken, *The Art of Jewish Prayer*. Jerusalem: Jason Aronson Inc., 1991.

Lamm, Norman. *The Shema: Spirituality and Law in Judaism*. Philadelphia: Jewish Publication Society, 1998.

Millgram, Abraham. *Jewish Worship*. Philadelphia: Jewish Publication Society, 1971.

Munk, Elie. *The World of Prayer*. New York: Philipp Feldheim Publisher, 1963.

Petuchowski, Jakob J. *Prayerbook Reform in Europe*. New York: The World Union for Progressive Judaism, 1968.

Shach, Stephen R. *The Structure of the Siddur*. London: Jason Aronson Inc., 1996.

Sperber, Daniel. *Why Jews Do What They Do*. Hoboken, N.J.: Ktav Publishing House, 1999.

Steinsaltz, Adin. *A Guide to Jewish Prayer*. New York: Schocken Books, 2000.

Prayer Books

The ArtScroll Siddur. Brooklyn: Mesorah Publications, 1987.

Birnbaum, Philip, ed. *Daily Prayer Book*. New York: Hebrew Publishing Company, 1949.

Ha'Avodah Sh'Balev. Jerusalem: The Movement for Progressive Judaism in Israel, 1992.

Likrat Shabbat: Worship, Study, and Song for Sabbath and Festival Evenings. Bridgeport, Ct.: The Prayer Book Press, 1998.

Sabbath and Festival Prayer Book. New York: The Rabbinical Assembly and the United Synagogue of Conservative Judaism, 1999.

Service of the Heart. London: Union of Liberal and Progressive Synagogues, 1967.

Siddur Rinat Yisrael. Jerusalem: Murshat, 1976.

Siddur Sim Shalom. New York: The United Synagogue of Conservative Judaism, 1985.

Stern, Chaim, ed. *Gates of the House: The New Union Home Prayer Book*. New York: Central Conference of American Rabbis, 1977.

_____, ed. *Gates of Prayer: The New Union Prayer Book*. New York: Central Conference of American Rabbis, 1975.

_____, ed. *Gates of Prayer for Assemblies*. New York: Central Conference of American Rabbis, 1993.

_____, ed. *Gates of Prayer for Shabbat and Weekdays*. New York: Central Conference of American Rabbis, 1994.

_____, ed. *Gates of Prayer for Weekdays*. New York: Central Conference of American Rabbis, 1975.

GLOSSARY

The Hebrew words used in the book are listed below. They appear in alphabetical order of the transliterations accompanied by the page number where they are first discussed in the commentary.

ACHEIR. Another. 62 אַחֵר

ADAR SHEINI. Adar II. 203 אֲדָר שֵׁנִי

ADAT. Congregation of. 40 עֲדַת

ADON OLAM. 234 אֲדוֹן עוֹלָם
"Eternal Lord."

AHAVAH RABBAH. 38, 49 אַהֲבָה רַבָּה
"[With] Great Love."

AHAVAT OLAM. 52 אַהֲבַת עוֹלָם

AL HATZADDIKIM. 91 עַל הַצַּדִּיקִים
"For the Righteous."

ALEINU. "It Is Our 215 עָלֵינוּ
Duty."

ALIYAH. "Going up" to 190 עֲלִיָּה
read from the Torah,
also immigration to
Israel.

ALIYAH L'REGEL 190 עֲלִיָּה לְרֶגֶל
Pilgrimage to Jerusalem
for the festivals of
Pesach, Shavuot,
and Sukkot.

AMIDAH. Standing 78 עֲמִידָה
(the Eighteen Benedic-
tions recited while
standing).

ARBA KANFOT. Four 5 אַרְבַּע כַּנְפוֹת
corners (small four-
fringed garment).

AVEILEI TZION. 141 אַבְלֵי צִיּוֹן
Mourners of Zion.

AVODAH. "Worship." 138 עֲבוֹדָה

AVOT. "Fathers" 102 אָבוֹת
or "Patriarchs."

B'RACHAH, B'RACHOT 17 בְּרָכָה, בְּרָכוֹת
(pl.). Blessing(s).

BAAL KOREI. The trained 190 בַּעַל קוֹרֵא
reader of Torah.

BAR'CHU. "Praise 38 בָּרְכוּ
[the Lord]."

BARUCH SHE-AMAR. 26 בָּרוּךְ שֶׁאָמַר
"Praised Be the One
Who Spoke."

BARUCH SHENATAN. 183 בָּרוּךְ שֶׁנָּתַן
"Praised be the One
who has given."
(From "At the Ark.")

BIKUR CHOLIM. Visiting 84 בִּקּוּר חוֹלִים
the sick.

BINAH. "Wisdom." 80 בִּינָה

BIRCHOT HAMITZVOT. 19 בִּרְכוֹת הַמִּצְוֹות
Blessings before
doing a mitzvah.

BIRCHOT HANEHENIN. 18 בִּרְכוֹת הַנֶּהֱנִין
Blessings before
partaking of pleasures.

BIRCHOT HAPRATIYOT. 19 בִּרְכוֹת הַפְּרָטִיּוֹת
Blessings recited
before personal or
private occasions.

KADDISH. 224 קַדִּישׁ
"Sanctification."

KADDISH D'RABANAN. 227 קַדִּישׁ דְּרַבָּנָן
Rabbi's Kaddish.

KADDISH L'ITCHAD'TA. 227 קַדִּישׁ
Kaddish of Renewal. לְאִתְחַדְתָּא

KADDISH SHALEIM. 225 קַדִּישׁ שָׁלֵם
Full Kaddish.

KADDISH TITKABEIL. 225 קַדִּישׁ תִּתְקַבֵּל
Kaddish of Acceptance
(another name for
Kaddish Shalem).

KADDISH YATOM. 225 קַדִּישׁ יָתוֹם
Mourner's Kaddish.

KADOSH. Sacred. 124 קָדוֹשׁ
(See KEDOSHIM).

KAVANAH. Devotion, 10 כַּוָּנָה
purpose.

KEREN Y'SHUAH. 95 קֶרֶן יְשׁוּעָה
"The Messianic Hope."

KIBBUTZ GALUYOT. 86 קִבּוּץ גָּלֻיּוֹת
"Gathering of Exiles."

KIDDUSH. The blessing 124 קִדּוּשׁ
over wine.

KIDDUSH HASHEM. 63 קִדּוּשׁ הַשֵּׁם
Sanctification of
God's name.

KIDDUSH L'YOM SHABBAT. 239 קִדּוּשׁ לְיוֹם
Kiddush for Shabbat שַׁבָּת
Day.

KIDDUSHIN. Marriage 69 קִדּוּשִׁין
ceremony.

KIPPAH. Skullcap. 3 כִּפָּה

KOHEIN, KOHANIM (pl.). 189 כֹּהֵן, כֹּהֲנִים
Priest(s).

KOTEL MAARAVI. 142 כֹּתֶל מַעֲרָבִי
Western Wall.

L'HACHAYOT HAMEITIM. 115 לְהַחֲיוֹת
"To revive the dead." הַמֵּתִים
(From "Gevurot.")

L'HITPALEIL. To pray. 11 לְהִתְפַּלֵּל

L'VAVCHA. Your heart. 66 לְבָבְךָ

LEIVI, L'VIYIM (pl.). 189 לֵוִי, לְוִיִּים
Levite(s).

LEV. Heart. 66 לֵב

M'CHALKEL CHAYIM 113 מְכַלְכֵּל חַיִּים
BECHESED. "Who in בְּחֶסֶד
loving kindness
sustains the living."
(From "Gevurot.")

M'CHAYEIH HAKOL. 115 מְחַיֶּה הַכֹּל
"Who sustains all life."
(From "Gevurot.")

M'CHAYEIH HAMEITIM. 115 מְחַיֶּה הַמֵּתִים
"Who revives the
dead." (From
"Gevurot.")

M'NUCHATEINU. 132 מְנוּחָתֵינוּ
"Our rest." (From
"K'dushat Hayom.")

M'TURG'MAN. 191 מְתוּרְגְּמָן
Translator.

MAARIV. Evening 4 מַעֲרִיב
service.

MACHNIA ZEIDIM. 90 מַכְנִיעַ זֵדִים
"Humbling the
Arrogant."

MASHIACH. The 96 מָשִׁיחַ
anointed one;
messiah.

MEZUZAH. A small case 65 מְזוּזָה
of metal or wood
containing a roll of
parchment upon which
are inscribed the first
two passages of the
Shema.

MI CHAMOCHAH BA'EILIM. 72 מִי־כָמֹכָה בָּאֵלִם
"Who is like You
among the mighty?"
(From "Geulah.")

MINCHAH. Afternoon 4 מִנְחָה
service.